Violin Dreams

VIOLIN DREAMS

Arnold Steinhardt

HOUGHTON MIFFLIN COMPANY

BOSTON · NEW YORK 2006

For information about permission to reproduce selections
from this book, write to Permissions, Houghton Mifflin Company,
215 Park Avenue South, New York, New York 10003.

Visit our Web site: www.houghtonmifflinbooks.com.

Library of Congress Cataloging-in-Publication Data

Steinhardt, Arnold.

Violin dreams / Arnold Steinhardt.

p.   m.

ISBN-13: 978-0-618-36892-1

ISBN-10: 0-618-36892-2

1. Steinhardt, Arnold. 2. Violinists—United States—
Biography. I. Title.

ML418.S737A3 2006

787.2092—dc22   2005037777

Printed in the United States of America

Book design by Robert Overholtzer

M P 10 9 8 7 6 5 4 3 2 1

The illustration on page xiv, Components of the Modern Violin,
was taken from the *New Dictionary of Music and Musicians* (figure 703),
John Tyrrell, ed., copyright © 2003 by Oxford University Press, Inc.
Used by permission of Oxford University Press.

For Dorothea,
even though she
doesn't play the violin

I only heard a singing, a sighing, a weeping, a sobbing, a talking, a roaring — all sorts of strange sounds that I had never heard in my life before. Sounds sweet as honey, smooth as oil, kept pouring without end straight into my heart, and my soul soared far, far away into another world, into a paradise of pure sound. — "The Fiddle," SHOLOM ALEICHEM

ACKNOWLEDGMENTS

This book would never have seen the light of day without
Jill Kneerim, my friend and literary agent, who guided and
encouraged me with unflagging enthusiasm. Deanne Urmy,
my editor, exercised great patience and resourcefulness
in getting a traveling violinist to put his story together
with some kind of coherence. Verlyn Klinkenborg offered
invaluable advice. My son, Alexander, provided thoughtful
comment as did Alan and Arlene Alda. Liz Duvall kept me on
the path to good grammar and clarity of thought. Emanuel
Batshaw, Ralph Berkowitz, Paul Childs, Donald Collup,
Virginia Dajani, Michael Gilbert, Francis Kuttner, Hiroshi
Iizuka, Sandy Noyes, Marianne Wurlitzer, and Samuel
Zigmuntowicz made valuable contributions. I am grateful
to Tom Casey for his translation of Lao-tsu, and to Lee Koonce
for his translation of "La Cumparsita." Finally, to my wife,
Dorothea, who often realized in mid-sentence by the glazed
look in my eyes that I was off somewhere in fiddle land,
I offer deep thanks for her patience and understanding.

CONTENTS

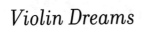

Violin Dreams

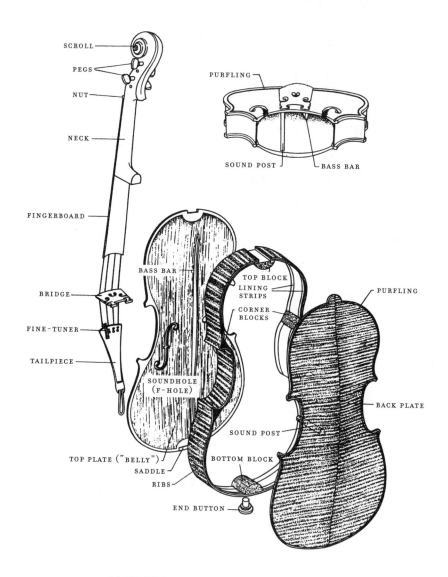

SCROLL

PEGS

NUT

NECK

PURFLING

SOUND POST — BASS BAR

FINGERBOARD

BASS BAR

TOP BLOCK
LINING
STRIPS

CORNER
BLOCKS

PURFLING

BRIDGE

FINE-TUNER

TAILPIECE

SOUNDHOLE
(F-HOLE)

BACK PLATE

SOUND POST

TOP PLATE ("BELLY")

SADDLE

RIBS

BOTTOM BLOCK

END BUTTON

COMPONENTS OF THE MODERN VIOLIN

Survival of the Fittest

Onstage, please," someone called out in the half-light. Standing in the wings of Carnegie Hall, I felt my heart racing and the palms of my hands turning clammy. The stage door swung open slowly, framing the broad expanse of hardwood floor where, in a matter of seconds, I would play Johann Sebastian Bach's Chaconne for solo violin. Doubts rushed at me like a fetid wind. Would I play well? Would the listeners, music lovers with exacting expectations, be pleased? Or might I be booed for a less than stellar rendition of the great Chaconne? Then I thought the unthinkable: *Just don't play.* It was my choice, after all. Either cross the Rubicon onto the heady but risky concert stage or cancel the performance entirely, something akin to jilting your bride at the altar.

As if by alchemy, a delicious anticipation unexpectedly rose up in me, quelling my fears. Of course I would play! I strode onto

Carnegie's stage, savoring tiers of seats stacked dizzyingly one on top of the other. The hall's grandeur swept any lingering nerves away, but the applause that I expected to float forward was absent. An eerie silence greeted my entrance from the wings, and when I looked out over the stage, my heart sank. There was no audience at all. Carnegie Hall, lit on every level by strings of shimmering lights, stood empty, like a great ocean liner at dock awaiting passengers before a voyage. Only when lowering my gaze a notch did I notice that a few people were indeed occupying the front row's center section. Curiously enough, they all had writing pads and pencils ready.

"Thank you for coming, Mr. Steinhardt," a man with a salt-and-pepper mustache who sat on the aisle called out. "We would like to ask you questions about the violin." Before I could respond, a woman with a cigarette in her hand leaned forward and spoke. "Would you tell us about the violin's early history?" Apparently this self-appointed jury was bent on going through with some kind of examination. Better to humor these people and get on with my recital. After all, the audience had not yet arrived.

I began to think out loud. "Let's see. Antonio Stradivari was the most famous. He studied with Nicholas Amati. Amati was one of the early violinmakers. Then there was Maggini. Was he the first?" The woman eyed me coolly and chose not to answer. A frigid silence lifted off the entire group as I stood at the front of the stage looking down on them.

The man spoke again. "Please tell us about the string instruments leading up to the violin — the rebec, the hurdy-gurdy, and the crwth."

The names were familiar to me, but I was forced to admit the truth. "I can't tell you anything about the rebec, the hurdy-gurdy, or the . . ." Without a vowel to move the consonants along, my tongue snagged on *crwth* as if I were afflicted by a speech impediment. My face flushed with shame.

This must have been the last straw, for the entire group of judges rose and began to talk among themselves. I searched frantically in my mind for a way to dispense with these people who had entered my life like a rogue asteroid.

Then the obvious occurred to me. I would simply play the Chaconne as planned. Let Bach's noble opening strains answer the criticism of my tormentors and banish them from the hall! But when I tried to lift the violin onto my shoulder, it became unbearably heavy, and the bow refused to move across the strings, as if a quick-setting glue had been applied to its horsehair. The Chaconne's opening three- and four-note chords should have been easy enough to play, but to my mounting consternation, only a strangled croak came out of the violin. From the corner of my eye I saw the man with the mustache collecting pads. He mounted the stage steps slowly.

A feeling of suffocating dread rose up in me, and then I awoke. Carnegie Hall, my violin recital, even the panel of judges who moments earlier had held me hostage, were gone. To my immense relief, the concert-exam was only an anxiety dream, one of dozens I've had over the years.

The bright morning light nudged my sleep-laden eyes open and I slowly got out of bed. Even in my early-morning stupor, I understood one thing. I had dreamed about the Chaconne because I was about to play it. A dear friend, Petra Shattuck, had just died unexpectedly, leaving a large family grieving for her. A few days ago, her husband, John, had called and asked me to play at her memorial service. Bach's Chaconne, solemn and ceremonial, seemed a fitting choice for all of us who mourned her. Whether played separately or as the last of the D Minor Partita's five movements, the Chaconne stood out as a towering and emotion-charged work. It reminded me of a mighty cathedral — imposing in length, moving and uplifting in spirit, and exquisite in its details.

To prepare for Petra's service, I had been practicing the Chaconne every day — fussing over individual phrases, searching for better ways to string them together, and wondering about the very nature of the piece, at its core an old dance form that had been around for centuries. After the many times I had heard and played the Chaconne, I had hoped it would fall relatively easily into place by now, but it appeared to be taunting me. The more I worked, the more I saw; the more I saw, the further away it drifted from my grasp. Perhaps that is in the nature of every masterpiece. But more than that, the Chaconne seemed to exude shadows over its grandeur and artful design. Exactly what was hidden there I could not say, but I would lose myself for long stretches of time exploring the work's repeating four-bar phrases, which rose and fell and marched solemnly forward in ever-changing patterns. The upcoming performance for Petra clearly weighed on me. Why else would the Chaconne worm its way into my nocturnal wanderings?

An hour later, hurrying down the hall of Rutgers University's Mason Gross School of the Arts, where I have taught for many years, I passed the studios of Susan Starr, concert pianist, and Doug Johnson, music historian. Ah — the woman with the cigarette, the man with the salt-and-pepper mustache! We faculty members recently had lobbed questions at a squirming violinist undergoing his final oral exam. Most of what we had asked covered ground I knew intimately about the repertoire for the instrument, but some questions about the violin itself had stumped me. I emerged from the exam room feeling vaguely uncomfortable. If I myself knew so little about the violin's origins, what right did I have to judge this young student?

Was my life too busy, was sheer sloth the culprit, or did the violin interest me only as a conduit for the music I played? After all, nobody expected a carpenter to know the hammer and saw's history. Odd, though, wasn't it, for me to be so ill-informed about an instrument that demanded such intimacy? When I hold the violin, my left arm stretches lovingly around its neck, my right hand draws the bow across the strings like a caress, and the violin itself is tucked under my chin, a place halfway between my brain and my beating heart. Instruments that are played at arm's length — the piano, the bassoon, the tympani — have a certain reserve built into the relationship. *Touch me, hold me if you must, but don't get too close,* they seem to say. To play the violin, however, I must stroke its strings and embrace a delicate body with ample curves and a scroll like a perfect hairdo fresh from the beauty salon. This creature sings ardently to me day after day, year after year, as I embrace it. Shouldn't I want to know something about it?

But these are grownup thoughts, whereas my violin study began with a child's perspective. At the age of six, the dawn of my awareness, I accepted all the wonders of life — my beloved toy train, the fairy tales that frightened me, a butterfly's miraculous flight, and even the first magical sounds of my violin — at face value. When I rode my bicycle down the block, the thrill of its motion and the joy of having finally learned to ride it were what interested me, not the bicycle's design or history. Why would I think any differently about the violin when I was learning to hold it and make it do my bidding? Unlike a lawyer, firefighter, or bus driver, who begins and ends his or her career as an adult, I am still inhabited by that unquestioning child who began violin study many years ago.

All morning long that day at Rutgers I worked with my violin students. I heard the things that violin lessons are made of — scales, études, Bach, Mozart, Paganini. Hanfang Jiang, a gifted student from China, played Bartók's First Rhapsody for me. Hanfang played well, very well, and I was pleased with her progress, but did *she* know when the violin had come into being and who the first violinmakers were?

When lunchtime arrived, I walked over to the school library with my sandwich and thermos and began pulling books about stringed instruments off the shelves. Reflexively, I looked around for my dream's tormentors. *Isn't it a little late?* I imagined my anxiety-dream judges snickering at my attempts to learn about the violin some sixty years after taking it up.

I came across illustrations of two early bowed instruments from India, the ravanastron and the omerti, each made of a hollowed cylinder of sycamore wood and played in the manner of a cello. The primal simplicity of the violin's ancestors was breathtaking: a sounding box, a stick attached to it, and a couple of strings stretched across the structure. Any one of us could approximate it with some spare wood, a knife, and a little time to kill. It seemed only a step or two removed from the most primitive attempts at an instrument. The early hunters could not have failed to notice the twang of a bowstring as it drove the arrow toward its unsuspecting prey. I imagined the hunting party later that evening, gorged on the kill, recounting stories of its conquests by the campfire. Some sated cave dweller, motivated perhaps by idle curiosity, stretched a thin strip of cast-aside animal skin over a hollow gourd and plucked it absentmindedly with one finger. He raised his eyebrows in mild astonishment at the reverberant sound. A new musical instrument, the prototype of the guitar, the banjo, the mandolin, the balalaika, might have been born that evening as the fire's embers died away.

The ravanastron illustration also showed its mate, a bow of the most basic kind — nothing more than a slender, curved piece of wood with a string attached at both sides, but still recognizable as a distant cousin of today's violin bow. It has been said that the history of the violin is really the history of the bow. When I draw my bow across the violin's strings and coax out a sustained sound, a small miracle takes place. As if by magic, my gesture is able to produce an astonishing range of sounds akin to the human voice. The bow is a magic wand that sets the violin apart from plucked instruments. The accomplished guitarist creates the illusion of sustained sound by grouping notes together that individually die. But if my bow arm is in good working order, I need no such subterfuge. Germans call the violin a "stroke" instrument, an apt name, considering what the bow does.

But I have more difficulty imagining a script for the bow's Eve than the violin's Adam. Back at the same campfire after the hunt, how did the tribe's musical-instrument inventor get the idea of stroking his musical string rather than plucking it? In response to his mate's complaints about that awful twanging sound, he might have taken a smooth piece of cane or reed left over from a woven basket and drawn it across the strings. Perhaps he even notched it, if the sound proved insufficient — one of the innumerable little breakthroughs, along with myriad failures and dead ends, that culminated in the elegant object made of pernambucco and ebony wood, ivory, silver, mother-of-pearl, and horsehair that I hold in my right hand every time I hold the violin with my left.

I glanced again at the ravanastron illustration and realized with a start that I'd seen something like it recently in the New York City subway, of all places. While changing trains at Times Square station in rush hour, I thought I heard a violin above the din. A small crowd had gathered around a young Chinese man who sat between the express and local train tracks, playing with great energy on a cellolike two-stringed instrument. It sounded like a violin run amuck — the pitch rising and falling wildly, the vibrato frenzied, the music passionate. Despite his instrument's foreignness, the sliding connections between notes and minute inflections of bowing were the completely familiar gestures of my string world. I stood transfixed in the crowd, listening to what was unmistakably virtuoso playing. When the music came to an end, the crowd clapped enthusiastically and began to disperse.

I lingered out of something more than curiosity. We belonged to the same fraternal order, so to speak. We were both string players. When our eyes met, I mimicked the motions of a violinist and then pointed to my own body. The man's face lit up. "I play the urheen, an ancient instrument from China, where I was born," he said in clear English. "Here you sometimes call it a Chinese fiddle. Sit down!" With that, the man abruptly stood up and pulled me over to the stool on which he had been playing. "No, no, no," I protested, but to no avail. In a series of deft motions, he pushed me onto the stool and handed me his instrument and bow. "Play," he commanded, grinning widely. "No, no," I repeated more urgently. More or less the same group of people again collected around us to see what the fuss was about. It had taken only several seconds, ten at most, for me to be transformed from amused by-stander to the main attraction. What had I gotten myself into?

I do not play the cello and I certainly don't know how to play the urheen, but the man seemed unconcerned about those insignificant details. He gave me a lesson on the spot — even as I said "No, no" for the third time — by guiding both my hands on the instrument with his. To my amazement, a passable sound came out of the urheen and the crowd clapped once again.

The rumble of an approaching train provided the excuse I needed to hand the instrument back and get up. This time it was the urheen player's turn to say "No, no," and we both laughed as I boarded the N train. An American violinist and a Chinese fiddler eyed one another with a sense of newfound familiarity through the closing doors.

I returned to my book and flipped the page. As if by command, an illustration of the urheen stared up at me. Next to it was a picture of the modern Turkish or Arabian kemangeh a'gouz, a ravanastron-like instrument. I looked at the kemangeh, meaning "ancient bowed instrument" in Persian, and wondered why it was familiar to me. After all, I had never paid much attention to any of the instruments featured in this dry textbook. Then I remembered the Azerbaijani taxi driver who had recently picked me up at La Guardia Airport. He looked at my instrument case as I got into the cab and asked what was inside. Half an hour later, I paid him in front of my apartment building. Once again he looked at the violin case in my hand, and then he glared at me accusingly. "Can you *crrry* on the violin?" he demanded to know. I was taken aback. "In my country they have such a *crrrying* instrument, the kemangeh. You can really crrry on it. Can you crrry on that?" I assured him that I could, would, and have cried on the violin. The driver must have realized as we stood facing one another by the still-open trunk of his taxi that a winner in the crying contest would never be decided this way. Suddenly he opened his mouth wide and began a vocal imitation of his native instrument, accompanied by the flailing arm movements of a kemangeh player. If you believe the taxi driver, and I do, the kemangeh and its relatives may have been crying for millennia.

The afternoon sunlight gradually moved across the library's walls and my book's cast of musical instruments marched in a slow processional toward the birth of the violin. There were the instruments of my anxiety dream, the three- and six-string Welsh crwths, dating as far back as the ninth century, and the pear-shaped rebec from Arabia. The musicians in Shakespeare's *Romeo and Juliet,* Hugh Rebeck, Simon Catling (Catgut), and James Soundpost, were undoubtedly rebec players. Then came the Arabian rabab, the Gothic fidula or fiddle, and the French vielle, followed by the enormously successful family of fretted viols that appeared in Europe only a few years before the violin. They had the appearance of small, mischievous animals that could be kept in line only by the bows that played on them.

The Italian Renaissance inspired a flurry of new ideas and experiments in all fields, but especially in the arts. Large-scale musical events now took place in the open air, creating a need for a louder bowed instrument with a soprano voice. Makers of lutes, a fretted plucked instrument whose body was in the shape of a pear cut lengthwise, must have contributed significantly to the violin's genesis. To this day violinmakers are called luthiers — literally, lute makers. Did the experimentation going on in each instrument maker's shop gradually, inevitably lead up to the violin? Or was there one person who rose above the title of craftsman — an artist with the vision to collect these countless experiments and consolidate them into a vision of aesthetic and tonal perfection? None other than Leonardo da Vinci had an inventor's interest in wind instruments. Some have claimed he played the violin. The thought that he might have been the violin's creator is tantalizing. Nonetheless, the violin's origin around 1530 remains obscure, and candidates for the honor of having made the first are many.

The violin was a dramatic improvement over its distant relatives. It had significant new features: the curvature of both top and back to spread the sound vibrations, and openings in the top in the shape of an *f*. The instrument's proportions were wonderfully balanced. Unlike its cousins the viola, the cello, and the double bass, which came in a variety of successful sizes, any slight alteration in the violin's dimensions caused a marked change in the quality and fullness of its sound. I had assumed self-centeredly that the violin's fixed measurements were a thoughtful gesture to performers, allowing us to switch easily from one instrument to another. But no less a master than Stradivari, who experimented briefly with a "long" model, soon realized its drawbacks and returned to a more traditional measurement.

The violin caught on quickly. It is known that in about 1555, the French court imported a dance band of Italian violinists, and in 1573, when Catherine de Médicis put on an elaborate affair in which sixteen of the most beautiful ladies and young girls represented the sixteen provinces of France, "the music was the most melodious one had ever seen and the ballet was accompanied by some thirty violins playing very pleasantly a warlike tune," wrote an observer. About the same time, Andrea Amati was already making violins of such quality in Cremona, Italy, that he was able to found a family dynasty, and Cremona quickly became a center of violinmaking, where the greatest makers of all time, Antonio Stradivari and Joseph Guarneri del Gesù, soon thrived.

According to Anthony Wood, a seventeenth-century Oxford University historian, musicians who played viols, the refined fretted instruments of the court, looked down their noses at this brash newcomer called the violin. Wood wrote that "the gentlemen in private meetings I frequented played three, four, and five parts with viols, a treble viol, tenor viol, countertenor and bass, and they esteemed a violin to be an instrument only belonging to a common fiddler, and could not endure that it should come among them for fear of making their meeting to be vain and fiddling." The two competitors, one aristocrat, one commoner, managed to exist uneasily side by side for more than a century until the violin's power, versatility, brilliance, and singing nature turned the viol into an endangered species. In 1640, G. B. Doni summed up the instrument's power succinctly: "In the hand of a skillful player, the violin represents the sweetness of the lute, the suavity of the viol, the majesty of the harp, the force of the trumpet, the vivacity of the fife, the sadness of the flute, the pathetic quality of the cornet; as if every variety, as in the great edifice of the organ, is heard with marvelous artifice."

The violin's story struck me as downright Darwinian. Call it survival of the fittest. Just substitute rebecs, crwths, viols, and fiddles for apes, Neanderthal man, and Lucy. And the parallel goes further. Darwin was a strict adherent of the ancient motto *Natura non facit saltum* — Nature does not make big leaps. He believed that ancestors and descendants must be connected by "infinitely numerous transitional links" forming "the finest graduated steps." But fossil records show few indications of gradual change, just as there is very little to link the lute and viol makers inhabiting fifteenth- and sixteenth-century Italy with the first recorded violinmakers. Paleontologists are still arguing over whether new species only seem to appear suddenly because fossil records are so scant, an argument easily applied to the violin's breathtaking arrival in a near-finished state.

Much of what I read that day in the library will probably make no lasting impression on me. I am a violinist, not a historian. What difference does it make that either Gaspard Tieffenbrucker or Gasparo da Salo might have made the first violin around 1530? What remains indelible is the miracle of this little box with four strings that emerged from the ferment of the Renaissance. The violin has essentially remained the same since its origins almost five hundred years ago. It has seventy parts, seventy-two if top and bottom plates are each made from two pieces of wood. Each of its separate parts is indispensable.

We will probably never know the violin's exact birthdate or whether the honor of first maker should be awarded to Gaspard Tieffenbrucker, but his portrait and a verse were supposedly found in one of his instruments: "I lived in the woods, until I was slain by the relentless axe. Whilst I was alive I was silent, but in death my melody is exquisite." I leaned back in my chair in the library to ponder this sentimental nugget. My own violin was made from a tree that was probably felled over one hundred years before it was crafted into an instrument. The melodies I play on it probably come out of a three-hundred-year-old piece of wood. If any living thing has claim on immortality, it would be that tree.

My reverie was broken by the realization that I had a student violin recital to hear. I hurried back to the music building feeling a little better. In just an hour's reading, I had exorcised most

of my postdream ghosts. Still, in the hope that dreams are sometimes something more than a dubious fringe benefit of sleep,
I did not want to forget this one. Dreams are not reality, yet they
must have some significance. Mine had just sent me to the library. But what might the dream offer other than a dry history
lesson? Was it my guidance counselor, spiritual adviser, psychic,
Greek chorus, bridge to the subconscious, deliverer of unvarnished truths, doomsday seeker, frivolous entertainer? Or was it
merely a purveyor of nonsense? I tried to match my dream with
this menu. "Unvarnished truth" rang true. When I thought about
the Chaconne, the unvarnished truth was that Bach's intricacies
had yet to be solved.

CHAPTER 2

Photo Gallery

I SLIPPED INTO the music building's concert hall and sat down just as Valissa Willworth walked onstage, violin and bow in one hand, lecture recital paper in the other. She bowed to a smattering of applause emanating from fewer than a dozen people who sat willy-nilly in the small hall — I (her teacher), two other faculty members, Valissa's adoring new husband, who eagerly manned the video camera, and a few of her most faithful friends. Try as we might to simulate a large crowd, our clapping sounded more like popcorn popping, and a small bag's worth at that. These recitals, a graduate degree requirement, were seldom well attended, and I felt sorry for Valissa, who had worked so hard to perform for so few. As famous a musician as Béla Bartók had once played in this hall — for a bigger audience than today's, I hoped.

Valissa placed her instrument and bow gingerly on a table, cleared her throat, and announced her subject: "Eugène Ysaÿe's

Sonata for Solo Violin, op. 27, no.2: The Implications of the Bach Quotation." I nodded my head in approval. Ysaÿe was one of history's most innovative and charismatic violinists. He had even made it into the photo gallery of violinists I keep inside my own violin case, his massively chiseled head sunk in contemplation.

The little exhibit sandwiched into the satin strips alongside my bows came about more or less by accident. Years ago, my friend and mentor, the violinist Alexander Schneider, sent me a postcard portrait of Niccolò Paganini. Sascha, as Schneider is called, scrawled on the back of the card for my entertainment: "If you want to be the next Paganini, why are you reading this? Go practice!!" Sascha had sent me dozens of curious items over the years, some zany, some off-color, almost all amusing. But when I stopped smiling over his admonishment (undoubtedly true) that I should practice more, I looked again at Paganini. The portrait by Delacroix was full of atmosphere and mystery. Here at last was something other than Paganini's music that seemed to capture some of the man people called the greatest violinist who ever lived.

Paganini was the stuff of legends: the wizard violinist who played on one remaining string after the other three mysteriously broke, the gambler who lost his priceless violin in a card game, the man who was whispered to be in league with the devil. Something told me not to put the postcard in my bottom drawer with all of Sascha's other outrageous offerings — pictures of seminaked ladies, boxers, Orthodox rabbis; a photo of four grim, uniformed South American generals with the caption "The Guarneri String Quartet after 25 Years" (our quartet had just celebrated its silver anniversary); the postcard from Japan of a man in a white uniform supervising cows being milked in stainless steel stalls at a high-tech dairy farm (Sascha had written underneath, "Daniel Barenboim auditioning musicians for his orchestra"). No, there was too much substance in this rendition of the great Paganini, wickedly undulating as he played, to be relegated to a drawer, so I slipped him between my bows. He peered out, framed by Brazilian pernambucco wood and horsehair. Maybe Sascha was only half right. Practice, yes, but a role model awaiting me every time I opened my case might also come in handy.

Soon Paganini's portrait had company, a publicity shot of Jascha Heifetz I picked up somewhere in my travels. There were great violinists in the twentieth century, and then there was Heifetz. In the hundreds of hours I spent listening to him on records and the few times I heard him in person, he made my heart palpitate, my palms sweat, and my mind struggle to grasp how the instrument could be played with such ease, daring, and unearthly beauty. Perhaps, like Paganini, Heifetz had sold his soul to the devil. Heifetz the violinist, and even Heifetz as a concept of perfection, seemed beyond my grasp.

Keeping Heifetz's picture in my case had a hidden price I had not reckoned with. The photograph seemed to speak when I lifted my violin out: *I, Jascha Heifetz, with the best training possible, an uncommon musical talent, and magical violinist's fingers, nonetheless consider it my duty to practice obsessively every day of my life. What about you?*

When members of an audience came backstage after a performance, they occasionally noticed these photos of Paganini and Heifetz, star fiddlers of the nineteenth and twentieth centuries, respectively. Waiting their turn to congratulate me, they would nudge each other and point to the open violin case. "Keeping the competition in your sights, are you?" one of them once asked.

The competition soon had another addition — a 1962 photo of my teacher the Hungarian violinist Joseph Szigeti, in front of his home in Switzerland, with me posing proudly by his side. The conductor George Szell had sent me to Szigeti in the hope that at twenty-five I might benefit from the seventy-year-old master's wisdom. If Paganini was the sorcerer and Heifetz the bewitching stylist, then Szigeti was the poet. Tall, slender, and with a high-domed forehead that called to mind the evolved, futuristic humans in science fiction movies, Szigeti was revered by other musicians. In a violin world often inhabited by self-involved virtuosos, he stood somewhat alone, a man whose brain, heart, and soul interlocked as if he sought a direct line to the composer. At summer's end I looked through the just-developed photographs of my Swiss adventure and came across one of Szigeti and me, old master and eager young professional. What splendid fortune to have worked with him for two uninterrupted months! I placed the photo next to Heifetz and Paganini in my violin case. The collection was growing.

I saw a great deal of Heifetz, Szigeti, and Paganini in the next months. The 1963 Queen Elizabeth International Violin Competition was one year away, hardly enough time for me to bring several hours of required repertoire to a polished state. Every time I opened the violin case to practice, Jascha, Joseph, and Niccolò were there — not so much as stern taskmasters but more as subliminal role models looking me over as I began my daily workout. The three violinists went everywhere with me that year: to rehearsals, to concerts, and finally to Brussels for the competition.

An unexpected diversion from the competition's high-stress nature came in the form of a mystery man named Philip Newman who often appeared backstage and played the violin for us during breaks. He seemed to be a fixture of the competition that Queen Elizabeth had established in honor of her dear friend, the great Belgian violinist Eugène Ysaÿe. It was rumored that Newman was Ysaÿe's illegitimate son. His renditions, warm and touching in the way I imagined Ysaÿe himself would have played, gave credence to the gossip.

Newman approached me in the green room after my performance of Bartók's Second Violin Concerto. He extended a few kind words about my playing and gave me a photograph of Ysaÿe. I looked down at Ysaÿe's leonine head and the mane of hair that flowed almost to his shoulders and then glanced back up at Newman. The resemblance was striking. In that moment I had the feeling that Ysaÿe stood before me, his aura permeating the green room and his playing miraculously available through the medium of Newman, who, I saw, had signed the photograph.

Yehudi Menuhin described Ysaÿe's playing as exuberant, flamboyant, elegant in its phrasing, and incredibly charming and alluring. Szigeti remembered his "unthrobbing" pure cantilena, or melodic line. The Catalonian cellist Pablo Casals reportedly said that he never heard a violinist play in tune until Ysaÿe. George Bernard Shaw, the British playwright and music critic, called his playing "bumptious." The violinist Josef Gingold, who studied with Ysaÿe, told me that besides being a supreme artist and a great virtuoso, he possessed an extraordinary personal magnetism. Composers stood in line to write music for him. César Franck's Violin and Piano Sonata, Chausson's *Poème*, and Debussy's String Quartet were all dedicated to this mountain of a man.

And now I was speaking with Newman, who only thirty-two years earlier had played for Ysaÿe on his deathbed and then used his own violin strings to bind the wreath he placed on the master's grave. Was Newman really Ysaÿe's son? I never learned the truth, but the precious photograph he gave me went directly into my violin case with Heifetz, Szigeti, and Paganini. Now four great violinists dwelled there, a fiddler's Mount Rushmore.

The sound of Valissa's voice interrupted my reverie and banished the Rushmore gang back to their velvet-lined quarters. "As one of the greatest violinists of all time, Eugène Ysaÿe enjoyed a magnificent concert career that spanned Eastern and Western Europe and the United States," Valissa was saying. "He also composed numerous works for violin, taught some of the most notable violinists of the twentieth century, and conducted orchestras in Belgium, London, and Cincinnati." She quickly proceeded to the heart of her lecture. "One of Ysaÿe's most lasting contributions was the composition of six sonatas for unaccompanied violin. These works are both technically brilliant and artistically rich, and are considered vital to any concert violinist's repertoire. It is important to note the dedicatees of each of the six sonatas. Ysaÿe chose six of his most promising violinist friends of the younger generation and dedicated one sonata to each. He then subtly patterned the character of each work after the corresponding violinist. The first was given to Joseph Szigeti, who was the catalyst for the entire set." I had completely forgotten this. "Upon hearing the violinist perform a Bach sonata in concert in 1923, Ysaÿe was struck by his supple and distinguished playing, by the originality of his interpretation, and by the loftiness of his aesthetic concept."

During the summer I worked with Szigeti, including the study of Ysaÿe's sonatas, he had divulged nothing of this great honor. Ysaÿe's name certainly came up often enough. Szigeti once stopped me during a lesson and with his aged, shaky hand scrawled a trill sign over a single note in my music and then wrote Ysaÿe's name beside it. Fifty years earlier he had heard Ysaÿe add this small but spirited embellishment in a concert. Occasionally he would tell stories about Ysaÿe, a man who dwarfed most others in girth, height, and the relishing of food, drink, and romance. He once told me with a poker face that ten years after Ysaÿe left Cincinnati, Ohio, as conductor of the orchestra, every second child in town looked like him.

Valissa told us about the powerful influence that Bach's six Sonatas and Partitas for Solo Violin had had on Ysaÿe and how the genius of Bach had frightened him as he contemplated following in the master's footsteps. Then she traded her lecture paper for violin and bow and launched into Ysaÿe's Second Sonata. Anyone wandering into the hall at that moment who knew Bach's Partita in E Major but not the Ysaÿe sonata might think Valissa had gone slightly mad. The music was instantly recognizable as Bach's Preludium, the partita's celebrated first movement, but something was wrong. Valissa played the first fourteen notes not with their customary vigor but quietly, as if playing for herself, and then stopped. Had she lost her place? If so, then only briefly, for without warning she attacked the violin in a fifteen-note parody of the Preludium, setting her curly blond hair aquiver. Then she stopped as abruptly as she had started. I could see her husband clutching his video camera for dear life. Again a short silence — curls at rest — and again another hushed Bach quotation, this time twenty-eight notes that came to a halt as if Valissa's energy source had been cut off. She stood motionless one last time, exploded again in a flurry of notes, and then seemed to change her mind. The passage subsided into a long and winding narrative that referred to the Preludium again and again. Ysaÿe was doing the talking, but unquestionably Bach was whispering in his ear.

Ysaÿe called the movement "Obsession" in homage to Bach's genius, yet you can literally hear the composer railing again and again at the sheer folly of the task he set for himself in the master's shadow. It is hard to imagine a violinist who has passed through Bach's gravitational field untouched. Bach was first my chore, gradually my interest, and finally my quest. After all, why did I still struggle with his Chaconne in my Carnegie Hall dream? Jascha Heifetz, who performed regularly for U.S. troops during World War II, used to tell them in his clipped Russian accent, "Bach is like spinach. You may not like it, but it's good for you." Whatever Heifetz may have thought, the passage of time changed my feeling about the thicket of notes that had once mystified me. Spinach might be good for you, but Bach's seemingly improvised slow movements, the intricate fugues laid out in formal, architectural detail for the ages, and the playful dances behind which darker feelings sometimes lurked all fed the soul.

Valissa came to the end of the sonata, and we clapped enthusiastically for an excellent performance and lecture recital. Yet having brought us this near Ysaÿe, she had only piqued my curiosity. What did Eugène Ysaÿe actually sound like? I have known four people who knew him — Szigeti, who heard him play, the violinists Josef Gingold and Jascha Brodsky, who studied with him, and the pianist Arthur Rubinstein, who often played chamber music with him. All had delicious stories to tell about Ysaÿe. During a break in rehearsals with the Guarneri String Quartet sometime in the 1970s, Rubinstein leaned back on his piano bench, gazed upward, as if to travel back in time, and reminisced about his life as a musician in the early days of the twentieth century: "There were no summer music festivals, you know. We gathered at the estates of wealthy music lovers and played for sheer enjoyment. Casals was there. So were Kreisler, Thibaud, the violist Lionel Tertis, and Ysaÿe. Ah, Ysaÿe. What a violinist! He made them all sound like children — even Kreisler, if you can imagine that."

But that was the trouble. I found it hard to imagine Ysaÿe's playing, even though Rubinstein, remarkable raconteur that he was, had intoxicated us with his description of a great musician in an age whose traces have all but vanished. I had played for — and with — Casals and listened to Thibaud and Tertis on recordings. I could say with some assurance that I knew the distinguishing characteristics of their artistry. But Rubinstein's description left me with no feeling about Ysaÿe other than that his playing was remarkable. When I looked in my *Grove Dictionary*, the musician's bible, it described Ysaÿe's playing as "full-blooded," "intense," and "magisterial." Contemporaries, even Rubinstein, may have agreed that he possessed those qualities, but the word *magisterial* makes no musical sound whatsoever. I could not imagine the great man's style.

What a pity. Truth be told, I yearned to hear not only Ysaÿe but all the great violinists, stretching back to the beginning of violin time. What did the virtuosos Arcangelo Corelli, Giuseppe Tartini, Pietro Locatelli, Antonio Vivaldi, and Niccolò Paganini sound like? Something of their capabilities can be gleaned from the dazzling works they created, assuming that what a violinist composed he could also play. But when I read about them in books, the familiar wall separating words from music remained as impenetra-

ble as ever. I learned that Corelli, the first important violin virtuoso, in the seventeenth century, played as a soloist at an early age
with great success and that he was a passionate collector of pictures. Not much to chew on there. Corelli's pupil, Locatelli, unquestionably advanced violin technique with his book *The Art of
the Violin.* He was so popular with the public that the Dutch upper
classes went into mourning when he died, in 1764. This sheds no
light whatsoever on the quality of his playing. The first epoch in
Italian violin playing ended with Tartini, who was born in 1692.
Celebrated musicians of the time said that Tartini had the most
beautiful, animated tone and the highest degree of dexterity, us-
ing all his fingers with equal ease. With every word, the ancient
violinists seem to recede further and further from my ears.

Several months later I sat in the same concert hall for yet another lecture recital. The topic? Eugène Ysaÿe! My student Hisami
Iijima started off in a familiar vein: "Eugène Ysaÿe is one of the
most important figures in the history of the violin. After Paganini,
who contributed modern technique to the violin literature, many
violinist-composers left important works for the violin. But it was
Ysaÿe who made the next dramatic step in violin technique and
violin literature." I smiled. Hisami would do well in the next hour,
but there probably would be no surprises in a second lecture on
the same subject. "I will now play *Rêve d'enfant,* op. 14, written for
Ysaÿe's young son Antoine," she announced. "Ysaÿe's wife sent a
telegram informing him that Antoine, who was ill, had taken a
turn for the worse. On tour after a concert, Ysaÿe waited in his
hotel for a second telegram and wrote this piece to 'Mon petit
Antoine.'"

Hisami, holding the violin as delicately as if it were a baby, rendered this dreamy morsel beautifully, and as we clapped, the old yearning came over me. How would Ysaÿe have played it? As if to answer, Hisami headed across the room to a small CD player. "And now Eugene Ysaÿe will play his *Rêve d'enfant*," she announced. I held my breath, not quite able to believe that an artist consigned to the sealed-off realm of history was about to cross the divide into my consciousness. Hisami turned her CD player on, and through the scratch and hiss of the original 78 rpm recording, now remastered, Ysaÿe played for us. I sat absolutely rapt. His vibrato was fast and tight, he often slid from one note to another in the way singers of that era did, and his sense of pulse was exquisitely supple. I know of no living violinist who would want or dare to sound like that today — styles in performance have changed that much — yet Ysaÿe gave me goose bumps. His playing was indeed full-blooded, intense, and magisterial, but I would easily add other adjectives: assertive, extravagant, emotive, but also tender and intimate. As it turned out, *Rêve d'enfant* did its work well. Little Antoine recovered quickly.

The record miraculously took those of us in Hisami's audience back almost a century, to February 1, 1913. On that day, Hisami told us, Ysaÿe walked into the recording studios of Manhattan's Woolworth Building and played two of his compositions, *Mazurka* and *Rêve d'enfant*, into a large, conical horn. A photograph of the event shows Ysaÿe, dressed in a rumpled three-piece suit, playing into one of those horns while several other horns of various sizes stand behind him on the floor like so many dunce caps. In that era of acoustical recording, the sound vibrations were transmitted to a recording stylus, which then cut a groove into a large master disk made of beeswax.

Ysaÿe played on his beloved Joseph Guarneri del Gesù for

these recordings. Guarneri, who stands next to Antonio Stradivari as one of the two greatest violinmakers of all time, made this instrument in 1740, four years before his death. I heard the Ysaÿe Guarneri often in the hands of the great virtuoso Isaac Stern, who owned it for a significant part of his career. But it was mainly Stern the artist I listened to in concert, not his Guarneri. Only when my violin rubbed shoulders occasionally with Stern's in chamber music rehearsals and performances did I take real notice of it. All the players brought outstanding instruments to these sessions, but his Guarneri's characteristically dark and husky tone stood out from the others' voices. The violin, whose back had a most striking chipped and mottled varnish, possessed a powerful and resonant tone, but also something more elusive. Its sound was luminous. Whether the music demanded silken murmurs, a soaring lyricism, or something stentorian, its layered overtones seemed mysteriously to rearrange themselves accordingly. I was in the presence of a great violin but could not quite explain to myself how or why its sound touched me deeply. No wonder Ysaÿe loved his del Gesù. He went so far as to have the luthier Joseph Hel of Lille insert a label with the inscription "This violin is the most faithful companion of my life." What must Ysaÿe's two wives and many mistresses have thought of this unlikely competition! As remarkable as the violin was, one might think that the primitive recording methods available to Ysaÿe would destroy any sense of its voice, but some of the instrument's quality shone through the recording's nasty scratch and hiss. It was a tribute to both violin and violinist.

Only thirty-six years earlier, in 1877, Thomas A. Edison had conceived of the idea that the vibrations made by sound waves could be recorded as a pattern by means of a vibrating needle attached to a diaphragm. He shouted "Mary had a little lamb" into the horn of his newly invented tinfoil cylinder phonograph. Hearing Edison speak from the grave, or for that matter Johannes Brahms squeak in a comically high-pitched voice "Ich bin Herr Brahms," is an eerie curiosity, but recordings have also miraculously retrieved musicians' souls from the past and saved them from extinction. Tinfoil was soon replaced by wax and then by Emile Berliner's flat disk, from which duplicates could be stamped. Finally the advent of electrical recording eliminated the problems of acoustic reproduction, in which the speaking voice tended to lose its sibilants, orchestral music sounded muffled, and lower strings simply disappeared. Only the voice and the violin seemed to come off decently in those early acoustical recordings.

"Your recordings are the best I have ever listened to. Your method of perpetuating the characteristic tone of the violin undoubtedly excels all others," boasted a 1914 publicity blurb by Eugène Ysaÿe from the company that had just recorded him. Thanks to Edison and the many inventors who followed, we are able to hear in the twenty-first century remastered records of such artist-violinists as Joseph Joachim, Jacques Thibaud, Franz Drdla, Franz von Vecsey, and Maud Powell, who began to record in the very first hours of the twentieth century. We can listen to what has been called the golden age of violinists, whose playing was intrinsically linked to the vocal art of bel canto — beautiful, sustained tone, fine phrasing, and a style that stressed individual personality and musical outlook. Ysaÿe was one of the lucky ones who made it across the threshold before death shut the door irrevocably on his artistry. Whenever I so desire, Eugène Ysaÿe will play *Rêve d'enfant* for me from the Woolworth Building on February 1, 1913.

My unexpected encounter with the performance by Ysaÿe meant that I now knew the playing of three of the four violinists in my instrument case. Only the fourth, Paganini, was closed off to me forever. I railed against the thought. If only Edison had invented the wax cylinder a few decades earlier, one of my students might have ended a lecture recital by saying, "But words are so inadequate. Let Paganini himself play the *Witches Dance* in this 1822 recording on the Pasta e Fagioli label." Ah, then I would hear Paganini, know Paganini.

Sadly, I could only read about the man. Born in Genoa, Italy, in 1782, he was tall, emaciated, and deathly pale, with a striking hooked nose, feverish eyes, and long hair flowing to his shoulders. Onstage, Niccolò Paganini gave the impression of a skeleton whose loose limbs were about to clatter to the floor. It was said that when he made his acknowledgments, he bowed like a camel and grinned like a mountain goat. Some in the audience tittered at this oddly comical figure, but their amusement was short-lived. Thrusting his left shoulder and right foot forward so that his body formed a triangle, he produced sounds from the violin that had never been heard before. At first bold and fiery, then giving way to scales and runs at dazzling speeds, his playing took away the breath of his listeners. Then came improbable sounds resembling bird whistles. Paganini had devised a way to adopt harmonics, the natural overtones of the open strings, by stopping them, making unimaginable sounds in artificial harmonics, even double harmonics, at will. The audience was dumbfounded, overwhelmed, hysterical. As the wild applause finally subsided, Paganini would begin playing a long and noble theme as if he and his violin were a human voice. Leigh Hunt, an English writer, said, "Paganini's bow perfectly talked. It remonstrated, supplicated, answered, held a dialogue."

The ability to sing like a human voice, the violin's most compelling feature, was one thing, but I found it hard to get my mind around the idea that Paganini could bring off a brilliant dialogue. It reminded me of Gypsy violinists I had heard in Europe who could mimic an array of bird calls, an impressive trick done as an improvisation during a set piece but pale compared to the accounts of Paganini's acrobatics.

I read on in the story of this great violinist. At the home of a certain Lord Holland, someone asked Paganini to improvise on the violin the story of a son who kills his father, runs away, becomes a highwayman, falls in love with a girl who will not listen to him, leads her to a wild country spot, and suddenly jumps with her from a rock into an abyss, where they disappear forever. Paganini listened quietly, and when the story was at an end, asked that all the lights be extinguished. He then began playing, and so grand and terrible was his musical interpretation of the story that several ladies fainted and the salon, when relit, looked like a battlefield.

The best I could do under the circumstances was to hope that I would dream about Paganini. Who cares that dreams are counterfeit? If Paganini played for me, his flaming virtuosity, the very sound he made, and even the sway of his body would *feel* authentic. And when I recalled later on that his playing was wild and fast, his violin literally smoldering, it would come back to me as no less vivid than reality itself. I would have *heard* Paganini.

My eyes refocused on the present. Time to practice. I took out my violin and began to tune. Let's see. Scales first, then a little Bach. Bach was always a good thing to start with. In the lid of my case, I caught sight of the four violinists, my permanent lodgers. Perhaps I'd play the Chaconne for them once again today, only it would be different from the usual. It would be a little too fast, a bit wild, and full of heat! Niccolò would understand.

CHAPTER 3

Thump, thump, thump, thump, thump

A table, a chair, a bowl of fruit, and a violin; what else does a man need to be happy? — ALBERT EINSTEIN

As TIME WENT ON, images of other violinists moved into my instrument case. First, the photo of a smiling David Oistrakh, the Russian violin virtuoso, with two compatriots, the composer Dmitri Shostakovich and the pianist Sviatoslav Richter, caught by the camera as they reemerged onstage after a performance. Next, a tattered postcard featuring the leading German violinist of his day and a close friend of Brahms's, Joseph Joachim, seated solemnly with the other bearded members of his string quartet. Also a picture featuring the youngish, mustached, and already avuncular-looking Austrian violinist Fritz Kreisler. Then a faded photo of the cellist Pablo Casals, acknowledging applause in front of his orchestra, with Sascha Schneider as concertmaster and me, a bearded young man, standing next to him.

I looked from one violinist to another in this crazy quilt of photographs and realized that all had some things in common. Musical talent, of course, and a natural aptitude for the instrument, but if the film of each of their musical lives were rewound to day one, you would undoubtedly see a small violin, more like a toy than anything else, being tucked under the chin of a very young child. There is simply no other way to master the awkward hand and arm positions and to cultivate coordination along neural pathways than to start when the body is still a lump of wet clay waiting to be sculpted. But what five- or six-year-old is aware of anything about the instrument except that it might be fun to play? How can he or she know that one has to begin young and practice daily, and that starting violin at the ancient age of, say, thirteen will most likely be a losing battle? A child can't know this, but his parents must. Mama and Papa must love music, understand the importance of an early start, have the discipline to keep the child's nose to the grindstone, and be inured to the fact that the endeavor will set the youngster apart from other children and a more normal life — very special parents indeed. Perhaps a portrait collection celebrating famous violinists' parents would have been a good idea for my violin case.

Whatever their motives, parents are the first-stage engine in the launching of a career. Paganini's mother dreamed that her son was destined to become a great violinist. Heifetz's father, a violinist himself, gave Jascha his first lessons — hiding the violin when he was not at home so the young boy's practicing would take place only under his strict supervision. Sascha Schneider's father beat him when he didn't practice four hours a day. When Eugène Ysaÿe was four, his father, Nicholas, also a violinist, began teaching him. Ysaÿe said, "His hand was heavy, but without his strict attitude I should never become what I am today." It was Ysaÿe's father who taught him the most efficient hand positions and correct bowing and developed in him a taste for a singing and expressive tone. "What!" he once admonished Eugène, then five or six. "You already use vibrato? I forbid you to do so! You are all over the place like a bad tenor. Vibrato will come later, and you are not to deviate from the note. You'll *speak* through the violin."

But if Ysaÿe's father was responsible for guiding young Eugène's violin studies, who and what gave *him* the motivation to do so? Ysaÿe's grandfathers and great-grandfathers were village nailsmiths, his uncle a mason, his father a tailor, but they all played the violin for village festivals, weddings, and other occasions.

A legend was handed down in the Ysaÿe family, famous for generations as craftsmen in the Ardennes. It told of a boy whom some woodcutters found in the forest and brought to the village. The boy grew up to be a blacksmith. Once, at a village festival, he astonished everyone by playing the viol beautifully. From then on the villagers took pleasure in dancing and singing to the strains of his viol. One day an illustrious stranger stopped in front of the smithy to have his horse shod. The count's servant saw the viol inside and told the young smith that he had heard a new Italian instrument played by some minstrels at the count's court. That instrument, called the violin, was much better than the viol — its tone was like the human voice and could express every feeling and passion. From that moment the young man no longer took pleasure in his viol. Day and night he was thinking of that wonderful new instrument that could express joy and sorrow and whose tones went straight to the human heart.

Then he had a dream: he saw before him a young woman

of indescribable beauty, not unlike his own love, Biethline. She came to him and kissed his brow. The young man awoke and looked at the wall his broken and neglected viol used to hang on and could barely believe his eyes: there, instead of the viol, was a new instrument of beautiful proportions. He put it against his shoulder and drew the bow over the strings, producing sounds that were truly divine. The violin sang in a heartwarming tone; it rejoiced and wept for happiness — and so did the musician. Thus, goes the legend, came the first violin to the Ardennes and to the Ysaÿe family.

There were no such legends or dreams in my family background, but my parents loved music passionately. They were devoted concertgoers, and if music was not coming from the radio or record player at home, it came from their own mouths. They sang folk songs in English, Yiddish, Hebrew, Polish, and Russian spontaneously and anywhere — at the dinner table, in the car, or by a gurgling mountain stream. They loved music, but they adored the violin. My father remembers being taken to hear Jascha Heifetz, then a child prodigy of about his own age, perform near his hometown in Poland. Dad was so overwhelmed by the sound of the violin and by Heifetz's wizardry that he wanted to play himself, but as one of ten children in a family of limited resources, he lost out to an older brother when it came to lessons. My father's love of music probably came from his father, Aaron, who, although untrained as a musician, composed Yiddish songs that he sang at home. One of these has passed from generation to generation — sung by my grandfather to his son, then sung by my father to my brother and me when we were young, and now ready to be handed down to my own children and grandchildren. Even on his deathbed, his body racked with cancer, my father listened to music, almost as a substitute for the food he could no longer keep down. With his eyes closed and his strength ebbing away, he sang his father's songs one last time. Music, a great friend in life, eased his exit from it.

At age six, my mother sneaked into a Jewish wedding in order to hear the klezmer band play. *Kley zemer,* literally "vessels of song" in Hebrew, came to mean the musicians who played this melding of dance tunes and folk music drawn from traditions from the Baltic to the Black Sea, and finally to an entire musical genre. Not long ago, Mother, at ninety-six, tried to describe the composition of the band whose music had mesmerized her some ninety years earlier in Dlugosiodlo, the Polish shtetl where she was born and raised. She recalled that there was a struck keyboard instrument (hammered dulcimer), a reed instrument played straight down (clarinet), loud blow instruments (brass), and a violin — an expressive, singing violin whose sound bewitched her. Every phase of the wedding, from the prewedding party hosted by the bridegroom to the ceremony a week later in honor of the bride and groom, was accompanied by klezmer music. As the wedding progressed, specific dances were played for family friends and guests, others to escort older members home afterward.

The little town of Dlugosiodlo had a small and tight-knit Jewish community. A young child at a wedding with no visible parents accompanying her attracted attention. When Mother was asked whether her family were friends of the bride or the groom, she had to admit the truth, and she was immediately thrown out. But the allure of the klezmer music and especially the violin was too strong for her to resist, and when the time came for the next wedding she was back again; and the next, and the next (this six-year-old had her ways). Each time she was ejected, but first she managed to wriggle past watchful eyes in order to hear music that made her want to laugh and cry and dance.

Not long ago the Guarneri String Quartet was scheduled to play in Warsaw. I telephoned Mother beforehand and asked how far Warsaw was from Dlugosiodlo. I thought it would be a nice idea to visit the place, after all the stories I had heard growing up. "Dlugosiodlo? Oh, more or less a whole day's trip by horse and wagon," she answered. I burst out laughing. "Horse and wagon?" Mother turned indignant. "Of course, horse and wagon. How else are you going to get there?"

Born in 1906, Mother lived an essentially nineteenth-century existence in a village with dirt roads, no electricity, and certainly no automobiles. For those with a little money who wanted to go to Warsaw, the horse and wagon probably took them only as far as the nearest train station, but Mother's family was too poor for that. Her father had gone to America to try to earn enough to send for the rest of the family. Meanwhile, her grandfather, Yankele Goldberg, was the family's sole means of support, selling oil made out of cottonseed for human consumption and the leftover mash shaped into bricks for animal feed. Mother described how Yankele led horses attached to a grinding wheel around and around his back yard in order to press the oil from the seed. Of course, everyone knew his last name, but in the village he was always referred to in Yiddish as Yankele the oil man. Yankele was no mere oil man, however. As a devoutly Orthodox Hasidic Jew, he sang praise to God — zmirot, Mother called it — in his ringing voice each and every day at the dinner table while Mother and her baby sister, Fay, listened in strict silence. Klezmer music was good for weddings, but zmirot was good for the soul. Throughout eastern Europe, Hasidism, under the guidance of the rabbi

Baal Shem Tov, was burgeoning. It encouraged Jews to express their piety through the ecstatic fervor of music and dance. The unintended consequence of Yankele's singing may have been that Mother wound up a music lover.

When Mother understood that I wanted to visit Dlugosiodlo, her mood soured. "Don't go there," she warned. "The town probably doesn't even exist anymore, and if it does, there are no Jews left. They killed all the Jews." Mother was one of the fortunate ones able to migrate to the United States, in 1920, before the Holocaust settled like the plague on European Jews. She had stayed in Poland long enough, however, to experience withering anti-Semitism firsthand and to know many people in Dlugosiodlo who were later shipped to the death camps.

I did not take Mother's advice. Not that I didn't understand her feelings — I had heard harrowing stories all my life about her narrow escape from Polish boys trying to stone her in a back alley, about severe hunger, illness, poverty, and the death of two younger brothers. But she also told stories that delighted me. There was cousin Meyer, a mischievous troublemaker who made Mother stand guard while he stole pears from a neighbor's orchard; their old horse, who had to be pushed from behind when going uphill with a load; and Yankele's goat, which followed Mother adoringly wherever she went.

But these stories were a side issue. The Yiddish songs Mother sang to me as a child, the first music I can recall hearing — songs that, whether happy or sad, always made me want to cry — came from Dlugosiodlo. Mother's eyes became liquid when she sang. The rise and fall of her voice seemed to carry mysterious and unnamed truths about the nature of things. The violin lessons I would later have, the inspirational artists I would hear, were vital to my musical education, but I knew instinctively that these songs — songs that the Jews carried across the diaspora in their aching hearts, along with a few belongings on their backs and the Old Testament in their hands — were the hard kernel of musical truth from which all else stemmed. I felt compelled to go to Dlugosiodlo.

A message was waiting for me several weeks later when I arrived at my Warsaw hotel, bleary-eyed after the long trip from New York City:

Dear Arnold,

Dlugosiodlo is a little more than an hour from here and I am happy to drive there with you. I have arranged for a Polish friend to come along as translator. She is only free at three this afternoon so call me if you want to go.

LOVE, ELA

My fatigue fell away. A casual remark on the telephone to my wife's cousin living in Warsaw had led to this. What a lovely thing for Ela to do! A mitzvah, my great-grandfather Yankele would have called it — a good deed.

Promptly at three, Ela Buschbeck pulled up to the hotel with her friend, and soon we were on the main highway headed northeast in the direction of Bialystok. An hour later the first signs for Dlugosiodlo appeared. Its impending reality made me nervous. Mother's stories unwittingly conjured up the idealized image of a rustic village filled with gingerbread houses, crooked streets — a sanitized and aesthetically pleasing poverty straight out of a Chagall painting. The real Dlugosiodlo would not, could not, be like that.

Gently rolling hills dotted with sparse stands of trees flanked our approach. Might this have been where Mother collected wild berries with her girlfriends in late summer? Then, without fanfare, our small, paved road crossed another and we were in the center of the village — a very plain village indeed, where cinder blocks and corrugated iron roofs seemed to rule.

Mother was wrong about Dlugosiodlo. It still existed — a place small enough to traverse by foot in any direction in five or ten minutes. But she was right about the Jews. We asked an old woman passing by about them. "The Jews? Of course I remember the Jews. They gave us bread when we were too poor to buy it from them. They lived over there." She waved her hand toward a group of one-story buildings. A few weathered wooden structures stood out from the cinder blocks. Perhaps Mother had lived in one of them, and perhaps Yankele's horses had gone around and around behind it. I spied a ramshackle barn. Might that have been where Meyer had dragged Mother by the hand when she asked where babies came from? "*That*," said Meyer, triumphantly pointing to a sheep bleating in great pain as it gave birth to a lamb, "is where babies come from, and *that* is what's going to happen to you."

But what about the weddings? The klezmer music? Where exactly did that fiddler mesmerize my mother almost a century ago? These were my burning questions for the old lady. Again she gestured: "Over there. The building was over there, but it's long gone. Everything is gone, even their cemetery." She pointed to the edge of some woods that lay beyond a field a quarter mile away. Gone. Everything gone.

Ela and her friend probably felt sorry for me to have come so far for so little, but to my surprise I was overcome with emotion. The physical signs of Jewish life had completely vanished from this drab little town, but they seemed to hang everywhere in the air, like the pungent smell of my grandmother's carrot and prune tzimmes, which lingered long after the last bite had been eaten. My mother was one of the very last living witnesses to the rich Jewish culture that had spread across eastern Europe. You could read about it in the loving tales of Sholem Aleichem, see it in the evocative photographs of Alter Kacyzne, but I was one of the lucky ones who had heard about it directly from someone who had lived it. I stood there, deeply moved. Dlugosiodlo's Jewish soul survived not in buildings and gravestones but in the memory of Yankele singing at the dinner table, of his horses that went around and around, and of weddings celebrated joyously with klezmer music.

Ironically, if there was any physical sign at all of Jewish life in Dlugosiodlo at that very moment, it was I — not only because I was probably the only Jew there, but because I was a violinist. The Jews gave music a privileged status. Everything from circumcision to marriage was celebrated with music. The Jews even sang on an infamous death march to one of the Nazi concentration camps: *Zog nit az du gehst der letzten weg* — Don't say that you are taking the last road. In the synagogue, the cantor and the congregation sang, and Hebrew prayers themselves were chanted in a lamenting, emotion-laden, singsong voice. Perhaps Jews believed that only music could give these prayers wings strong enough to deliver them directly to God. The music of the cantor, as a representative of his community, spoke for and to its members, bringing out their sense of identity. The cantor was expected to sing not only with religious fervor but with great artistry as well. Sascha Schneider's father, not a religious man, took his son to hear the cantor of Vilna sing the Kol Nidre service on Yom Kippur. His renditions were tinged with the krehktz, a kind of moan, which left the congregation moved to tears. Sascha never forgot it.

Great cantors were undoubtedly the inspiration for a huge number of Jewish musicians in the late nineteenth and twentieth centuries. And perhaps because no other instrument could capture the cantor's voice better than the violin, most of the great violinists of those years were Jewish. Their names spill out of my head: Joseph Joachim, Leopold Auer, Efrem Zimbalist, Mischa Elman, Jascha Heifetz, Nathan Milstein, Toscha Seidel, Bronislaw Huberman, Joseph Szigeti, Yehudi Menuhin, David Oistrakh, Szymon Goldberg, Alexander Schneider, Joseph Roisman, Erica Morini, Isaac Stern, Oscar Shumsky — the list goes on and on. Many of them came out of the shtetls of eastern Europe, and some even had fathers who were klezmer fiddlers — the violin transformed from lowly dance instrument to aristocratic concert violin in a single generation. An old joke has two Jews meeting on the street. One says to the other, "If I were Rothschild, I'd be richer than Rothschild." "What kind of nonsense is this?" the other exclaims. "Rothschild is the richest Jew in the entire world. How could you possibly be richer than him?" "I'll tell you how," says the first Jew. "I'd be richer than Rothschild because first of all, I would have all his money, and second, I'd give violin lessons on the side." Indeed, for the longest time, when I heard the expression "a practicing Jew," an image of a violinist hard at work on his scales and etudes came to mind rather than someone praying at the local synagogue.

On one of my parents' first dates, they went to hear the child prodigy Yehudi Menuhin play the violin in Carnegie Hall. And when Mother was pregnant with me, she attended concerts regularly and played her record of the Beethoven Violin Concerto over and over in the hope that it would instill a love for music and the violin in me. When Dr. Hollombe, our family doctor, heard about this concert hall in the womb, he threw back his head and roared with laughter. "Mrs. Steinhardt," he said, "I doubt if it will do anything for your child, but it will definitely do wonders for you." Mother, of course, had the last laugh. When the nurse looked at my large hands at birth and remarked that I would make a fine bricklayer, Mother responded politely but firmly that no, I was going to be a violinist.

These stories about Mother's single-mindedness were amusing to me at first blush, but also somewhat disturbing. What if I showed no talent, or what if the talent was there but I had no real interest in music? What if, God forbid, I wanted to be a bricklayer? For every child whose parents mastermind his or her trip to the concert hall there are a dozen others — wrecks littering the path — who suffer the effects of parents obsessed with fulfilling their own unanswered dreams rather than the inchoate ones of their progeny. I once heard about a boy who was pushed by his parents into playing the violin, sent to the best teachers and schools, and finally coerced by them into a Carnegie Hall debut. Afterward the young man collected the reviews from his concert — all of them raves — and paid a visit to his parents: "Mom, Dad. Here are the reviews of my Carnegie Hall concert. I hope you enjoy reading them. And here is my violin. Now that I've satisfied your dream for me to be a fine violinist, I'm going back to school to become a lawyer."

My violin-loving parents incarcerated me in not one but two distinct prisons, now that I think about it. One was constructed from their own desires; the other was genetic, in which relatives such as Yankele singing to God and Aaron composing Yiddish melodies took charge of my DNA over a century ago. What choice did I, or for that matter my younger brother, Victor (who became a pianist and composer), really have?

Indeed, the first time I remember hearing a violin, I also remember that my eyes filled with tears. I was no more than five or six, an age when scraped knees or a stern reprimand is more likely to jog the tear ducts. The violin's sound was pure and radiant, adjectives that I might have only dimly understood but whose essence seemed already to reside in my small frame, waiting to be discovered. In my sixty-year-old memory of that day, I wandered into my parents' living room, where they sat listening to one of their many records. The music began with five gentle tympani beats: thump, thump, thump, thump, thump. But to my child's ears those initial thumps could just as easily have been heartbeats, or perhaps the tapping of a hollowed log in a distant glade. Then a whole orchestra of sounds amiably filled the room. In my wondering innocence I coupled the sounds of woodwinds and strings with scenes of nature — forests, gently flowing brooks, and distant mountain ranges.

A family friend, Tartikoff, was probably responsible for those images. Whether Tartikoff was his first or last name I did not know. My parents would say things like "We're late to see Tartikoff" or "I wonder what Tartikoff has in store for us." Later I came to realize that my parents followed a Central European tradition of calling good friends by their last names. Tartikoff, whose first name I never learned, was an amateur painter and music lover. We would usually be treated to his newest painting, inevitably accompanied by music coming out of the radio or record player. On our most recent visit, Tartikoff had showed me his just-finished painting of an imposing mountain range. He called it *Eroica*. Tartikoff must have realized that the name meant nothing to me, for he put his arm around my shoulders and explained that *Eroica* was the name of a symphony by Beethoven. He began to sing the opening theme, all the while tracing with his index finger the mountain's profile. The rise and fall of each were in perfect synchronization. "You see," he said quite proudly, "they are the same." In my youthful estimation, Tartikoff was a genius for having come up with the idea, and the coupling of sound and images stayed with me.

As I listened intently in our living room along with my parents, the music gradually faded to the barest thread of sound, a fragile runway of sorts on which the violin made its first entrance. Starting modestly, almost inconsequentially, and then ascending in ever more emboldened steps, the violin finally burst with joy onto its high plateau and exulted over and over again before fluttering momentarily back to its starting point. Then, with newfound energy, it made a more forceful rush to the high ground and tapered firmly but gracefully to an end. Five more heartbeats or thumps from that distant glade acknowledged the violin's tale.

I stood there transfixed, having no idea that this disembodied sound possessed a name, violin, much less a size, weight, and material. If someone had shown me a real violin at that moment, I would have been amazed that such a small instrument, one no bigger than some of the toys I played with, could produce this array of intoxicating sounds.

The music moved on, orchestra and violin interweaving sometimes peacefully and solemnly, sometimes with deep sadness. I sensed that a story of unusual length and importance was being told, the sounds accompanied almost subliminally before my inner eye by more images from nature. After a time the orchestra dropped away entirely, allowing the violin more freedom to run, pirouette, and hesitate at will. Here I no longer needed Tartikoff's visual aids. The violin seemed independent, self-sufficient, and capable of so many different moods. Sometimes it showed off with a shower of notes, then behaved wickedly in clusters of angry pitches, and just as suddenly melted into angelic beauty.

Then a familiar melody appeared in yet another incarnation. Supported by no more than a skeleton of harmony, the violin played this tune one last time with the bare-bones simplicity of a children's song that I myself might have sung. At this moment I felt my chest involuntarily tighten. The song's childlike nature was not what undid me. It was the melody's transformation, first delivered cheerfully by woodwinds and solo violin, then with aching melancholy by the strings, and now distilled into a simple, unadorned collection of notes played humbly and quietly by the violin alone. The violin's sound was touching, silken, human, almost as if the voice were raised a notch to some level of more abstract beauty. The weight and fullness of this moment, presumably the domain of grownups, unsettled me. There was nothing in my insular world of nurturing parents and neighborhood playmates that prepared me for Beethoven's concerto and his messenger, the violin — nothing unless you took stock in the songs sung long ago in Yiddish by my ancestors and my mother's trips during her pregnancy to the concert hall.

The names of the next-door children and the games we played fell away long ago, but the feeling of that Beethoven moment remains firmly etched. Unlike a photograph, which becomes less clear with each duplication, my response after hearing the concerto innumerable times refuses to budge. And what if I've been tricked by the violin's siren voice? What if my perception has moved a notch every time the final children's song is spun out? It is still my truth, my memory; and memory, as Proust says, is the only reality. Each time the fireworks of the violin cadenza melt into that last hushed refrain, I am invariably transported to a shrouded place where one's deepest feelings reside, unnamed except as a lump in the throat, unseen except for a pair of moist eyes. That is the miracle of music and the power of the violin.

CHAPTER 4

Violin 101

It was the shape of a turkey and the size of a goose, and he
turned it over on its back and rubbed its belly wid a stick,
and och! St. Patrick, how it did squale!
— An Irishman describing the violin he heard at a fair

I DON'T REMEMBER starting the violin. I don't even remember asking to play. A curious amnesia cloaks the arrival of a violin and bow in my six-year-old life. My vivid emotional encounter with the Beethoven Violin Concerto some months earlier undoubtedly set the scene for the instrument, but I have no recollection of any lessons that first year. The violin's sweet sound certainly caught my attention, but going to the trouble of learning to play it must have seemed a squandering of time meant for more important things: playing hide-and-seek with my neighborhood friends, chasing monarch and swallowtail butterflies that settled on the bushes in front of our apartment house, and playing with the bow and arrows my parents had recently given me for my birthday. This was the bow I adored, and this is the bow that remains in my memory, rather than the one linked to the violin.

I do know from my parents that Mr. Singer, the music teacher at Logan Street Elementary School, came to our door and asked whether I would like to study an instrument and play it in the school orchestra. There was no question, of course, what that instrument would be. The violin was provided by the Los Angeles public school system for a two-dollar deposit.

I regret not having even a lingering, faded impression of my first lesson with Mr. Singer. He must have begun by showing me the violin, probably a "quarter-size," and by describing its four pillars of sound, the E, A, D, and G strings. What did it feel like to hold the violin, reach around the instrument's neck with my little paw, and tuck it up under my chin for the first time? And what was my initial sensation of holding the bow — that feather-light wooden stick — in my right hand and trying to draw its horsehair across the instrument's strings? My memory of these first halting steps in what was to be a lifelong journey has simply vanished.

Sentimental parents bronze their baby's first shoes, but to the best of my knowledge one does not do that to violins and bows. At the end of the school year, my parents returned the violin and got their two dollars back. Instruments of that era in the California school system were usually mass-produced in Czechoslovakia. They were plainly made and cheaply varnished, but they did the job. My violin could easily have been used by dozens of beginning students before and after me. The irony was that many such violins sported labels inside that were copies of the ones found in genuine Stradivarius instruments; *Antonius Stradivarius*

Cremonensis, fecibat Anno 1715 was a typical example. Without re-gard for the famous violinmaker's Italian heritage, *Made in Czecho-slovakia* was often shamelessly printed underneath, perhaps in the spirit of a foreign subsidiary to the parent company.

Although memories of my Czech Stradivarius have disap-peared, I take some comfort in knowing that I am not the only musician afflicted with juvenile instrument amnesia. The violin-ist Ida Bieler once told me that when she was accepted as a stu-dent by Nathan Milstein, the Russian virtuoso, he said, "There are three facets of your technique you need to work on. Two I can help you with, but you'll have to go elsewhere for the third. That's the one my mother taught me when I started violin lessons with her, and I don't remember how she did it or what she said."

I assumed that those first fiddle memories of mine were as irretrievable as Milstein's, unless I underwent deep hypnosis. But in the summer of 2000, Roberta Guaspari, a brilliant violin teacher who works with youngsters in Harlem, asked me to serve as a guinea pig. Her organization, Opus 118 Harlem School of Mu-sic, is dedicated to making music lessons available to schoolchil-dren. Roberta was hosting a string institute workshop for forty music teachers, and she asked me to submit to a lesson as a so-called left-handed violinist in order to demonstrate her teaching methods with a beginner: me. Anyone who has tried to write a sentence or throw a ball "wrong-handed" knows that all previous experience is virtually useless, and playing the violin and bow with opposite hands is no different. The right and left sides of our brains apparently refuse to communicate with each other. As an active member of Opus 118's board of directors, I would have been hard-pressed to refuse Roberta, but there was also a hidden at-traction in the prospect of making a fool out of myself in public.

Roberta was giving me the opportunity to have my first violin lesson all over again, fifty-eight years later. Naturally, I accepted.

Roberta began the class by having several of her youngest students play "Twinkle, Twinkle, Little Star." After an admirable performance, she told the teachers, "I hope to give these kids the tools to play the violin and to make a beautiful sound on it. They're going to be so glad if I succeed. It's just as hard as ever to get kids to focus and accept the need for discipline, but they need to believe in their heart that they can do it. Your part as a teacher is to give that child the confidence that he can learn anything — math, reading. The violin for some is a tool, a vehicle."

A teacher asked Roberta how to start the very first lesson. "I tell them: open the case. I talk about the latches. Then I play for them. Nothing goes fast. You have to tell them how many times to do something. They don't know anything. Do that exercise seventeen times, I tell them." Standing off to the side, I wondered whether Mr. Singer had shown me the latches on my case.

Roberta motioned to me. "I'm going to teach Arnold to play the violin on the wrong shoulder. He really doesn't know how to do this." I picked up the violin and bow clumsily and waited. "Let's see if you can do it well or not. You'll do everything I tell you. You are floppy, completely floppy. You're my puppet now."

The teachers tittered. This was the approach Roberta used successfully with her five-, six-, and seven-year-olds. I smiled. Roberta and I might play at being puppeteer and puppet, but as a grownup and especially as a professional violinist, I would be in charge of my own arms, hands, and fingers.

"OK. Go down your neck with the violin. Let it feel right under your chin, only don't move your torso, Arnold. Actually, you need to come down to your shoulder. Land the helicopter. Now relax."

But that was the problem. I stood with my elbow and wrist in a completely unnatural position. The violin felt like a foreign object in my right hand, and with every command I felt it become more alien. My assumption that I would have at least *some* control of the situation was clearly misguided, and I stiffened with panic.

Roberta looked me over coolly. "This hand feels tight. Arnold, you gotta loosen up." The teachers broke out laughing.

"Easy for you to say, Roberta," I muttered. The lesson was no longer a game.

Roberta showed me how to put each finger down on the string. "There. Gotta aim the first finger at your nose so the fingernail points . . . Don't squeeze it, just feel that it's on a balance beam. That looks good." That did feel more comfortable, I had to admit. "Now put two down, OK, and three. Leave your pinkie relaxed. You don't look half bad, Arnold. Now hold the bow against your belly and then lift it up. Put your fingers over the bow. Make a floppy waterfall. Watch the wrist. Flop the dinosaur." Roberta was adamant about the way beginners should hold the violin and bow. "Look through the opening in the bow made by your fingers. That's your tickle tunnel. Roll the bow away from the bridge a little bit. OK. Good."

By this time, feeling quite helpless, I had no choice but to follow Roberta's instructions slavishly. This puppeteer had a sixty-four-year-old puppet on her strings. Roberta played a tune to the rhythm of "I like chocolate ice cream" and then nodded for me to join in. Obediently, I pulled the bow back and forth across the strings, expecting almost nothing in my diminished condition. Strangled sounds came out of the violin — but they *were* in the correct rhythm. "I did it. I *did* it," I squealed, very pleased with myself.

"You don't look half bad, Arnold."

"Yes, but I'm stuck."

Roberta stepped back and regarded me with a professional eye. "Put your bow back in your belly, Arnold. Put your feet together. And now, take a bow." The teachers clapped, and I was on my way as a left-handed violinist.

My first lesson with Roberta — strictly speaking, my *second* first lesson — failed to revive my memories of the first first with Mr. Singer, but it did capture the strange feel of beginning violin. The motions of both arms are quite foreign to everyday life. Nothing else calls for me to twist my left arm up and to the side, and I don't iron a shirt with my right arm at eye level. When people mime playing the violin in jest, they rarely look normal, because the motions are so unnatural. The Robertas and Mr. Singers of the world are severely challenged every time they teach that first stretch of fingers around the strings and the skating glide of the bow's horsehair across them.

Roberta's images of waterfalls, dinosaurs, and tickle tunnels did serve to revive long-forgotten memories of lessons with my second violin teacher, Carl Moldrem, a well-known children's teacher in the Los Angeles area. By the time I got to him I was a big seven-year-old and had graduated to a half-size violin. "Watch your mouse hole," Moldrem warned when I held the violin so tightly that there was no space between my hand and the instrument's neck. It was hard to relax in such a contorted position. Moldrem had a special harness devised for tense left thumbs that refused to stay still. He fitted part of a glove to the guilty digit and tied it with a string to the nearest peg. A fellow student, Richard Maury, remembers that his grandmother was furious to discover a piece of her best leather gloves missing.

Moldrem was also clever about teaching music's basic rhythms. Dividing a whole note into two half notes and a half note into two quarter notes was not hard for me to grasp, but the idea of a triplet — three notes played within one quarter note — sent me into a panic. It seemed impossible to use my fingers like scissors in order to cut a unit of time into three sections — three exactly equal sections. Mr. Moldrem put his hand on my shoulder soothingly. "Think of the notes as fruits, Arnie. A long note is a pear, two shorter ones are an apple, four fast ones are a watermelon, and as for the triplet, why, that's just a pineapple." The forbidding triplet was instantly transformed into something benign. It was easy to say *pineapple*. Had I not done it many times in my short life? I mouthed the word *pineapple* as I peered anxiously at the triplet figure printed on the music page before me and then dared to play. The triplet came out well enough for Moldrem to compliment me and go on to the next subject. In Moldrem's rhythm-by-fruit world, the lyrics to Cole Porter's "Night and day, you are the one" would simply be "Apple pear, pineapple pear."

By the time I began studying with Mr. Moldrem, I must already have learned to put my four fingers down on the open strings and play first-position notes, for he soon assigned me, one by one, successive volumes of *A Tune a Day.* Melodies such as "Go Down, Moses" and "Drink to Me Only with Thine Eyes" fascinated me because as short as they were, they told a complete story, with a beginning, a middle, and an end. To this day, if I hum to myself "Drink to Me Only with Thine Eyes," it has a rightness about it that defies alteration: Part A, rising and falling, Part B, literally repeating Part A for emphasis, Part C veering off in a new direction yet rhythmically tied to Parts A and B, and Part D, repeating Part A for one last time — a melody governed by an incal-

culable yet very real logic of up and down, of motion and repose. I
would come to recognize that sense of inevitability, of iron-clad
form, in all my musical touchstones, whether "Taps," "America
the Beautiful," or the iconic melody of Beethoven's Ninth Symphony.

But just because I responded to the perfect little melodies of *A
Tune a Day*, that did not mean I could play them well. I knew how
to put my fingers on the strings, but little anarchists that they
were, they wouldn't necessarily land in the right places. There
were no markers on the fingerboard to guide me to each note, and
the consequences of my fingers wandering on this uncharted sea
were often painful to anyone in earshot. Once, years later, at a
benefit concert, I stood backstage with a member of the Kingston
Trio. As we chatted, he with his guitar, I with my violin, he looked
down at the violin and shook his head. "How can you play without frets?" he asked. "The person who thought up an instrument
without frets was like the first cow who looked at grass and said, *I
wonder if that stuff might be good to eat?*"

As if in response to the violin's fretless nature, Mr. Moldrem
placed strips of white tape in the places where notes should be, so
that I could see as well as hear, and finally feel for good measure.
But even though I was improving, the sound I coaxed out of my
instrument was far removed from what I heard on my parents'
violin records. The stick I held in my right hand slipped and
slid uncontrollably one moment and then seemed to smother the
sound the next. Mr. Moldrem showed me a kind of secret highway
on each string, where a magical sound existed, waiting to be found
by the bow. On either side of this treacherously narrow road lay
danger and disaster. Even in my second year of study, I often
brought forth a series of strange squawks and strangled sounds

when I drew the bow across the strings, but with Moldrem's guidance I began to produce a decent tone. Occasionally I would stumble onto the secret highway for a moment, only to have it inexplicably vanish. All the violinists in my parents' record collection — Jascha Heifetz, Mischa Elman, Fritz Kreisler, and Nathan Milstein — knew the highway's secret, although I could already tell that each one traveled on it in a slightly different manner.

The culmination of my first year with Moldrem was his annual student concert, in which I performed themes from both the Beethoven Violin Concerto and the Brahms First Symphony. Unfortunately, Moldrem failed to warn me about stage fright. One by one, he singled out students huddled backstage and ordered them out onto the stage. I was seized by an unfamiliar and intense terror as my turn to walk out alone into this ominous wasteland approached. To my mind, it seemed like an execution. Looking desperately for relief, I begged the woman overseeing us for a glass of water. When she gave it to me, my hand was trembling so badly that I dropped it on the tile floor. The glass shattered, and just at that moment Moldrem pointed to me: my turn had arrived. I shook my head. A flurry of words followed as Moldrem and his assistant coaxed, cajoled, and finally lured me onto the stage. The assorted group of parents and friends who came to see their darlings perform clapped enthusiastically. As I looked around the little union hall filled with smiling faces, my fear fell away. Rather than an execution, this was a chance to show these people what I could do. I launched into the Brahms symphony with gusto and played it surprisingly well.

Soon Moldrem was introducing me, age eight, to vibrato — the slight shake of the left hand that somehow breathes life into the violin's sound. At first I couldn't understand the combination of motions he wanted me to make. Moldrem patiently explained, demonstrated, and manipulated my arm, hand, and fingers back and forth mechanically. Even when I began to grasp the separate components of this gesture, I still could not combine them in anything other than an irregular wobble. For weeks my dutiful attempts seemed only to ruin the simple but adequate sound I was already able to produce. How frustrating! The piano didn't vibrate; neither did the clarinet. Why should the violin have to? But one day the necessary elements of muscle strength and coordination unexpectedly coalesced, as if several parties in a dispute had finally reached agreement, and miraculously I now possessed an almost even and pleasing vibrato. Learning to ride a bicycle a few months later gave me the same kind of thrill — a sense of things coming together as if by magic. Not to say that my vibrato was beautiful — I had no inkling of the infinite varieties of speed and width that an artist-violinist employs. But as making vibrato became increasingly comfortable, I succeeded in steering more often onto that highway Moldrem spoke of. Now I could play the melodies he assigned me with a certain amount of expression.

At about the age of nine, I graduated to a new book, simply called *Standard Violin Pieces*. Its selections were longer and more involved and had piano accompaniment. Simonetti's "Madrigal," one of my first assignments, was a lovely melody followed by a somewhat contrasting little middle section and ending with a coda reminiscent of the beginning — perfection, in my eyes, on a much grander scale than *A Tune a Day* could ever offer. At this point I realized something that I am still at a loss to explain: music engendered emotions, and different groups of notes elicited different feelings. Why did "Drink to Me Only with Thine Eyes" make me nostalgic, Simonetti's "Madrigal" content, "Taps" solemn, "America the Beautiful" upbeat and hopeful, and the "Ode to Joy" recklessly happy? Music was a receptacle of powerful moods and emotions, a fact constantly driven home by my parents, who would call out for me to play with more feeling if my practicing sounded lackluster. "Old songs are more than tunes," the playwright Ben Hecht once said. "They are little houses in which our hearts once lived."

Since my father usually worked during the day, Mother was the one who took me after school to my lessons with Mr. Moldrem at G. Schirmer's music store in downtown Los Angeles. Afterward we often had lunch at Clifton's Cafeteria, a few blocks away. Without the tables and chairs, Clifton's could have served as a set for a Tarzan movie. It was decorated in a jungle motif, with grottos, palm trees, and waterfalls. If my luck held, we would find a spot to eat in one of those enticing grottos. An electric organ, ensconced in a bamboo cage on the second floor, was barely audible above the sound of falling water.

One day Mother and I noticed a sign posted on the bamboo cage: TALENT CONTEST EVERY THURSDAY AFTERNOON. We climbed the steps and spoke to the very plump lady who played the organ week after week. Telling us it didn't matter that I was only ten years old, she encouraged me to enter. Several weeks later, when my lesson fell on a Thursday, we rushed to Clifton's immediately afterward. Accompanied by the nice lady on the organ and the sound of a fake waterfall, I played Monte's "Czardas," an intermediate-level show-off piece. To my amazement, I won a prize of five dollars.

Though I was thrilled with the money and the recognition, the prize marked no turning point. My career goal of the moment was to become either a fireman or, better still, a fighter pilot. After my parents tucked me in at night, I would pull the sheets up around my eyes to simulate goggles and became Ace Steinhardt, World War II performer of daredevil and heroic airborne acts. The fantasy always ended the same way: I dismounted from my airplane triumphantly and kissed the girl who stepped forward out of the adoring crowd — as it happened, Rosemary, the girl in my fourth-grade class whom I had a crush on.

Even if I had taken the violin more seriously, there was a significant barrier to a possible career in music: I hated to practice. The idea that the neighborhood kids were outside playing while I was condemned to violin prison was more than I could bear. I took every step within my power to cut my sentence short or even avoid practicing entirely. If my designated practice time was four to four-thirty, I would move the clock on the mantle back five minutes when I started and forward five minutes twenty minutes later, saving the grand total of ten odious minutes of practice. If my parents were occupied in another room, I would surreptitiously trade comic books for *Standard Violin Pieces* on the music stand and read about the heroic exploits of Superman or Captain Marvel while improvising Rubinstein's "Melody in F" as best I could. As my parents uncovered each ruse, they would scold me and I would cry in repentance. I did love the violin, and my parents considered music important in my education, but as they repeatedly said, they were not going to throw out their hard-earned money on a *vilde chaya,* the Yiddish term for a wild animal, who resisted practicing as if it were the plague.

My parents were right, of course, about their *vilde chaya.* No matter how many times they threatened to stop lessons and no matter how many times I promised to mend my ways, playing in the fields near our house with my friends was always more attractive than practicing. I, a ten-year-old child, stood guilty of being undisciplined and of lacking the dedication necessary to become an accomplished violinist. My parents, however, understand all too well that though I was only ten, my biological clock was ticking away. If certain neural connections had not been made and muscular development had not occurred by this time, no amount of later practice would make up for it. This was war, and my parents were winning. They were the ones who insisted on practice five minutes every day when I began studying the violin, then ten, then fifteen, and once I had graduated to a three-quarter-sized instrument, a whole half-hour each and every day.

The fact that I could play Monte's "Czardas" well enough to win a prize meant that certain things were already in place. I moved the fingers of my left hand quickly and quite accurately, and I could shift positions decently. I was also able to draw a nice sound and make the bow bounce when fast passages needed to sparkle. Mom and Dad kept my nose to the grindstone, and Mr. Moldrem, with his deft touch and quiet ways, taught me well. Together they produced a solid little violinist. "Your son has talent, Mrs. Steinhardt," my teacher assured Mother after she complained about my lack of interest in practicing. "But what can I and my husband do to make him work?" she implored. Moldrem, a self-appointed teacher of children, possessed a rare quality — knowing when to let a student go. "Your son needs to have someone light a fire under him, Mrs. Steinhardt," he said. "I think he needs a new teacher."

CHAPTER 5

Mischa, Jascha, Toscha, Sascha

Moldrem's parting words must have stuck in my parents' minds. They chose Peter Meremblum as my next teacher, a fiery Russian who had studied at the Imperial Conservatory in Petrograd with the great Hungarian pedagogue Leopold Auer. Being a student of Auer's gave Meremblum tremendous cachet, since Auer had taught some of the most famous violinists of the era — Efrem Zimbalist, Mischa Elman, Jascha Heifetz, Toscha Seidel, and Nathan Milstein. As a sought-after teacher, Meremblum commanded such a high fee that my father, earning a modest income as a diamond setter, could afford only one lesson every other week.

We dubbed Meremblum "Professor Half Auer." Unlike kindly Mr. Moldrem, he flew off the handle frequently. At my very first lesson, he shook his head unhappily while I played. "No, no, no. Out from tunn." Tunn? I had no idea what that meant. To make matters worse, the man was practically yelling at me. I regarded Meremblum nervously. "Out from tunn!" he repeated, even louder, this time pointing to his right ear. Ah. Out of tune. Flustered, I offered a lame excuse. "Mr. Meremblum, I think it's my violin. My violin's out of tune." Meremblum gaped at me, grabbed the violin from my hands, turned the pegs willy-nilly up and down so that the instrument was truly off pitch, proceeded to play the passage in question pristinely, and then handed the violin back to me without comment.

Everything about Meremblum was exotic — his temperamental outbursts, his mangled English served up with a thick Russian accent, even the smell of his after-shave lotion, Aqua Velva, which he applied not only to his face but also to his violin fingerboard as a rosin remover. But above all he was an excellent teacher who pushed my violin technique forward and introduced me to new repertoire. The student concertos of Seitz, Accolay, and Bériot that Moldrem deemed necessary for my development were replaced by music of enough import to be heard on the concert stage — Saint-Saëns's *Havanaise,* the Bruch and Mendelssohn violin concertos, and Wieniawski's *Scherzo Tarantelle.*

Shortly after I began studying with Meremblum, my parents took me to hear Mischa Elman play a recital in Philharmonic Hall, across from Pershing Square in downtown Los Angeles. My parents revered Elman. When we listened to his records at home, an aching melancholy laced his playing — playing that reminded me of the way Mother sang Yiddish songs. As we awaited his entrance onstage, I imagined how he would look. He would be handsome, perhaps, but certainly imposing, and with a shock of wavy, long hair that my parents might deem "artistic." This was how the conductor Leopold Stokowski looked in the foot-high plaster-of-Paris replica of him that stood on the bookcase in our living room — his arms and long, spindly fingers poised sensitively in the act of leading an orchestra, his head lifted nobly as if contemplating the meaning of life itself. Elman would have to look just as impressive. Didn't all artists look the way they played?

But the man who finally emerged was short, bald, and homely, and he could have been mistaken for the house manager about to make an announcement. Elman held a violin and bow in his hands and bobbed up and down comically as he acknowledged the audience's applause. Another man trailed him onto the stage, deferring to him as if he were Elman's butler, and sat down inconspicuously at the piano. Elman tuned his violin, lifted it to his chin, and together they began to play, Elman weaving awkwardly both sideways and up and down. How disappointing that he wasn't more like Stokowski! I looked around curiously at the packed house of people listening raptly. No one seemed amused by his demeanor. One phrase after another emanated from Elman's violin and wafted across the hall to our cheap seats in the very back. I had never heard a great violinist in the flesh before. Elman's playing was ravishing, but his sound itself commanded center stage — a sound like fine lacquer that you could look into without ever quite seeing bottom. His sound was legendary. His father and Jascha Heifetz's, both violinists themselves, were once overheard bragging about their sons. "My Jascha's technique is so perfect that when he plays, all other violinists sound like children," boasted the elder Heifetz. "But that's just technique," countered Papa Elman. "Sound is what's important, and my Mischa's sound is to melt the heart. Take pizzicato, for example. When others pluck the string you get *plink,* but with my Mischa, what you hear is *plunnnk*."

Only one specific work from that recital remains in my memory. The piano was moved to the side of the stage and Elman reemerged alone to play Bach's Chaconne for unaccompanied violin. Bach's music was not new to me; Meremblum had recently assigned me the Sonata in G Minor, but learning it had been far from a rewarding experience. The music seemed dense, forbidding, and bewildering to look at on the printed page — a mass of thickly grouped notes that twisted and turned like a nest of worms suddenly uncovered. I could not make sense of the sonata, and Meremblum, probably realizing that he had given it to me too soon, quickly went on to something less difficult. Elman, looking even less imposing than before as he stood alone on a stage bereft of pianist and piano, launched into the Chaconne. He played a series of chords with sweeping bow strokes that made the single violin sound almost like an entire orchestra. The music seemed to have a pattern that endlessly renewed itself. At the outset it was solemn and stately, as if a procession were taking place, later hushed and intimate, sometimes angry and even defiant, and finally, with the return of the opening chords, triumphant. When it came to an end, Philharmonic Hall erupted in applause and Elman received a standing ovation. The instrument I reluctantly practiced every day — deliverer of sweet tunes and showpieces — had been transformed suddenly into a veritable force of nature. I strained to catch a glimpse of Elman through the wall of grownups clapping wildly in front of me. How strange. For the past quarter of an hour he had turned himself into a sorcerer, but now that music no longer streamed from his violin, he was once again merely a bald little man, bowing awkwardly to the cheering public like a well-oiled puppet.

Later, safely tucked into my bed, I felt the concert whirling around in my head. Mischa Elman was certainly a magician and the Chaconne his magic brew — but the violin! Elman's violin, hardly bigger than the one I practiced on, was able to play on my emotions as if I myself were an instrument. Being a fighter pilot was beginning to lose its allure. About to nod off, I wondered what it would be like to be a concert violinist standing on the stage and performing the Chaconne.

After Elman's concert, I gradually rearranged my priorities. Superman and Captain Marvel comic books lost their dominance on my music stand, and I began to practice on my own initiative. Now when relatives and friends of my parents asked me what I wanted to be when I grew up, an answer rolled with naive ease off my tongue: "Concert violinist." Other than playing the Chaconne in Philharmonic Hall, I wasn't sure what being a concert violinist entailed, but saying it gave me a sense of purpose and pride.

Around this time, at the end of one of my lessons, Meremblum got up from his chair, peered at my three-quarter-sized instrument, and said, "Why you play toy wioleen?" He made a face. "Bed. Very bed." It was true. My violin had a small, nasal sound that I had accepted for years but that now grated on my nerves. Meremblum picked up his own violin, placed it under my chin, and motioned for me to play. Tentatively I drew the bow across the strings, my arms just barely long enough to handle the violin's added length. A strong, full sound emerged. Meremblum nodded in approval. "Ees good. Fool size, fool sond."

With Meremblum's help, a grownup's violin arrived in our

house some weeks later. I was proud to be playing such a big violin, the size of Mischa Elman's. Full size, full sound: when I resumed work on the Mendelssohn Violin Concerto, my latest assignment, each phrase had just a little more authority, just a little more boldness than I could muster before.

My parents incessantly pointed out the importance of practice. They had the habit of trotting out appropriate clichés. "Practice makes perfect," they reminded me. "One percent inspiration, ninety-nine percent perspiration." The maxim attributed to the great Polish pianist Paderewski impressed me most of all: "If I don't practice one day, I know it; if I don't practice two days, musicians know it; and if I don't practice three days, the whole world knows it."

I now grudgingly admitted that, yes, the more I practiced, the better I would probably sound. The results of my practicing could easily be tracked at school. When I first auditioned for the Bancroft Junior High School orchestra, Maurice Ives, its conductor, judged me proficient enough to sit next to the concertmaster, Clementina Hewitt — unquestionably the school's best violinist. Any change in the seating order was then decided at regular intervals by so-called challenges. A player could bid for another's seat at challenge time. From day one I coveted Clementina's seat. Not just the public acknowledgment that its occupant was the best violinist there, sitting proudly at the very front of the violin section and directly under Mr. Ives's nose, but the title itself: *concertmaster.* What status and glamour *that* carried! Foolishly, I challenged Clementina at the first opportunity. She accepted, we both played, and the orchestra voted overwhelmingly for her to keep her seat. Clem was simply a better violinist than I was. As the semester progressed, though, driven by the sense of competition, I continued my quest, and although Clem inevitably won, the vote began to narrow. Even with a full school load, I was able to practice one to two hours a day, three hours on weekends, and it showed. Not long before the end of school that year, the vote tipped just barely in my favor. For the next couple of weeks I basked in the glory. Concertmaster! Clem, still sitting next to me but now on my left side, took her loss like a good sport. But when one last challenge came before summer vacation, she fought back. Playing unusually well, she recaptured the concertmaster's chair.

Smarting, that summer I took my parents' adage "practice makes perfect" to heart and began to put in four to five hours daily, a regime I could never have endured before. When school opened again in September, my playing had improved so much that I was voted concertmaster by a hefty margin. Not that there was any question of Clementina's ability. She became an outstanding violinist and now plays in the Buffalo Philharmonic Orchestra.

One reason for my new work ethic was that concerts were actually beginning to come my way. My parents belonged to several Jewish charity organizations that clamored for music to spice up their regular fundraising events. What could be better than having the fiddling son of one of its members play after the rice pudding but before the appeal for money? Ernest Bloch's *Baal Shem Suite (Three Pictures of Hasidic Life)* was a favorite at these functions. Hasidism — literally, "pietism" — and its father, Israel ben Eliezer (c. 1700–1760), better known as the Baal Shem Tov ("Master of the Good Name"), believed that unlearned men could approach God directly through prayer and worship. Cleaving to

God, as it was called, was a joyous, ecstatic experience. God was everywhere and to be found in every act of life: prayer, the book of knowledge, song, even dancing with the Torah. When I began practicing the *Baal Shem Suite*'s second movement, called the Nigun, Dad interrupted me in midphrase by pounding his fist on the dining room table. "Two thousand years of Jewish suffering are in those notes. The Nigun is a cry to God himself. You must put more *feeling* into it!" This self-proclaimed atheist was pleading with me to talk to God!

But in truth the Nigun (which means "song" in Hebrew) was its own best teacher. It lamented, it wailed, it suffered, it despaired, and soon I began to feel the Jews' tragic but inspiring story. I had never tried to speak directly to God, but the violin seemed the perfect vehicle. I began to learn how I could use it to cry, to sob, to sing, to moan by altering the speed and width of my vibrato and occasionally slipping slowly from one note to another in the style of the great cantors of old. Dad maintained that my performance of the Nigun would be successful only if people in the audience cried. Later that summer, after I played the Nigun at a benefit for the young state of Israel, he came backstage and told me that he had cried himself. His reaction was cause for elation, yet I also felt a vague unease with what I had just accomplished. A large but ill-defined presence suddenly resided in me, with unimaginable power. What other emotions might it unleash when I played the violin?

With the growing belief that I might someday become a serious musician, one particular virtuoso began to infiltrate and finally dominate my evolution as a young violinist. Born in Vilna, Lithuania, on February 2, 1901, Jascha Heifetz first studied the violin with his father, Reuven Heifetz, and later with Leopold Auer. Heifetz made his American debut in Carnegie Hall in 1918. Word must have spread about the young firebrand, for everybody who was anybody in music turned out for the concert. During intermission, Mischa Elman turned to the pianist Leopold Godowsky and complained, "It's hot in here, isn't it?" which prompted the now famous retort, "Not for pianists."

My new teacher, Meremblum, had gone to school with Heifetz in Russia, and their friendship continued decades later halfway around the world in Los Angeles. (Heifetz even appeared with Meremblum's orchestra in the 1939 film *They Shall Have Music*). Hardly a lesson went by without Meremblum's making a comment about him. "Heifetz practices six to eight hours a day. Heifetz plays two hours of scales before he even looks at a piece of music." The Heifetz campaign continued at home. My parents urged me to work harder so that I might become the next Heifetz, and when I slacked off they shook their heads sadly. How could I expect to be a Heifetz when I wasted time playing ball? At student concerts, "He's no Heifetz" from my dad was the kiss of death for an untalented fiddler.

The steady flow of comments was a testament to the breathtaking scope of Heifetz's playing. The violin is so difficult to play that only a precious few have truly mastered it. Their brilliance and appealing musical personalities fill concert halls with eager listeners. Yet Heifetz had something beyond this. They say that an accident takes place when several unlikely things converge at the very same moment. Heifetz was the most perfect example of a statistical improbability, or better said, a divine accident — the confluence of an ideal violinist's body, an uncommon musical gift, and an obsessive need for perfection at every level. But there was more. Heifetz seemed to have the nervous system of a humming-bird: he could execute the minutest details at breakneck speed, shift moods in a split second, and recklessly dare all where others were prudently cautious. I listened to his recordings in disbelief. It was simply not possible for a human being to play with such wizardry. I despaired of ever even remotely approaching his level.

For a brief time as a teenager, though, I dared to think other-wise. I liked to play a little game with Mr. Heifetz, putting my as-signed music on the stand and his rendition on the record player. It might be any one of a number of pieces I worked on — Tchai-kovsky's Violin Concerto, Saint-Saëns's *Havanaise,* or Sarasate's "Gypsy Airs." First I listened to Heifetz, shaking my head in won-der. Then I practiced the same piece myself. At the outset, the gap between us seemed too immense to cross, but with work I im-proved, and with improvement my spirits soared. I was catching up. Why, I was almost as good as Heifetz! Time to swagger over to the record player and listen to him again — Heifetz, whose fingers moved so effortlessly, whose phrasing was like liquid mercury, whose playing seared with white heat one moment and teased playfully the next. "Jascha, Jascha," I muttered despairingly as the record ended. Heifetz reigned over every would-be violinist, in-spiring the industrious, crushing hope for those not supremely gifted, and stalking the lazy.

Finally I heard Heifetz in person, on the very same stage where Elman had captivated me years earlier. The contrast be-tween the two was remarkable. Heifetz, a small, slender, immacu-lately attired man, stepped onto the stage with a minimum of gesture but the bearing of royalty. He did not accept our welcoming applause with deep bows as Elman had. He merely tilted his head in our direction. As he stood in front of the Los Angeles Philharmonic Orchestra waiting for his solo entrance, he hardly moved, and even when he began to play, there were no excessive gestures, no grandstanding for the public, only those motions absolutely necessary to play the violin. Visually, Heifetz gave off a feeling of reserve, even aloofness, and yet the perfection of his delivery and the range of expression were astonishing. Heifetz challenged the most difficult passages by rushing headlong into them — a display of fearlessness that made my heart beat faster. Yet the lyrical moments had such tenderness and sensitivity that I wanted to weep. It was a performance of fire and shimmering light delivered in a container made out of ice. At the end of the concert, I stood in line to shake Heifetz's hand in his dressing room. One by one he greeted his devotees with the same cool reserve he had displayed earlier onstage. When my turn to greet him came, I was momentarily tongue-tied. What could I possibly say to the man-god who now regarded me almost clinically? Then I found my voice and blurted out that I too played the violin. The barest trace of a smile crossed Heifetz's face as he shook my hand. "Good lawk," he said.

Meremblum assigned me a new concerto at about that time, the Symphonie Espagnol, by Edouard Lalo. No less than Peter Ilich Tchaikovsky wrote in 1878 to his patron, Mme. Von Meck, "Do you know the Symphonie Espagnol by the French composer Lalo? The piece has been recently brought out by the very modern violinist, Sarasate. It is for solo violin and orchestra, and consists of five independent movements, based upon Spanish idioms. It is so fresh and light, and contains piquant rhythms and melodies which are beautifully harmonized." I loved the Symphonie Espagnol, especially after listening to Nathan Milstein's recording over and over to gain some idea of the piece. Milstein's playing had an effortless brilliance, suave and playful, yet it was hard to parlay what I heard into a conception of my own. If I had only thought about the concerto's title or examined Milstein's record album cover, displaying two Spanish dancers and a bucolic rural scene embedded in the outline of a violin, I would have been better served. Instead I showed up for my lesson more preoccupied with the notes themselves than with the irresistible melodies and colorful harmonies that laced the work.

Meremblum considered it his duty to teach me how to get into the music's character. "Filling. You mawst play wit filling," he insisted. Impulsive mood changes, hot-blooded brilliance, outbursts of reckless freedom, moments of coquetry and flirtation — these were the qualities that he tried to draw out of me. Yes, play the violin well, he insisted, but Symphonie Espagnol would rise or fall with my ability to step out of modern American clothes and into those of nineteenth-century Spain.

Eventually I did begin to play with "filling" — enough so that Meremblum gave me the green light to audition for the Los Angeles Philharmonic Youth Concerts as soloist. When I was chosen by the orchestra's conductor, Alfred Wallenstein, to play the last movement of Symphonie Espagnol shortly after my fourteenth birthday, it was official acknowledgment that I was truly on my way to becoming a concert violinist. The Symphonie's last movement, a lively tarantella, begins with sounds akin to the pealing of bells followed by a bustling syncopated rhythm that repeats over and over again, first rising gradually in volume, then subsiding until the violin joins in to frolic with the orchestra. I waited for my entrance on the very stage where both Elman and Heifetz had played.

The Philharmonic performance was a significant benchmark in my young musical life — one for which Meremblum deserved a great deal of credit. I had learned a lot from him in four years, but much of what he said at lessons was becoming old hat. My parents began to look for a new teacher for me. In all fairness, four years with any teacher tests the limits of what he or she can offer in the way of technique and musicianship. Perhaps a new teacher would emphasize some of the same basic things — good intonation, clean shifting from one position to another, a healthy sound — but Meremblum played solely as a studio musician for films, and my parents and I thought it was time to find someone with the perspective of a concert performer, who could introduce me to another level of artistry and the mysterious craft of communicating with an audience.

Two attractive candidates presented themselves: Sascha Jacobson, an outstanding violinist with a solid reputation as both musician and teacher, and Toscha Seidel, the fiery virtuoso, said to be Leopold Auer's favorite pupil, now concertmaster of Paramount Studios Orchestra. George and Ira Gershwin's tongue-in-cheek song "Mischa, Jascha, Toscha, Sascha," about four Russian violinists who acquired fame in the United States, was becoming my own personal story. Mischa inaugurated my violin journey, Jascha provided inspiration in transit, and now either Sascha or Toscha would lead me further along the path.

It is hard to know what kind of violinist I would have become if I had studied with Jacobson. In my adolescent state, the choice of a good teacher and one well matched to my needs was crucial. But what were my needs? I had no idea, and my parents, music lovers, to be sure, but untrained in the world of violin pedagogy, knew no more than I did. Certainly Seidel was glamorous. Featured on a number of Hollywood soundtracks, he had recorded the violin solos for the film *Intermezzo,* starring Leslie Howard and Ingrid Bergman. When we listened to Seidel's recording of the movie's signature theme, I imagined that the disk would melt from the heat of his glowing tone. The record, an irresistible siren song, came to an end and my parents called Seidel.

Born in Odessa on November 4, 1900, Toscha Seidel began learning the violin from his uncle at the age of three. In 1912 he entered the violin class of Leopold Auer at the St. Petersburg Conservatory. Seidel and Heifetz were Auer's star pupils at the time, and the teacher often presented the two boys in concert together. Heifetz was called "the angel of the violin," whereas Seidel was "the devil." In 1918 Seidel came with Auer to New York City, where he made his recital debut in Carnegie Hall on April 14. In the 1930s he moved to California, where he remained until his death, in 1962. Seidel was regarded as one of the premier violinists of his generation, but somehow he never received the international recognition he deserved. The violin pedagogue Carl Flesch once remarked, "It is an injustice of fate that Seidel is not considered the third in a triumvirate with Heifetz and Elman."

Seidel's fate, just or not, was my good fortune, for his position at Paramount Studios kept him more or less rooted in Los Angeles. That fall I had my first lesson with him in his upscale

Beverly Hills home. Seidel settled down in a rocking chair across the living room from where I stood by the piano, lit his pipe, and then motioned for his accompanist, Denise Coppin, to begin. A B minor chord, the beginning of Saint-Saëns's Third Violin Concerto, rumbled from the piano, and I made my solo entrance. Out of the corner of my eye I could see the motion of Seidel's rocking chair and a lazy trail of smoke lifting from his pipe.

As the opening violin statement came to an end, he suddenly yelled "Stop!" in such a loud and raspy voice that my bow jerked off the string. Seidel continued to rock and smoke in complete silence, all the while glaring at me. Finally he got up and walked over to me. He was very short, and I in my fifteenth year had recently grown a great deal. I looked down at him nervously and he up at me with displeasure spread plainly across his face. "You play like a dead fish," he said with a scowl. Then he whacked me over the shoulder with his bow for good measure and ordered me to sit down. He signaled Coppin to start again. It was a terrible moment. Meremblum had yelled at me occasionally, but Seidel did him one better, yelling *and* hitting. What kind of monster had me in his clutches?

Out came that B minor chord once again, and then Seidel picked up his own instrument to attack the Saint-Saëns himself. The effect was so electrifying that I forgot about his abusive treatment. Auer was right to dub Seidel the devil of the violin. His rendition, intense and passionate, was hellishly hot, and yet the man could also make the violin sing ever so sweetly. "There," he said, glaring at me once again. "Now you play."

The formula was almost always the same in future lessons. I would play. Seidel would order me to sit down. Then he himself would play whatever I had brought in.

Was Seidel a terrible teacher? In certain respects, yes. And yet I learned a tremendous amount from him — by example, of course, but also because there was no holding back with him. Before each lesson I checked my inhibitions, if reluctantly, at the door. What teenager wants to appear excessively emotional? On the other hand, who wants to be accused of playing like a dead fish?

Over time Seidel and I covered a tremendous amount of repertoire — a great swath of concertos, all twenty-four Paganini caprices, and a number of virtuoso works. Whether by inspiration, intimidation, or threat of violence, I improved. But it never ceased to be unnerving to be dueling with my teacher for supremacy at each lesson. He was an artist at the zenith of his powers; I was a work in progress. Also, Seidel played a magical violin, a Stradivarius, I my mouse-brown, plain-sounding, no-name violin. It was the first time that I saw and heard a Stradivarius up close — golden in color, as I remember it, and with a sweet, sweet sound. Even its pegs, boxwood with ivory rings and buttons, spoke of royalty. How could I be expected to go mano a mano with the master under such circumstances?

As if to answer the question, Seidel announced one day that I needed a new violin and that he would help me pick it out. My parents and I met him at Callier's Violin Shop in Hollywood, where Mr. Callier led us to cabinets filled with dozens of violins hanging from hooks like so many sides of meat in a butcher shop. At the far end of the room sat a workman bent over a large, worn-looking wooden bench. Parts of violins and various tools were spread out in great disorder before him. The scene had a storybook quality to it. The workman might have been Gepetto, the pieces of wood Pinocchio in the making. The smell of the place — a mixture of cut wood, varnish, rosin, and simmering glue — tweaked my nasal passages oddly. Callier pulled down instruments one by one for Seidel to try. I could hear small differences in them, but the trouble was that Seidel made them all sound appealing with his lustrous tone.

Finally he chose an instrument made by Giovanni Dollenz. It was much more refined in tone than mine and, for want of a better description, old-sounding. My previous violins had been harsh or just plain dull, but this one was almost silvery in quality, as if age had smoothed out some of its rough edges. Seidel looked through one of the f-holes and then motioned to me. It took some doing to get the light to fall just right on the label inside, but there it was, barely discernible through the dust that had accrued over time: *Giovanni Dollenz, Fecit in Trieste Anno 1830.* Stumbling onto an ancient cave painting could have had no greater effect on me. I was holding a violin made over 120 years before in Trieste, Italy.

"But how do we know the violin is what it says it is and is worth the price?" my worried father asked. Mr. Callier was asking five hundred dollars, the very outer limit of what my parents could afford. Callier handed Dad a certificate of authenticity, folded in three to allow for front, back, and side-view photographs of the violin — mug shots, really, like the ones you saw of gangsters on the wanted posters at the post office. On the other side of the certificate was a description of the instrument:

> The one-piece back is fashioned from attractive rootstock maple, marked by strong flames of irregular growth, slanting mostly downward from left to right; the ribs show soft, narrow figure. The head bearing its original neck is boldly carved from sparsely flamed maple. Plentiful, thick, golden red-brown varnish is of brilliant texture and all original.

Giovanni Dollenz, working in Trieste from about 1800 to 1850, was probably a pupil of Lorenzo Storioni and a very gifted maker. This violin, reminiscent of the style of Michelangelo Bergonzi, is built on a flat pattern and is in an excellent state of preservation.

March 11, 1950
ERICH LACHMANN
Violin expert

I had never heard of Giovanni Dollenz, but no matter. The violin sounded much better than mine, looked far more beautiful, and even came with a certificate of authenticity from a violin expert. Phrases from Lachmann's description echoed in my head: "boldly carved," "strong flames of irregular growth." The words sounded almost poetic. My parents huddled in a corner with Seidel and Callier, and after a few moments of negotiation, Dad wrote a check and I walked out of the shop with my very own Giovanni Dollenz. I have owned and played six different violins since the Dollenz was eventually put to rest, all significantly better and with more distinguished pedigrees, yet acquiring none of these matched the feeling of that moment — the feeling that comes only with first love.

The new violin made playing far more interesting for me, but not necessarily easier. I could draw a more pleasing sound out of the Dollenz, but that in turn broadened the spectrum of colors and nuances available to me. Every work that Seidel placed before me now demanded more resourcefulness, more imagination. At the same time, I had to learn the violin's eccentricities. Some notes required more speed, some more pressure than on my old instrument. On the Dollenz, the D above middle D on the G string, the one I depended on for one last cry of despair before the Nigun ended in abject resignation, emitted a flutter rather than a pure sound — a "wolf," as it is called. Then I remembered David Oistrakh's advice: "I do three things to avoid a wolf. I press my left shoulder tightly against the violin, I vibrate more, and I pray." Oistrakh's tip kept the wolf from the Nigun's door.

Although the Dollenz was sweeter than my previous violin, I still could not even come close to matching Seidel's incandescent sound in my lessons. He had a magnificent Stradivarius valued at approximately $25,000 in that year, 1952, I an obscure Giovanni Dollenz bought at one fiftieth the price. But of course it wasn't only the violin, by a long shot. Seidel had a fast and narrow wrist vibrato and a way of drawing the bow across the strings close to the bridge that produced a sound of unusual lushness and intensity, a sound that was soon to be the major object of my attention.

In 1953, director George Stevens's legendary rendition of the archetypal Western myth, *Shane,* appeared in movie theaters. Of course I had to see it. Alan Ladd played the role of Shane, a drifter and retired gunfighter, Jean Arthur and Van Heflin played Marian and Joe, the homesteaders, and Jack Palance the hired gun. In the film's denouement, Shane, who has come to help Joe and Marian in their new homestead, realizes reluctantly that the only way to stop the old ranchers from terrorizing these newly arrived pioneers is to have a showdown with the ranchers' hired gun.

(Soft strings play in the background.)

Marian: Shane, wait. You were through with gunfighting.
Shane: I changed my mind.
Marian: Are you doing this just for me?

Shane: For you, Marian — for Joe — and little Joe.
Marian: Then we'll never see you again?
Shane: Never's a long time, ma'am. Tell him [Joe] I was sorry.

There is clearly much feeling between them, but because Marian is married, propriety stops them from saying too much. A solo violin begins to play ever so softly and sweetly on the soundtrack — that of my own teacher, Toscha Seidel.

Marian: No need to tell him.

She looks at Shane tenderly and shakes his hand, but somehow it is more than a handshake. Toscha plays on.

Marian: Please. Take care of yourself.

Marian, standing helplessly in front of their homestead, watches Shane mount his horse and slowly ride away toward the inevitable gun duel that will follow. Toscha's violin gently fades away. I sat spellbound in the theater. Alan Ladd and Jean Arthur had delivered the scene to perfection, and yet few would have been aware of a third and perhaps equally important actor present. Toscha Seidel, whose name was not even listed in the film credits, had played a barely discernible little melody like an intimate and loving caress as a stand-in for Shane and Marian's feelings.

Seidel was one of a select group of violinists who lived lavishly in Southern California by dint of being able to supply on demand a few seconds of poignant sound and throbbing vibrato for that heart-melting moment in a love scene, enacted innumerable times in innumerable films — the one that essentially said *I love you.* I listened to Seidel somewhat differently from then on — thrilled to know that the violin had such power and anxious to glean its secrets. Absolutely no one produced a smoldering tone like Seidel's. Standing next to him at lessons, I hoped that at the very least, a spark might jump from his violin to mine and I would then be able to smolder too.

"Bring in the Bach Chaconne," Seidel ordered unexpectedly at the end of a lesson one day. The Chaconne. Elman. Philharmonic Hall. Since that moment years earlier when I had first heard the Chaconne, I had come across it surprisingly often — on the radio, in student recitals, and on the Heifetz record of solo Bach my parents brought home. It had gained a permanent berth in the violin repertoire; now it was my turn to embrace it. I placed the volume of Bach's six Partitas and Sonatas for Solo Violin on the music stand. There was my old nemesis, the G Minor Sonata, whose opening Adagio had befuddled me years ago. That old Bach feeling came over me again. How could I make sense out of all that black ink spread chaotically across the page? The swirling chains of stubbornly dense and turgid notes made me feel unable to breathe. Sometime in the not too distant future, I would breathe easier. I would realize that Bach had actually provided me with a splendid example of improvisation on the movement's skeletal frame — a collection of scales, arpeggios, fanciful turns, discreet pauses, and a final little cadenza that any decent Baroque fiddler would have been expected to summon up on the spot but that most modern violinists would not or could not.

I began turning the pages until the D Minor Partita appeared: Allemande, Corrente, Sarabande, Gigue, and finally the Chaconne.

Seidel had sidestepped the first four movements and asked for only the Chaconne. Such was the Chaconne's weight and length that violinists often played it as a separate piece. Hoping to outdo all those other fiddlers, Jascha Heifetz once performed it twice in a single recital — once on the violin, once a fifth lower on viola, with an intermission separating the two renditions.

The Chaconne, filled with page after page of tightly packed notes, did not look like any other music I knew. In the Mendelssohn Violin Concerto, for example, the soloist plays the opening statement, rests during the orchestral tutti, plays a few minutes more, rests again, and so on. Concertos by Brahms, Beethoven, and a host of others, plus dozens of works with piano, follow a similar pattern. But the Chaconne went on and on without interruption. Of course, it had to. Bach deemed that there would be no keyboard instrument to harmonize or provide a dialogue with the violin. A single naked violin told the Chaconne's story.

I decided to read through the entire piece as best I could in order to get an overall impression. The opening chords formed a four-bar phrase, more or less mimicked by the next phrase of four bars — two joined halves of a single entity. The next eight bars were again split in two, as were the next and the next. The complementary sets of four bars were like couples on promenade that continually changed their garb. Heavy chords gradually became more transparent and then dissolved into winding passages of single notes. They in turn, as if having had a change of heart, began to gather in strength, becoming more florid and slowly increasing in brilliance. The four-bar phrases continued inexorably, but in the excitement of a new marchlike figure that called out angrily, I lost track of the parading couples and simply reveled in the richness and variety of each phrase. A long section of arpeggiated chords slowly swelled in intensity, burst into angry chains of swirling notes, and then returned to the opening chords.

For a moment I thought that the piece was at an end, but the Chaconne only hesitated in order to shake itself loose from the tonality of D minor, and then continued ever so quietly in the new key of D major. The effect of this transformation from declamatory chords to hymnlike two-part harmony — music that would be at home in a church service — was striking. It spoke of deep peace, of simple gratitude, of something meditative. My parents had not raised my brother and me with any sense of religion. When I first heard Elman at age eleven, I doubt that I had ever been in a place of worship, and yet that is exactly what the D major section evoked then and now — a private sanctuary where I could commune with the unknown and unnamed.

I moved on, stumbling often over difficult passages. Again I thought I recognized those pairs of four-bar phrases, and again they slowly evolved in character. At one point Bach introduced a note repeated three times in succession — da-da-da — as if he were mocking his own seriousness. The figure repeated over and over, each time a little more insistently. But this was no lighthearted banter. I had the odd impression that another layer of meaning had been woven into the music, a feeling that Bach was trying to say something. The figure unexpectedly picked up a note — da-da-da-da — four hammered notes that were now intrusive, contentious. I loved those repeated notes, which sounded almost like Morse code. But what might da-da-da-da mean that da-da-da didn't?

The music gradually rose in pitch, arriving at a plateau of solemn broken chords, then took a deep breath and returned to its home key. This served as a signal for phrase after phrase to wind down, eventually reaching a place drained of everything except sadness and profound resignation. Against an ever-repeating single tone, a gentle wave of notes lifted up and down, up and down, each group descending step by step. It was a moment that I remembered from Elman's performance, a moment in which Bach seemed to be passing on some ancient and deep-seated truth about the human condition. Then the music slowly lifted itself out of this minimalist landscape and began to gather confidence in ever greater, ever more swirling patterns. It landed briefly on a single note and plunged majestically one last time into the opening chords of the Chaconne before coming to a climactic end on a long, drawn-out double D.

The Chaconne had lost none of its magic since Elman's performance. A procession of ever-changing four-bar phrases, each adding its own short story to the ones before, bonded together to form a grand mosaic of emotion — even at this sight-reading level of missed notes and shaky intonation. The Chaconne was exhilarating; it was also exhausting. I had never played a piece that went on for fifteen minutes without interruption, a piece in which the violinist had to wear two hats — one as soloist, in the sustained melodic lines, and one as accompanist, in the many two-, three-, and four-note chords that laced the piece. My arms and back ached from the exertion. I would have to tame my fingers and build up my strength in the days to follow. As for how to stitch together those endlessly repeated phrases so that they sounded coherent and natural, I merely shrugged my teenage shoulders. Seidel would have to help me with those things.

One week later I knocked nervously on Seidel's door. He let

me in with a curt nod of the head. He was always a loose cannon at lessons. He might yell at me one day, praise me another, sometimes allow me to play for moments at a time, or just as easily tell me to shut up for the duration. Today there would be none of Denise Coppin's piano playing to hide behind.

"Chaconne," Seidel growled. The rocker moved back and forth, smoke curled from his pipe, but not a word came out of his mouth as I played. In the best of lessons, he would shout words of encouragement to spur me on, but on that day I played the entire Chaconne without interruption from him. When I drew out the last sustained note to its end and then dropped the violin and bow to my side, Seidel remained gently rocking back and forth. I feared that this was merely the eye of the storm and that hurricane Toscha would follow in a torrent of abuse.

But when he finally spoke, his voice was uncharacteristically reflective. "Not bad," he said, almost as a question. "That was not bad at all. Now let me play it for you." Seidel got up (he was not much taller standing than sitting) and began. His eyes glinted triumphantly as he engineered one exciting phrase after another. *You see,* those eyes proclaimed, this *is how it should be done.*

Seidel's Chaconne was certainly exciting and far fierier than Elman's version. It was almost too exciting. One musical storm unrelentingly followed another, without the relief of an occasional oasis of peacefulness. I was impressed but somehow left dissatisfied when he finished. Seidel's ardor and tempestuousness always took my breath away, but those very qualities seemed to work against him here. The Chaconne had something important to say. That much I knew, but the few comments Seidel offered when I played through it again were less than helpful: clean up this passage, play that one a little louder, make more retard here, etc. About the parading couples, that special moment in church, not to speak of *da-da-da* and *da-da-da-da,* he had little to say. The man who week after week solved the *Los Angeles Times* Sunday chess problem could not or would not show me the moves necessary to organize the Chaconne successfully. When he decided that I had "learned" the Chaconne and assigned me something else, I assumed that the work's secrets were simply off-limits to ordinary mortals.

The sad truth was that Seidel was far better at demonstrating his ideas than actually explaining them with words. Perhaps if I had studied with the more thoughtful Sascha rather than the tempestuous Toscha, I would have understood the Chaconne better. Sascha Jacobson, with a reputation as a highly intelligent musician, could also draw a beautiful tone out of his violin, the Red Diamond Stradivarius — soon to make headlines when it floated out to sea during a flash flood and was miraculously restored after washing ashore some days later.

My study of Bach's Chaconne coincided with my last year in high school. Where I would continue my musical education was anybody's guess, but one thing was clear: I was going to be a violinist. My schoolmates who were college-bound might have already planned their majors, but what difference did it make if they cavalierly changed dream professions over and over again? Doctor, lawyer, investment analyst, then back to doctor again — it didn't matter. They were young, and the luxury of time was on their side. My fate, however, had already been sealed years earlier. I knew it, and so did my friends, who looked at me with a mixture of curiosity and admiration. In school I was the guy who played the violin, and when I graduated from both junior high and high school, my yearbooks were filled with best wishes from friends who almost always made reference to the violin.

> Roses are red
> Violins are blue?
> Here's wishing
> Luck to you.
> TOM HEIMBERG

The winner of the violin-playing contest is none other than Arnoldini Paganini. Good luck in high school Arnold. From your everlasting friend.

> JOHN MACK

Dear Arnie,
Please send me two tickets to your Carnegie Hall debut.
> Love,
> VICKY KELRICH

One was deeply philosophical:

Dear Arnie,
In a way, it will be your duty to mankind to contribute your music to as many people as possible and to enrich their lives as well as your own. I am confident that you will reach your goal if you think of it as a way in which you are contributing to others, not only gaining personal success. Good luck and love,
> MYRA JAGENDORF

And one in particular was truly heartfelt:

Dear Arnie,
I don't think there is a need to say much because we have been good friends for a long time and I'm sure you understand how much I value your friendship. The first time I heard you

play the violin I knew you were a wonderful person. Funny how music reveals the character of the person playing it. All the luck in the world. Love,

JUNE GOTTLIEB

They called me Arnold, Arnie, Arn, even Arnoldini, and to some I was a fiddler rather than a violinist, but it was hard to ignore the powerful messages sent my way: I had a special gift to pursue, a solid character to nurture, the heady possibility of future artistic fulfillment to strive for, the lure of fame to contemplate, and the expectation of service to humanity. All this on the shoulders of a teenager! Like Hester in Hawthorne's *Scarlet Letter*, I might as well have had a letter emblazoned on my chest: *V* for violinist.

CHAPTER 6

Music School

MUSICIANS ARE FOND of tracing their bloodlines to the great figures of the past. A pianist might boast that his teachers go all the way back to, say, the nineteenth-century virtuoso Franz Liszt, or a composer that he has a tenuous personal connection to the great Ludwig van Beethoven. Their secret hope is that some of the greatness passes on from one generation to another. I often wondered where the plaintive, almost sobbing quality of Yehudi Menuhin's playing came from until I heard his teacher, the Romanian violinist Georges Enesco. Their two recordings of Schumann's D Minor Violin Sonata reveal the old master's influence on the young Menuhin. And the lean and winsome sound of Joseph Szigeti that I cherish — a sound unique in the world, I used to think — is instantly recognizable in the rare recordings that exist of his Hungarian teacher, Jenö Hubay.

As a seventeen-year-old about to graduate from high school,

I felt that my own violin lineage was already quite impressive. Couched in Old Testament terms, Joseph Joachim, the distinguished German violinist, begat Leopold Auer, who begat Toscha Seidel, who begat me. Without doubt, I belonged to an illustrious family — one in which Auer's pupils Heifetz, Elman, and Zimbalist were in effect my uncles. If only some of that DNA would rub off!

As I prepared for the next step in my musical education, it looked for a while as if I might remain in the Auer family. Two of his "children" had stayed close as grownups — my previous teacher, Peter Meremblum, and his old schoolmate Efrem Zimbalist, now the director of the Curtis Institute of Music in Philadelphia. Meremblum wrote a letter of recommendation on my behalf to Zimbalist, and such was the bond between them that I was admitted to the school without audition — something almost unheard of to this day.

Los Angeles, my hometown, is a sprawling city — a collection of suburbs connected by plumbing, the old joke goes — while Philadelphia, thanks to the vision of its founding fathers, is laid out thoughtfully. City Hall, at its center, is framed at equal distances by four squares, each an oasis of grass, trees, statuary, and fountains. The Curtis Institute of Music overlooks one of them — Rittenhouse Square. In a previous era elegant townhouses rimmed the square, but by the mid-1950s they were almost all gone, replaced by hotels, commercial buildings, and high-rise apartment houses. On a blustery day in the early fall of 1954, wearing something foreign to my native Southern California — an overcoat — I climbed the steps leading to the Curtis Institute and entered the school for the first time.

But was this really a school? I stood in an oversized oak-paneled room filled with opulent oriental rugs and old-looking oil paintings. A staircase flanked by massive wooden pillars ascended magisterially to the second floor. Curtis, which resides in three of the very few remaining townhouses left on the square, has never quite relinquished its character as a home where well-heeled families once lived. On October 1, 1924, Mary Louise Curtis Bok (later Mrs. Efrem Zimbalist) founded the all-scholarship school and opened its doors with the chartered purpose "to train exceptionally gifted young musicians for careers as performing artists on the highest professional level."

Jane Hill, the school's registrar, emerged from her office. "Hello, child. You must be Arnold." Mrs. Hill called all students "child," even those who had graduated and gone on to become renowned musicians. She directed me upstairs to Mr. Zimbalist's office and studio. Zimbalist, a white-haired, compact man who seemed ancient in my adolescent eyes but who in reality was no more than sixty-five, greeted me cordially and ushered me into a large room that looked out onto Rittenhouse Square. Even in the excitement of the moment — my hands trembling slightly as I tuned up — I could not help but notice the photographs of musicians and artists lining the walls, almost all signed and dedicated to Zimbalist. There was his teacher, Leopold Auer, the composers Nikolai Rimski-Korsakov, Aleksandr Glazunov, and Arnold Schönberg, the conductors Arturo Toscanini, Leopold Stokowski, and Fritz Reiner, the pianist Sergei Rachmaninoff, the poet Edna St. Vincent Millay, the scientist Albert Einstein, and, most astonishing of all, the violinists Zimbalist, Kreisler, and Heifetz, swimming in the ocean with only their smiling heads visible above water. The room was a gallery of world-famous figures — most of them dead and already consigned to history books — all connected in one way or another to the man dressed in a conservative gray business suit who now spoke to me with a Russian accent that reminded me of Meremblum and Seidel.

The similarity ended there, however, for Zimbalist in speech and gesture gave off an air of reserve and cultivation. What a privilege it would be to work with an artist who consorted with the giants of music! Zimbalist listened attentively to the concerto, some Bach, and a Paganini caprice that I had prepared, made some nice comments about my playing, and then delivered the bad news: his studio was already full and he would have to recommend me to Ivan Galamian, the other principal violin teacher at Curtis. Zimbalist shook my hand, wished me luck, and ushered me to the door.

In one stroke I had been orphaned from the Auer clan. Had Zimbalist not liked my playing? And who exactly was this Ivan Galamian? I knew only that he was the teacher of Michael Rabin, the brilliant young violinist, exactly my own age, who already traveled the world as a highly successful concert violinist. Jane Hill, who was waiting for me at the bottom of the stairs, immediately turned me around and sent me up to a third-floor studio where both Galamian and the celebrated harpist Carlos Salzedo taught. The sound of a violin wafted through the door, and I took advantage of a diamond-shaped window to peek inside. (Later I heard rumors that Salzedo's reputation as a womanizer had induced the school to install the window, in order to protect the virtue of the many attractive young women who studied with him.)

I could see a tall, swarthy man with black, tightly waved hair and dark, burning eyes regarding his student intently. He held a lit cigarette with thumb and first two fingers palm upward, as if he were offering it to his student. Galamian's looks were exotic, but something in his demeanor made me wonder — a minimum of gesture, a stillness in the way he leaned forward to listen, which suggested unshakable discipline and dedication. The lesson came to an end, the student emerged from the room, and Galamian motioned me in. He spoke with a Russian accent. Was there no violin teacher in the world without one? Galamian's voice, even more subdued than Zimbalist's, tended to trail off at the end of sentences, so the last words were often almost inaudible. Accustomed as I was to Toscha Seidel's tirades, the effect was striking.

Galamian wasted little time with small talk and asked me to play. Out came the same repertoire that Zimbalist had heard moments earlier. Galamian shook his head sadly when I finished. "You play quite well, but I don't know how. You have many bad habits. I will accept you as my student, but we have much work to do."

I left the studio in an uncertain state of mind. Zimbalist was out. Galamian was in. I was now officially enrolled in Curtis. But those words *bad habits* kept ringing in my ears. Perhaps this was the real reason Zimbalist had directed me to Galamian instead of accepting me himself and suffering the grueling work of stripping years of inefficient or awkward motions from my playing. Zimbalist had once said admiringly of Galamian that he could teach even a table to play the violin well.

A large group portrait of upper-class Dutch gentlemen in seventeenth-century garb gazed down on me as I descended the staircase. Their dour looks seemed to confirm Galamian's verdict: guilty of bad habits. His assessment should hardly have come as a surprise. My past teachers had remarked from time to time about the stiffness with which I held the bow. It was my bad luck that they had not had the discipline to keep after this problem, and I, a slothful teenager, was content to let matters slide.

The bow had never been much of a concern to me. The violin itself made the sound, didn't it, and the left-hand fingers made the notes — pure and simple. When Seidel insisted that I needed a decent bow to complement my newly acquired Dollenz, the Herman Pfretzschner he picked out, a solid German bow, seemed like mere window-dressing to me. It took an accident to make me even dimly aware of the bow's essential value. As an adolescent, I liked to charge into my room and take a flying leap onto the bed. On one ill-advised occasion, I leapt without looking and only realized when airborne that the Pfretzschner lay on the bed, poised to receive the full brunt of my body. The aerial journey, which seemed to last an eternity, ended with the bow broken in two. There was hell to pay from my parents, of course. They had invested the grand sum of fifty dollars in the bow and now would have to bear the additional cost of repairing it — glue plus a pin connecting the two parts would do the trick, Mr. Callier maintained. While I waited for the bow's return, my old one came out of storage. I was now proficient enough to notice that it reacted sluggishly — an object at repose dutifully remaining that way in accordance with the laws of physics. When the Pfretzschner came back a week later, miraculously in one piece and seemingly as good as new, its familiar qualities surprised me. This sturdy stick from the workshop of a family of solid bow-makers drew a much richer sound from the violin and sprang eagerly off the string on command. My disastrous flying leap should have produced a fresh understanding of the bow's importance, but I soon lapsed back into my old ways of thinking; a bow was nothing more than the dutiful servant of the violin.

At the school orchestra rehearsal preceding my very first lesson with Galamian, I found myself seated next to a friendly boy
named Jaime Laredo, who looked to be about thirteen years old.
Jaime had already begun his studies with Galamian and was happy
to show me how he held the bow. Unlike the great Auer-trained
players, who gripped it with fingers trailing behind the wrist as if
a powerful wind were driving them to the rear, Jaime merely lowered his fingers onto the bow, index finger slightly forward, in
what seemed a much more natural position. Then he demonstrated the basic motions that Galamian demanded of the fingers.
When I tried them myself, the wooden stick felt uncomfortably
alive in my hand and capable of flying off like some exotic winged
insect. Holding the bow tightly and stiffly gave me a much stronger sense of security. As the rehearsal progressed, I began to pick
out Galamian's students in the violin section by the distinctive
way they spread their fingers on the bow. Galamian's own teacher,
Lucien Capet, a famous violin teacher at the Paris Conservatory,
was the author of a well-known treatise called "Advanced Technique of the Violin Bow," and his method was unquestionably at
the heart of Galamian's strict regimen.

The next day I trudged reluctantly up the stairs to my new
teacher's studio, feeling somewhat as if I were paying a long over-
due and assiduously avoided visit to the dentist. Dentists pulled
teeth. Galamian eliminated bad habits.

Beneath the melancholy expressiveness of Galamian's eyes I
could sense an unassailable resolve. Clearly his life's mission was
to build solid violinists with the flexibility and strength needed to
negotiate the most difficult of passages with confidence and the
ability to produce a tone full enough to fill large concert halls. It

would be tempting to think of Galamian as the Henry Ford of the violin. But whereas Ford mass-produced identical automobiles, Galamian mass-produced fiddlers with the basic tools to enable their individual artistry to bloom.

The source of Galamian's character was something of a mystery to me, since he rarely spoke about his life. Born in Tabriz, Persia, in 1903 of Armenian ancestry, he was the son of a well-to-do merchant who moved the family to Moscow when Ivan was about two. In 1922, after the revolution, Galamian fled Russia and moved to Paris, where, despite being an excellent violinist, he began to perform less and teach more. One day a tiny four-year-old, the son of a Ukrainian violinist, appeared in his studio. According to Galamian's lifelong friend Jascha Brodsky, "When Galamian taught little Paul Makanowitzky, he would set him up on the table, much to the amusement of colleagues who might drop in." Under Galamian's supervision, the child prodigy improved so quickly that in four years he was ready to be presented publicly. In December 1929, Galamian invited several guests to hear young Paul in a private audition, which was shortly followed by a debut concert that garnered ecstatic reviews. Makanowitzky stood at the threshold of a brilliant concert career, and Galamian was hailed as a "professor magician." In 1937 Galamian moved to the United States, settling in New York City, where he lived till the end of his life.

Galamian spent my whole lesson going over hand positions and motions of the bow — making me repeat them over and over in front of a large mirror. When he was satisfied that I understood, he told me to go home and practice what I had learned in front of my own mirror. I stared at him uncomprehendingly. "No violin? No music?" Galamian nodded. "Leave the violin in the case. Practice with only the bow, and we will see how you do at the next lesson."

The Dutchmen looked down at me even more disapprovingly as I descended the stairs again. It did not matter in the least where or when or what I practiced in the next week. Not a single sound was going to come out of my violin — a bitter pill to swallow. Oh, the humiliation of it all! A violinist of my already significant stature — soloist with the Los Angeles Philharmonic Orchestra, I reminded myself — reduced to being a silent, one-handed violinist.

Los Angeles, big though it was, was far from the musical heart of the country. True, an extraordinary group of artists lived in Southern California, thanks to its seductive semitropical weather. Aldous Huxley shopped at our corner grocery store, and Jascha Heifetz, Gregor Piatigorsky, Arthur Rubinstein, Thomas Mann, Arnold Schönberg, and Igor Stravinsky all lived within twenty minutes of our house, as did many outstanding musicians lured to Los Angeles by the movie industry. But as a young player, I was a big fish in a small pond, with almost no idea of what it would be like to find myself in the concentration of talent drawn from all over the world to music conservatories in the East. Mary Curtis Bok Zimbalist, who arrived at Curtis almost daily in a Bentley driven by her chauffeur, Patrick, had the vision and wealth to fashion an intimately sized music school inhabited by the world's greatest teachers, and the best young players from all over the country and the world vied for the privilege to attend.

Those first weeks at school were painful. While I practiced with one hand, other student violinists whizzed up and down fiddle strings with both, the glamorous sounds of their efforts wafting out of practice rooms that I passed on the way to my own. Their playing set in motion a strange mixture of discouragement and inspiration in me. During that uncertain time, I went to New York to attend the Carnegie Hall debut recital of Toshiya Eto, the Japanese violinist, who had only recently graduated from Curtis. He dared to begin his program with Beethoven's notoriously difficult Kreutzer Sonata. Poised briefly in playing position as if in suspended animation next to his pianist, Billy Sokoloff, Eto suddenly pounced on the first chord with great force and almost instantly melted into a sustained and delicate melody that drifted up to Carnegie's highest seats, where I sat. What control, what confidence, what artistry! It was hard to imagine that a journey from my finger exercises before a mirror at Curtis to the stage of Carnegie Hall was even possible. For the first time since Mischa Elman's Chaconne inspired me to think that I wanted to be a concert violinist, doubt nibbled away at my dreams. Eto was already on his way, but where was I?

Blithely unconcerned about either the practical or the existential merit of this question, Galamian continued to drill me patiently but relentlessly week after week. Eventually he allowed me to begin playing again. He generally assigned only works from the standard violin repertoire, but their order differed mysteriously from one student to another. Galamian seemed unerringly to know a student's level and what music would move him or her forward. Unexpectedly, he asked me to prepare Tartini's *Devil's Trill Sonata*. The humiliation of the mirror exercises had led me to believe that I was only ready for "easy" music. But if so, why this piece, whose almost endless trills tire the left hand and defy clarity? Galamian allowed me to play the mournful beginning, a simple melody that gives no clue of the difficulties to come, without interruption, but when the trills began, he held up his hand. "You are an actor who just mumbled his lines." The thought must have tickled him, for he smiled and then repeated the sentence word for word as if he had marbles in his mouth. Galamian mumbled, but his point was crystal clear. Musicians are actors who deliver notes instead of words. The deft use of the bow would help bring my music to life.

He pressed on, unsure that I truly understood the music's essential character. "Do you know why Tartini called this his *Devil's Trill Sonata,* Arnold?" The *r* in my name fluttered lightly on his tongue in the Russian manner. I nodded. Every violin student knew the story: Tartini dreamed one night that he made a pact with the devil. In return for his soul, the devil promised to be at his side whenever he needed him. On a whim, Tartini handed him his violin to see what kind of musician he might be. To his astonishment, the devil's music was exquisite — a sonata of such unearthly skill and beauty that Tartini stood transfixed as he played. When he awoke, Tartini snatched up his fiddle and tried to recapture the sounds he had heard in the dream, feverishly noting down the music of a sonata. Although the *Devil's Trill* was, in Tartini's estimation, the best music he had ever composed, he claimed to regard it as a poor approximation of the devil's playing.

The story had the suspicious ring of a public relations fabrication, and yet it struck a chord in me. I often remembered my own dreams, many of them odd transformations of things that happened during waking hours. The devil had never appeared in my dreams, but recently a violin student I had taken to the school prom had. Julia was pretty enough in real life but radiantly beautiful in the dream. An angel, in effect, had visited me; why not the devil? The sonata's incessant trills were indeed odd, even menacing, and the firestorm of a cadenza that ends the work was heated, frenzied, almost out of control. It was easy to imagine that the devil had a hand in it somehow. When I had come to the end of the *Devil's Trill,* Galamian told me to bring the Tartini in again the next week, and "I want to hear more devilish sounds from you."

Galamian seemed to have little interest in my violin and bow. Presumably he thought that his job was to create violinists, not to worry about the tools of their trade. To some extent, a good fiddler would make his way in the world even on a cigar box. But my Curtis violinist friends and I, despite our relative inexperience, already knew that there was an enormous difference between instruments. Some were loud and brash, others soft and sweet, or dark, or bright, or any conceivable mixture of any of those elements. A singer was stuck with the instrument lodged in his or her throat, but my future depended to a significant degree in finding a good violin, the right violin. During orchestra rehearsals, instruments and bows were on display. My Pfretzschner, very low in the bow pecking order, was at least a known commodity, but no one had heard of a Giovanni Dollenz violin. One of the more knowledgeable students looked at my violin carefully during a break and burst out laughing. "Your violin is warped," he crowed. "Let's see! Let's see!" the others clamored. True enough, when I looked lengthwise down the violin's ribs, it was visibly warped. To my chagrin, I had never noticed it before. Who was this Dollenz character, anyhow? Someone took the trouble to look up Dollenz in the school library and learned that he was possibly a student of the great Cremonese maker Lorenzo Storioni. *Possibly a student of Storioni,* my friends repeated, chortling. Possibly! I took the ribbing good-naturedly. What did I care? The violin sounded sweet to my ears and I was making significant progress on it, wasn't I?

Winter arrived, and with it the bone-dry air of overheated Philadelphia apartments. Los Angeles, a city without significant seasons, had never been anything like this. My skin turned itchy and my violin slowly contracted under the relentless onslaught of dry heat. On one bitterly cold morning, an oddly thin and hollow sound dribbled out of my Dollenz, as if it were being played in the next room. I discovered that a section of the violin's ribs directly to the side of the chin rest had separated slightly from the back, to which it was glued — a common occurrence. The individual pieces of a violin are intentionally held together by relatively weak glue so that they will tend to come apart before a serious crack develops in the wood itself. The violin is a surprisingly delicate creature. Move the bridge or sound post just a tad and you could swear another instrument was under your chin. Even if it is perfectly set up, the ever-changing temperature, humidity, and air pressure ensure that an instrument sounds different every single day of the year. The unexpected opening in my Dollenz, barely wide enough to slip a razor blade inside, played havoc with the sound. Someone would have to glue the violin together. Perhaps I could have it done in one of the great string instrument centers of the world, New York City.

In my first years at Curtis, Galamian was often unwell, so his students had to travel to New York City, where he lived, for lessons. To this day my stomach shifts slightly when I pass his apartment building at 170 West Seventy-third Street. A small room adjacent to Galamian's studio, covered wall-to-wall with photographs and prints of famous violinists, served as a warmup area. Making us play our scales and exercises in front of the violin luminaries of the past — Tartini, Corelli, Paganini, Wieniawski, Vieuxtemps, Ysaÿe, and company — was undoubtedly Galamian's way of prodding us on. I can still hear his soft but firm voice in an endless mantra: *More bow. Out of tune. Clearer articulation.* And occasionally: *Good!*

None of us complained about the two-hour bus ride from Philadelphia and the subway trip uptown. When the lesson finished, the great city awaited us. It was time to meet friends for dinner, hear a concert, or perhaps visit the violin shops. Every city worth its salt had at least one or two topnotch luthiers, but New York had dozens. With the right money in your pocket, you could walk into a rare instrument shop and buy a Stradivarius or a Tourte bow. As a student with five dollars in my checking account, these were slightly beyond my means, but I did want to look and learn — something that cost no money at all. Word had it that Rembert Wurlitzer, one of the most important New York dealers, was friendly to students with little money. This was significant. Most fiddle shop sales personnel quickly spied, from our acne-spotted faces and tatty wardrobes, that we were probably a waste of time. The attitude was understandable, if shortsighted. Was I not a prospective client down the road?

I headed to Wurlitzer's shop on West Forty-second Street with my sick violin. For the very top dealers, repairing and adjusting instruments was a customer service necessary for the business. The real money, of course, was not in repairing violins but in buying and selling them. If a Stradivarius cost the price of a lavish home, the dealer's 20 percent sales commission was certainly worth a bedroom or two in it. As I entered the shop, Rembert Wurlitzer himself, tall, slender, and rather bald, emerged from the back room and cordially greeted me. He was a member of a family whose music company stretched back to seventeenth-century Saxony. He looked my violin over and said that it would be glued and ready for me to pick up by the end of the day. Almost as an afterthought, I asked whether he would appraise my Giovanni Dollenz for an instrument insurance update. The violin was certainly worth more than five hundred dollars, the sum my parents had paid for it years ago. If it was stolen, where would I find the money to replace such a fine Italian instrument? Mr. Wurlitzer, living up to his kindly reputation, agreed to look at the violin and to waive the customary appraisal fee.

When I returned, a repairman brought the violin out — now freshly glued, cleaned, and polished to a luster I had never seen before. As I held the glittering Dollenz admiringly in my hands, Mr. Wurlitzer appeared from the workshop with his brow furrowed. He had looked the violin over and judged that it was, regrettably, not a Dollenz but only a copy, not Italian but French, and fifty years younger than the label inside stated. My violin's good name had just been unceremoniously snatched away. The image of the Dollenz's certificate of authenticity, looking remarkably official with three accompanying photographs of the violin — front, side, and back — drifted before my eyes. That document bore the stamp of unshakable authority, and yet this esteemed expert judged my violin a fake. Wurlitzer, seeing that I was visibly shaken, offered an explanation for his opinion, pointing to the shape of the scroll, the makeup of the varnish, and the general pattern of the instrument.

During the bus trip back to Philadelphia, troubling questions gnawed at me. What made an expert expert? Which expert could I believe? And were there people, God forbid, who called themselves experts who actually were not?

In time I came to believe that Wurlitzer's opinion, shared by many other luthiers, was accurate. But this was only the first of many experiences of disputed opinions concerning violins I have owned. My Lorenzo Guadagnini was considered by some to be a Pietro Mantegazza, my Guarneri del Gesù was first thought to be a John Lott, and the violin I currently own was attributed at different times to at least four different makers. I once visited Emile Français's violin shop on the rue de Rome in Paris in order to buy some strings. Emile, the father of the New York City dealer Jacques Français, was a major Parisian dealer. Peering through the darkened windows of his shop, I could see no sign of life, but after I repeatedly knocked on the front door, Français, slightly stooped, let me in and turned on a single light. He looked me over mistrustfully through glasses that rested far down his nose. I introduced myself, placed my order, and, when the business transaction was completed, opened my violin case to put away the strings. Français, who had been rather uncommunicative until then, spoke.

"What is your violin?"

"A Lorenzo Guadagnini."

"May I see it?" Français held the instrument in both hands, looked it over, and handed it back. "This is no Lorenzo Guadagnini."

"Oh," I said, not able to come up with any other response to the unexpected news. As I put the violin away, he spoke again.

"What kind of bows do you have?"

"I have two — a Vuillaume and a Sartori."

"Let me see them, please."

Français carefully examined the first bow and then looked up darkly. "This is not a Vuillaume."

He examined the second bow, shaking his head. "And this is not a Sartori."

With each pronouncement, he glared at me as if I were some kind of con man trying to fence stolen goods. I put the bows away and Français spoke yet again.

"What did you say your name was?"

"Arnold Steinhardt."

Français held me suspiciously in his gaze. My heart sank. Was he going to tell me that I was not Arnold Steinhardt but merely a poor copy — that the real Steinhardt was shaped differently and had a two-piece back? I closed the case as fast as I could and fled from the shop.

They say that there is no such thing as history but only historians. Perhaps there are no violins either, only opinions about them; but opinions have consequences. As I left Wurlitzer's shop with my violin now stripped of the name Giovanni Dollenz, it had instantly lost easily half its value. Word spread quickly about Wurlitzer's appraisal when I returned to school. My warped violin was now only a copy of a Dollenz, who was only possibly a student of Storioni, who was only the last (and certainly not the best) of the great Cremonese makers. Now that my violin had lost its pedigree, I began to regard it with a cooler eye and ear. Its sound had been sweet as a nineteenth-century Italian violin. Now, suddenly fifty years younger and driven into French territory, was the sound not merely thin?

Thin or sweet, better or worse, this was my violin for the foreseeable future and the one I continued to play at my weekly lessons. Galamian, who considered the six Bach Sonatas and Partitas for Solo Violin a staple of the repertoire, began assigning me at least one or two of them every year, alternating between the so-called church sonatas, each with four movements — slow, fast (fugue), slow, fast — and the partitas, essentially each a collection of dance movements strung together. Galamian proffered musical advice regarding tempos, phrasing, and dynamics in teaching these works, but his principal interest was more basic — good rhythm, solid intonation, and a clean, healthy sound.

During the relatively brief period in which Galamian had performed in public, he had apparently been more than just a flashy virtuoso. Among the papers found after his death was a faded announcement of his concert from May 5, 1924 (including Bach's Chaconne), his Paris debut recital program of December 24, 1926, and several rave reviews. I could glean from the reviews that Galamian was a rare mix of sensitive artist and consummate violinist — qualities not often found together in one player — and yet in lesson after lesson he chose to emphasize matters of technique. This tack was initially disappointing to me. Of course rhythm, intonation, and sound were important, but if the Sonatas and Partitas were such giants of the repertoire, I expected Galamian to talk about their significance, their inner meaning, their profundity.

Even students who fared brilliantly with much of the repertoire seemed to stumble in Bach. It was as if two people resided in each violinist's body — one who could play difficult concertos admirably and one who lost both musical and technical courage in confronting the great Bach. In one of the very first Curtis Hall recitals I attended, a Galamian student performed Bach's Third Sonata in C Major. The performance was remarkably clean, healthy, solid — just the qualities that Galamian dearly prized. The intertwining voices were articulated so clearly that when I closed my eyes, it was not hard to imagine two, even three violinists playing together. Whether the performance was mature or only the work of a young, half-formed musical mind, I could not say, but it took my breath away. The young man played all the notes in a polished fashion, and that, coupled with the solid qualities of musicianship preached by Galamian, allowed Bach's genius to shine through. For the moment, if not forever, such an approach would be my most important goal.

Occasionally I tired of dense, turgid, sometimes unfathomable Bach. Three-voiced fugues were fine, but sometimes I longed for simplicity. My father sent me a package containing some of my old records. During one of my mother's periodic house cleanings she had threatened to throw them all out. Perhaps because I was experiencing the first stirrings of historical curiosity, I asked my dad to ship the records east. Among them were two recordings of the "Meditation" from the opera *Thaïs*, by Jules Massenet. The violin soloists were Fritz Kreisler and Mischa Elman. At midcentury there was no living violinist who did not revere both Kreisler and Elman. Kreisler's playing had a warmth, leisureliness, and freedom that brought forth the vanishing attributes of an earlier era. People loved his playing, and moreover, they left the concert hall content and thinking that the world wasn't half bad after all. Indeed, when Kreisler appeared onstage, his smiling and avuncular presence is said to have evoked minutes of applause before he even lifted violin to chin. As for Elman, concertgoers cherished how he sang on the violin, his lustrous tone, and the way he seemed to revel in it.

Despite Kreisler's and Elman's renown, the records of the "Meditation" did not interest me initially. The piece had suffered the fate of many pieces that are too successful for too long — first discovered, then performed, finally adulated, but then over-played, worn thin, and eventually ridiculed. After fifty years, Massenet's song had become the butt of jokes. At Curtis we called it the "Medication from *Thaïs.*" Kreisler's and Elman's artistry meant a great deal to me, but I wondered, as I pulled the solid-feeling yet very breakable 78 rpm records gingerly from their envelopes, why two famous violinists bothered to record the same treacly piece at more or less the same time. I loped down the stairs of my boarding house to see if I could use Mrs. Ewell's record player.

Mrs. Ewell, my elderly landlady, was finally speaking to me again. We had awakened her several nights earlier with our student version of the French film thriller *Diabolique.* Alarmed by the noise above her bedroom, she rushed upstairs in her night-gown, eyes swollen from sleep, only to find me submerged in a bathtub full of water with my shoes and clothes on — an attempt to enact the movie's most terrifying scene. The next morning Mrs. Ewell barred my way as I tried to leave. "Arnold," she said with a slight quiver in her voice, "you ought to see a psychiatrist." Secretly, I was pleased that my behavior provoked such a recommendation. We all lived for pranks and practical jokes. Indeed, they were just what music students facing an uncertain profession needed to let off steam.

I followed Mrs. Ewell into the living room, where the record player lived. My thirty-five-dollars-a-month rent covered the use of a small upstairs room for sleeping and practicing but certainly not the use of her private quarters. She seemed pleased, however, to be of service. Mrs. Ewell had been renting out rooms to Curtis students almost since the school's founding in the 1920s. I pulled the Kreisler out of its stiff paper sleeve and placed it on the turntable. Kreisler recorded two versions of the "Meditation," accompanied by Carl Lamson at the piano, on February 2, 1928, Kreisler's birthday. Such was the popularity of both the artist and the work that both takes were released. Mrs. Ewell joined me on the couch as the record player's arm and needle jerked sideways before settling onto the revolving platter's surface. The old record emitted a frightful collection of crackles, pops, and hisses, which yielded only reluctantly to the pianist's gently ascending introductory chords. Then Kreisler made his entrance. His tone was robust but with an underlying resonance that soared above the record's surface noise. His phrasing, supported by a narrow, pulsating vibrato, I can only describe as loving. When the record came to an end, Mrs. Ewell and I remained quietly sitting on her sofa. Perhaps because I listened with a person of Kreisler's generation rather than my own, I could drop the pose of opinionated swagger that students often display with one another in order to hide their inexperience and insecurity. I received the "Meditation" unselfconsciously and without preconceptions. A great poet had just spoken to us.

Kreisler's playing seemed to render Elman's version irrelevant. How could any violinist improve on the intoxicating beauty of what we had just heard? But Mrs. Ewell marched purposefully up to the record player and placed the other disk on the turntable. Again the scratchy surface, again the two-bar piano introduction, this time played by Percy B. Kahn. His tempo was faster than Kreisler's, allowing the solo line more freedom and impulsiveness. Elman sought out a very specific quality of tone. He was like a miner excavating the violin strings for veins of sound. The sheer opulence of his rendition bathed the senses. Elman's violin sang with an aching sadness. Where Kreisler had been noble, Elman was touching. Of the two versions, I could not say which affected me more. There was a devotional yet sultry magic in the way the winding melody was buttressed by a series of languid harmonies that rose and fell, sometimes precipitously. The composer Vincent d'Indy called it a "discreet and semi-religious eroticism." "Lovely. Just lovely," Mrs. Ewell finally murmured, her voice rustling in the incense-like air that lingered in the room.

Completely under the "Meditation's" spell, I gave it an unscheduled appearance at my next lesson with Galamian. He looked first at the music, then at me, and smiled indulgently. "I want to hear music that will make you a better violinist while your body is still young and malleable. The 'Meditation' is lovely, but you can play it anytime." I tried to hide my disappointment. Was there no room in the world for simple, heartfelt utterances? Did not bungalows reside alongside great cathedrals? Couldn't Galamian understand why I was so drawn to the scented, heady music of Thaïs, the courtesan who struggles to decide whether she should enter a convent or return to her lover?

Oddly enough, the one work of Bach's that Galamian had not yet assigned me, intentionally or not, was the D Minor Partita with its vaunted Chaconne. Schoolwork left little time to think about the Chaconne, but it hung in the back of my mind like a briefly visited place that beckoned insistently. In fact, my next encounter with the Chaconne was just around the corner.

For three years, from 1956 to 1958, I attended Meadowmount,

Galamian's summer violin camp in the Adirondack Mountains. Galamian had a strict idea about how the camp should be run: six to eight hours of daily practice, lights out at 10 P.M., and no private fraternizing with the opposite sex. "Keep out of zee booshes," he reminded us over and over again.

Aware of the danger of too much practice without musical direction or inspiration, Galamian invited distinguished violinists occasionally to visit the camp. One day Isaac Stern appeared at Meadowmount, and Galamian chose three students — Jaime Laredo, Jerry Rosen, and me — to play for him in a master class. The virtuoso Zino Francescatti had recently heard the same trio of students. In that master class, Francescatti seemed incapable of shedding his polished French manners to proffer a potentially unpleasant critique. "*Bon*," "Very good," and "*Magnifique*" were the only comments that left his mouth. I was not flattered. On the contrary, it was disappointing not to be able to profit from this once-in-a-lifetime encounter with the great artist. Somehow I had the cheek to corner Francescatti behind the concert hall afterward and demand to know what he *really* thought of my playing. Francescatti looked furtively right and left like a trapped animal, smiled synthetically, and uttered something preposterous. "No, no, young man. I loved your playing. Why" — here he smiled even more broadly — "I only wish I could play as well as you."

Isaac Stern had no such problem meting out criticism. Stern was smart, blunt, and probing. Rather than focusing on technical considerations, he chose to point out bad habits, question our musical choices, challenge us to think clearly and deeply about the music we were playing rather than the fiddle we were playing it on. Then he gave a lecture demonstration on Bach's Chaconne for the whole group of students. Stern first spoke of the Chaconne's origins as a four-bar dance, stressing the second of its three-beat pulse, the repetition of those four bars in endless variation, how Bach tipped his hand at the end of certain variations to reveal something about the one to follow, how variations could be grouped together cohesively, and finally the different characters of the work's three main sections. The information was interesting enough, but his manner of thinking especially caught my attention. Stern looked at the Chaconne the way I imagined an architect would analyze the structure and details of a building. If he could just understand how Bach had built the Chaconne, then and only then would he be able to render it himself. When the lecture came to an end, Stern performed the Chaconne for us — feet planted resolutely, chin jutting forward, eyes focused inward, his stocky, bull-like frame set as if for battle. His performance electrified us. We gave him a standing ovation.

Recently I ran into Michael Gilbert, a fellow Meadowmounter, at the Memphis airport. As we waited for our luggage, Michael and I reminisced about those good old days at Meadowmount — a prison camp in heaven, a gulag in paradise, we both agreed. "Remember Stern's lecture demonstration?" I asked. "Of course," he said. Michael and I reviewed step by step what Stern had said about the Chaconne as if it were yesterday. "Do you remember what he said when he finished the Chaconne?" Michael asked. Honestly, I couldn't. "When the applause stopped, Stern stepped forward and said, 'And as an object lesson for you, I was nervous!'"

What I do remember clearly is that as Stern bowed on the Meadowmount stage to feverish applause, my perception of the Chaconne and music at large underwent a change. From that moment on, I would try to look at all music through the composer's eyes. I also hoped that the Chaconne would stay with me as a companion, a point of orientation, and a source of bedrock wisdom.

Curtis was a well-insulated cocoon where we students could learn our instruments and the magical craft of music relatively undisturbed, but the real world began to clamor more and more for attention as the end of school approached. What exactly was I going to do with my life when I left those comforting oak-paneled walls? And how was I going to do it? Basically, four callings were available to me as a violinist — teacher, orchestra player, chamber musician, and soloist. There was no question where my heart lay. Like many of my friends, I wanted to be the next great soloist, and with Galamian's help I was doing my level best to rise to that rarefied level. But even if I were to become a superb violinist, who was going to know about me? Without a personal sponsor, one of the few routes that could lead to a career was the violin competition. Prizes consisted of engagements, sometimes money, and, perhaps most important, public exposure. In my third year of school, inexperienced and nervous, I tried out for the Philadelphia Youth Competition and didn't make the finals. Galamian's studio had been a benign sanctuary where the wounds of criticism healed easily from one lesson to the next. But competitions drew blood. There were winners, losers, and in my case the bitter fruit of defeat. Curtis offered no courses in how to deal with the insecurity of my profession, and even if it had, they would have been theoretical at best. On the verge of playing the violin at a high level, I now had to learn as quickly as possible how to excel under pressure, how to accept failure philosophically, and how to maintain some comfort level as I tried to find my way in a profession that by its very nature is filled with uncertainty.

The next year I entered the Philadelphia Youth Competition again. This time I won. The prize was an appearance with the Philadelphia Orchestra and its conductor, Eugene Ormandy. Sitting week after week in the box at the Academy of Music specifically reserved for Curtis students, I swooned over the orchestra's lush sound and admired Ormandy's supple gestures. Later that year I stood as if in a dream on the academy stage and performed Wieniawski's D Minor Concerto with the Philadelphia Orchestra.

There was, however, one significant blemish on this otherwise superlative experience. What I only suspected of my violin in the practice studio became magnified exponentially in this grand concert hall. The Wieniawski concerto's alluring melodies and virtuoso acrobatics seemed thin and monochromatic on my no-name instrument. Sooner or later my warped, identity-less, small-voiced violin would have to be put to rest.

The need for a fine instrument rose dramatically when, in the next and last year of school, I won the Leventritt International Violin Competition. The prize was no fewer than six solo appearances with several major American orchestras, including the New York Philharmonic. The competition's founder, Rosalie Leventritt, a doyenne in the cultural life of New York City, came to my rescue. She called her friend Gerald Warburg and asked him to lend me one of the Stradivarius instruments in his collection. Within a matter of days I found myself greeted affably by the balding, mustached, and middle-aged Gerry Warburg, a member of the distinguished banking family and an amateur cellist himself, in his East Side apartment. His father, Felix Warburg, had bought a quartet of Stradivarius instruments as a collector around 1900. When Gerry went to Vienna in 1925 to study cello, his father gave them to him. Warburg showed me these Strads — first his own cello, then a viola called the McDonald, one of only ten Stradivarius violas in the entire world, and finally a violin named the Spanish for its residence at one time in the Spanish court. Stradivari had made a quartet of instruments for Philip V of Spain as a gift. Philip was actually in Cremona in 1702 during the Spanish War of Succession, but Stradivari, advised not to make the presentation for fear of being branded a collaborator, ultimately decided to keep the instruments in the family. It took another three quarters of a century for the quartet finally to arrive at the Spanish court.

The violin Jerry Warburg placed in my hands almost fifty years ago had rich golden varnish, elegant looks, and a sap mark running lengthwise down the right side of the top. Apparently Stradivari had found one particular log ideal for his purposes and used it to make many violins, each with that characteristic sap mark. Jerry handed the violin to me carefully but somewhat matter-of-factly, as if it were an everyday sort of object. I had never held a Stradivarius in my hands before, a 250-year-old wooden artifact that was both history and art.

It would have been interesting to compare the Philadelphia and New York performances of the same concertos on different violins — one a commoner, one an aristocrat. The Spanish Strad's silvery tone had wings on it in my Carnegie Hall performance with the New York Philharmonic Orchestra. The violinist Adolf Busch once remarked about a Stradivarius that "when you hold such a violin in your hands, you might even think that you are talented!" A great orchestra, a legendary hall, a magical violin, and a very creditable performance of Wieniawski's D Minor Concerto! For days afterward the glow from this cocktail of ingredients lingered in my mind. Eventually I returned the Stradivarius to Warburg as planned. He shook my hand and wished me well, and I boarded the bus back to Philadelphia, having every reason to feel good. The future might still be unclear, but at least my New York debut had been a promising start.

I climbed the steps to my fourth-floor one-room apartment on St. James Street and opened my own violin case for the first time in several weeks. There lay the violin, my constant companion for the last seven years — jilted! I had callously, even joyfully abandoned it for another. Out of curiosity, I picked it up and played a few notes of the Brahms Violin Concerto, slated for my next lesson with Galamian. The sound was faded and pinched. It was, of course, that Spanish lady's fault. My old violin didn't stand a chance next to her. The glow of optimism that had bolstered me for days suddenly vanished. How was I to start a career without a good violin? And how was I to afford such a violin?

CHAPTER 7

I, Violinist

Having won a major violin competition, I now hoped to parlay my good fortune into the beginnings of a concert career. But the call I received several weeks later that would alter my life significantly was not from a manager eager to launch me into a soloist's orbit. George Szell, the conductor of the Cleveland Orchestra, whom I had met when he was judging the Leventritt Competition, invited me to join his orchestra as assistant concertmaster.

Szell had molded his orchestra into an ensemble that had gained worldwide admiration for its spit-polished and thoughtful interpretations of the great Central European repertoire. By age eleven Szell had already won success as a composer, pianist, and conductor, and such was his brilliance that he could sight-read a complex Richard Strauss orchestral score at the piano and even spontaneously transpose it to another key. Despite his erudition and renown, however, my initial reaction to the idea of sitting in an orchestra, even this great and admired one, was tepid. I wanted to be a soloist. That had been the plan since I'd heard Elman play the Chaconne long ago. Elman, Kreisler, Heifetz, Francescatti, Menuhin, Milstein, Stern — these were my heroes, not only for their ability to play brilliantly but also because they gave something of themselves to the music, something personal, individual, heartfelt, memorable. No matter how beautifully I might play, if I were buried in the Cleveland Orchestra, who would know?

I had heard a great deal about Szell — both good and very, very bad. He was brilliant but obsessive, deeply knowledgeable but rigid, candid to the point of cruelty, a shrewd collector of the very best players but capable of ruthlessly casting off those who did not meet his standards. On the phone, his clipped, immaculate English laced with a strong German accent was certainly intimidating. And the questions he asked made me feel as if he were preparing an FBI dossier on me: What education have you had? Who were your teachers? What kind of violin do you play? Where were your parents born? What do they do for a living? What are their names? Where do they live? (Two years later, Szell called me into his office and demanded to know why he could not locate my father's liquor store in downtown Los Angeles. He remembered my father's name, his business, and its location but had found only a place called Mitchell's; my father, Mischa, had Anglicized his name.)

Szell laid out his plans for me. I would play in the orchestra and sit next to the concertmaster, Josef Gingold, who had been my chamber music coach at Meadowmount and was an extraordinarily sensitive violinist. I would study and perform a concerto with Szell each season. Then came the clincher: Szell offered to arrange for me to study with his friend Joseph Szigeti, the great Hungarian violinist, who had just retired from the concert stage, and to pay for my trip to Switzerland, where Szigeti lived. Despite his reputation as an ogre, Szell presented me with an unparalleled opportunity. I mulled over the offer for a few days, then called Szell and accepted.

The phone was ringing as I climbed the steps to my Philadelphia apartment. "Ahneeee!" leaped out at me as I picked up the receiver. There was only one gravelly inflected voice like that anywhere in the world, and only one person besides my parents and childhood friends called me Arnie — Joe Gingold. "I'm so happy for youuuu! We will have a mahhhvelous time together. And by the way, I'll help you pick out a niiice violin at the end of the summer." As soon as the Cleveland Orchestra made the announcement of my appointment, Szell had called Joe to grill him about me and to lay his plans for me. I was a fresh lump of clay to be molded to his specifications. One of the items discussed was my violin. Joe described my fake Dollenz, which he knew from Meadowmount days, and Szell, aghast, ordered him to find a first-class violin for me. Cleveland had no major rare instrument dealers, but Philadelphia, the city I had called home for the past five years, certainly did. William Moennig & Son, a mere five-minute stroll from the Curtis Institute of Music, was located on Locust Street when I arrived at the school and is still there now, sixty years later. When I entered the shop in the 1950s to buy strings or to have my bow rehaired, three generations of Moennigs were working together — the diminutive and stooped older Moennig, about to retire; stocky William Moennig, Jr., running the shop;

and young, dapper Bill Moennig, Jr., slowly being initiated into the business.

Moennig's was the place where I bought my first outstanding bow — a Dominique Peccatte — as an early graduation present to myself. Now, only months later, I entered the shop with Joe Gingold at my side and a far more ambitious aim: to buy my first really good violin. Joe shook hands all around. "So goood to see you," he crooned right and left. Joe knew everybody there. He also knew exactly what he wanted. "Ahneee would like a violin with a strong and appealing sound in the twenty-five-hundred-dollar range," he said to William Moennig, Jr.

I gasped. In 1959 a bowl of soup cost three nickels at the Horn & Hardart Automat, the local butcher charged twenty cents for a pound of ground beef, and a good tweed suit might be fifty dollars. On a careful budget, I could manage all those items. But $2500! "Joe," I whispered, knowing that I had only forty-five dollars in my savings account at the moment, "isn't that too much?"

Joe looked at me sternly. "You need a good violin. You are now assistant concertsheister of the Cleveland Orchestra!"

I did the math as I smiled thinly. With only a thirty-week orchestra season, a violin that expensive would eat up half my yearly salary.

Moennig brought out several violins, which he laid on a table covered with soft velvet cloth. Realistically, the violin I ultimately chose would have to be much better than my own but far beneath the quality of Jerry Warburg's Spanish Strad. That left me in a no-man's land of possibilities.

Joe played the violins one by one, discarding all but two or three. Those he asked me to play. They sounded so different from each other and from my own that it was hard to know what I liked. "Niiice, niiice," Joe murmured. "Do you have anything in a slightly higher price range?" he asked Moennig.

My heart dropped. Joe was sending me to debtor's prison.

Moennig thought for a moment and then brought out another violin, red-brown in color and with a distinctive wide-grained spruce top. Joe played just a few notes on it and said "Ah" as he handed it to me.

From the very first note, the violin sounded more robust than the others and was instantly appealing. There was a pleasing woodiness to the tone, although I could not explain why I thought this.

"Italian?" Joe asked.

"Yes," Moennig confirmed. "Pressenda."

I looked inside the violin through one of the f-holes and tipped it until the light shone on the label. *Joannes Franciscus Pressenda; Turin 1823* was barely discernible.

Joe smiled at me and nodded knowingly. "Strong. Good quality. I think this is the violin for youuu."

I turned the violin over in my hands to look at its beautiful one-piece maple back. I loved it.

Joe turned to Moennig. "The price?"

"Thirty-five hundred, but we'll give you a professional discount of fifteen percent, which brings it down to three thousand dollars."

I tried again to tell Joe about the meager size of my bank account, but he waved me off. "Bill, you understand that Ahneee only starts his position with the Cleveland Orchestra in two weeks and that he will have to pay you in installments during the season."

Moennig nodded, and in a few moments a letter of agreement was drawn up. As I signed the document, nervous about the financial noose just put around my neck but elated to own my very first good violin, it occurred to me that I had never even heard of its maker. Moennig informed me that Pressenda learned his craft from Lorenzo Storioni in Cremona. Storioni? Giovanni Dollenz, the name on the fictitious label in my old violin, had only possibly been his student, but apparently there was no doubt about Pressenda. He was most definitely a student of Storioni's, and as I well knew by now, Storioni was the last of the great Cremonese masters.

Joe and I got into my 1947 Studebaker with the Pressenda resting on the back seat and began our trip to Cleveland. I was bursting with excitement. Seldom again would the world appear quite so fresh and full of promise. A new city, a new career, a new violin, and a new life awaited me.

Gingold belonged to that elite club of people who had never learned to drive an automobile, so I was the designated driver for the entire trip. I had just driven up to the Adirondack Mountains and back, a foolish all-night escapade in order to see a girl I liked. As Joe waxed poetic about my success in finding a violin whose sound would carry in a big hall, a hall with perhaps a thousand seats or more, my eyelids began to droop. Finally I could go on no longer and pulled into a rest stop. Joe eyed me questioningly, and I was obliged sheepishly to confess my predicament. In a matter of seconds I was fast asleep. When I awoke some time later, Joe was smiling. "Ahnee. Did you know you talk in your sleep? You said, 'Nicole, Nicole.' About this I won't ask. But then you said 'The audience . . . a thousand faces.' It was quite dramatic." Joe and I looked at each other as I shifted the old Studebaker into gear, and then we burst out laughing. Both Nicole and Pressenda had infiltrated my subconscious.

When we arrived in Cleveland, Szell quickly arranged to hear me play the Pressenda on the stage of Severance Hall, where the Cleveland Orchestra regularly performed. The violin's sound soared easily back to where the two men, Szell and Gingold, sat in the empty hall. I played one of the noble themes from Tchaikovsky's Fifth Symphony, slated for an upcoming concert, and then some Bach. Szell asked Joe pointed questions about the violin's capabilities and finally nodded his head in approval. Joannes Pressenda was accepted into the Cleveland Orchestra.

You would think that a world-renowned conductor had better things to do with his time than fuss about my instrument, but such was Szell's nature that he wanted to supervise every aspect of orchestra life, down to the smallest detail. He took a personal interest in me as a young musician with possibilities and was generous enough to have me solo regularly with the orchestra and to sponsor my trip to Europe. But he must have had some border collie in him, for he constantly herded me like a sheep. He advised me that the striped polo shirt I wore was inappropriate for rehearsals, that playing poker during intermission was corrupting, that I must wear garters so my socks would stay up during concerts (Szell lifted his pant leg in the privacy of his office and demonstrated), and that my summer beard would have to come off because he did not care for "a display of one's pubic hair in public." I was flattered and amused by the attention, yet maddened by the overdirection.

All was forgiven, however, when the orchestra played. Szell had a glittering array of talents. He was a supremely trained musician, an excellent pianist, a solid if somewhat derivative composer, a shrewd orchestra builder, and, when the spirit moved him, an electrifying conductor. The symphonies of Mozart, Beethoven, Schubert, Dvořák, Schumann, Mahler, and even Tchaikovsky were prepared to the exacting standards of a crack string quartet and then presented with all the authority of his powerful musical mind. Szell would tap the podium with his baton during rehearsals and say, "Good morning, ladies and gentlemen. I have some new ideas for Beethoven's Fifth." The orchestra would emit a collective groan under its breath. What new ideas could there be in a warhorse rehearsed and played to death for the last two hundred years? And yet Szell did come up with ideas — some good, some less successful, others very impressive. He usually kept performances strictly under control, often clamping down on the music's inherent suppleness. Sometimes he would stare coldly at individual members for their supposed failings, and occasionally we would be called into his office afterward for a musicological lecture or even a tongue-lashing. The lion tamer cracked his whip often; otherwise, God only knows what we wild beasts would do. But occasionally Szell would grant himself the freedom, and the orchestra the trust, to let the music soar without the usual restraints. Then there was magic in the air.

A seemingly endless parade of memorable soloists adorned the orchestra concerts. From my seat as assistant concertmaster, only inches away from the great violinists who played with us, I could see the sweat bead on their brows, hear them breathing heavily in the heat of a performance, and witness their private little exchanges with Szell during rehearsal. While Szell tried to be serious, Nathan Milstein cut up like a schoolboy; the Russian David Oistrakh, in contrast, was all business in the face of Szell's forced jolliness in trying to impress his cold war trophy soloist, and Henryk Szeryng behaved so pompously that by concert time Szell and he were not on speaking terms. Yet they all played stunningly. It was a distinct honor to join their ranks as soloist in my own right, playing concertos by Mozart, Glazunov, Wieniawski, and Bartók.

At the end of one rehearsal, Trogden, the orchestra's personnel manager, told me that Szell wanted to see me in his office. This worried me. We had recently finished a week of children's concerts in which I was acting concertmaster. At the Akron, Ohio, armory, we had been so tightly packed onto a highly waxed stage designed for military maneuvers that my extended foot inadvertently moved the podium an inch or two during a concert. Ernie Kardos, my stand partner, found this interesting. As Louis Lane, the orchestra's associate conductor, swashbuckled his way through Borodin's *Polovetzian Dances,* Ernie also placed his foot on the podium's edge, and together we pushed. The podium moved again, this time enough to cramp the violas sitting across from us. Abe Skernick, the principal violist, oblivious of our shenanigans, motioned for his entire section to move back. Ernie and I exchanged meaningful glances and pushed further. Abe, finding himself again in an unacceptably cramped position, looked perplexed for an instant and glanced in our direction. Then a light bulb went on. Abe whispered something to his stand partner, Fred Funkhauser, and together they pushed back. While Lane conducted, unaware of what was going on, a war took place underneath him — the podium sliding back and forth in slow motion.

A week later, the orchestra manager, A. Beverly Barksdale, called me into his office and showed me a letter he had just received from the Akron Parent Teachers Association complaining

about the disgraceful behavior of the concertmaster and first violist during their children's concert. I hung my head in shame.

I feared that this ignominious event was the reason for Szell's
summons. Szell had taken a fatherly interest in me from the start.
When I arrived early and well prepared at rehearsals and played
well in concerts, he beamed, but when I misbehaved or slacked
off, there was hell to pay. Discipline! Hard work! Despite Szell's
enormous musical gifts, these were the unbreakable rules he
himself lived by and demanded of others.

To my relief, he was smiling when I entered the room. He had
decided that I should next play the Beethoven Violin Concerto
with him. My anxiety gave way to sheer joy. This was the concerto I
revered above all others. Szell handed me a record he had made of
the concerto early in his conducting career with the Polish violinist Bronislaw Huberman. "Listen to this," he said with ill-concealed pride, "and especially to Huberman's solo entrance. He
is like Zeus storming Mount Olympus." With such a recommendation, I eagerly took the record home. By now I had heard the
Beethoven on record and in performance dozens and dozens of
times. Each rendition illuminated the concerto's contours more
clearly and brought yet another layer of meaning to the work I had
first heard as a five-year-old.

At the age of thirteen, Huberman had performed the Brahms
Concerto in Vienna with the composer attending. Brahms was
so moved that he inscribed a photo to him afterward "From his
grateful listener." Huberman's Beethoven concerto would be a
performance to remember! Through the record's crackly surface
noise, five opening tympani beats gently tapped for my attention,
followed by a chorus of woodwinds that sang out beckoningly.

But Huberman's entrance was anything but Zeuslike. The ascending octaves and the notes that followed sounded rough, his tone pinched. Most damning of all to me as a young violinist, his playing seemed hopelessly old-fashioned. Huberman slid rather than shifted from one position to another, in the accepted tradition of his era. I, a modern violinist of the second half of the twentieth century, found this style of playing amusing at best, especially in light of such polar opposites as Heifetz and Szigeti, whose polished performances of the Beethoven dazzled and moved me. I lied to Szell when I returned the record. I told him I loved Huberman's playing.

Private rehearsals began soon after. Szell sat at the piano and played the last few bars of orchestral tutti and then cued me to enter. "Zeus storming Mount Olympus" had become permanently stuck in my mind. The recipe I concocted to achieve this goal had two ingredients: immaculately clean octaves and unrestrained freedom — the precision of a modern violinist coupled with the abandon of a bygone age. To my delight, the octaves came off exactly as planned. "No, no, *no!*" Szell bellowed. "In time! The octaves must be strictly in time. You must always maintain a pulse." Each time I lingered on a note or phrase, Szell stopped playing and began to beat time with the tip of his pencil. "But, Mr. Szell, it's so . . . beautiful," I pleaded during the first movement's G minor section. Szell regarded me sternly. "There can be no beauty with anarchy," he pronounced. A talented but undisciplined violinist, a brilliant but dogmatic conductor. The result: Mount Olympus in a straitjacket. What was the harm in stopping along the road to pick a few daisies once in a while? But Szell demanded that the Beethoven concerto flow inexorably forward, even if (and here Szell made a sour face) I insisted on picking my beloved daisies.

Not long after, I walked onto the Severance Hall stage followed by Szell, bowed to the audience, and waited for him to give the downbeat. There was no orchestra in the world that played with the Cleveland's clarity, dynamic range, and musical taste. A concerto performance with them was always a special event, but the Beethoven resided in an exalted place: disarmingly good-natured, sweetly melancholy, ruminative, prayerful, majestic, noble. My heart beat loudly enough to provide competition for the opening "thump, thump, thump, thump, thump" of the tympani. I stood still as the eighty-eight bars of orchestral tutti unfolded, but a dizzying array of emotions roiled in me. Szell, given his nature, would have wanted to give order to them, but I could not. The satisfaction of having my dream of playing this concerto nearly fulfilled, the sensation of being within the sounds that Beethoven conceived rather than at a distance, and the feeling of having finally joined the cadre of violinists who lay their individually fashioned wreaths before this great work — all those emotions threatened to overwhelm me. The eighty-eight bars flowed by, and Mount Olympus in measured and stately steps drew near. Then I lifted my violin and bow and began to climb.

The Beethoven concerto performance was unquestionably a major milestone for me, but the way I regarded my role as soloist standing before a symphony orchestra began to shift. What kind of animal was a soloist, actually? Beethoven wrote this noble concerto for the brilliant twenty-six-year-old Viennese violinist Franz Clement, the kind of soloist who followed the very first performance by improvising a sonata on the violin on one string upside-down. Yet there was so much musical substance and organic interplay between soloist and orchestra that the concerto might just as well be conceived of as a symphony with solo violin rather than a concerto. Was I not at one point in the first movement merely weaving an obbligato filigree above the violins' mournful song, and at another in the third movement serving as a pliant accompanist for the amiable solo bassoon? None of those distinguished Cleveland Orchestra musicians stood while delivering the sonorous melodies that laced the concerto (except for the tympanist serving up those opening five notes), yet they were all truly soloists.

And this brought me to the great chamber music repertoire. Mozart's G Minor two-viola quintet, Schubert's two-cello quintet, Mendelssohn's octet, and a host of other magical works demanded an exhilarating degree of quick-change artistry. A chamber musician donned a soloist's cap one moment, became a humble accompanist the next, and just as abruptly melded into a choir of felicitous sound. The great chamber music repertoire offered an allure that snared my attention more and more.

To that end, the Marlboro Music School in southern Vermont was heaven-sent. Founded in 1951 by Adolf Busch, his brother Hermann, Adolf's son-in-law, the pianist Rudolf Serkin, and Busch's colleagues Marcel, Louis, and Blanche Moyse, Marlboro was conceived as a place where the artistic community would come together each summer to exchange ideas and study the great chamber music repertoire. Nineteen fifty-nine was the first of many summers I spent there. Inevitably, we learned from one another. Young musicians worked with older ones who were not only exceptional artists but also firmly tethered to the great traditions of the past. Rudolf Serkin, Marlboro's director, would tell us what Ferruccio Busoni had said to him about his music, as Felix Galimir would speak about Maurice Ravel, Alban Berg, and Anton

Webern and Marcel Moyse about Debussy. In studying Debussy's Trio for Harp, Flute, and Viola, Moyse, a renowned flutist who had played the work for the composer, leaned over my viola part and asked me to disregard one particular marking. "Debussy wanted it softer" was his offhand remark.

Blanche Moyse, violinist and conductor, regularly collected an intimate group of musicians at Marlboro to perform Bach's secular and church cantatas. I was enlisted, reluctantly at first. The church cantatas bore forbidding titles such as "Why Are You Saddened," "Come, You Sweet Hour of Death," "My Sighs, My Tears," "I Stand with One Foot in the Grave." The music affected me deeply in itself but also for what it stirred up. It was not easy to put a name to the inchoate spiritual feelings that I felt occasionally bubbling to the surface. I could talk comfortably with my friends about politics or baseball scores but only very reluctantly about grief or religious fervor. They had never directly touched my life. But Bach knew about these things — even the bedrock issues of life and death — from firsthand experience. At the age of eight he lost his uncle Christoph Bach, his father's identical twin, and a year later both his parents, Elisabeth and Ambrosius Bach. My own mortality stood in the back of my consciousness, waiting to be addressed. I was content to let the rest of my musical journey unfold in its own time and place, but in my mind there was a special urgency to the Bach problem. Perhaps Bach was a stand-in for the rabbi or priest I had never had — a prophet whose music moved me deeply but seemed nonetheless just beyond my grasp.

There were inevitably differing opinions about every phrase of every chamber music work we tackled at Marlboro. The evolution and alignment of those often clashing ideas was one of the principal reasons for rehearsals. The trouble with Bach, however, was that people often had dramatically opposing notions about his music. Play Bach freely and you were accused of overromanticizing; play it strictly in time and you belonged to the "sewing machine" school of interpretation. The world-renowned harpsichordist Wanda Landowska once said to a fellow musician, "Oh well, you play Bach your way. I'll play him his." But how should one play Bach?

Linked with never-ending interpretive issues was my choice of instrument and bow. Despite the violin's remarkably unchanging state over centuries, small alterations have inevitably occurred. Bach's violin works were written for an instrument with a somewhat shorter neck, lower bridge, and different strings than today's violin. The result was a relatively gentle and mellow sound. The modern violin, equipped with longer neck, higher bridge, and taut strings often made of synthetic material and wound metal rather than gut, is a more powerful creature. The convex bow of Bach's era was quite different from the one I play on today. It allowed the bow's horsehair to wrap more easily around the strings, making it possible for three- and four-note chords to be played simultaneously, the way they appeared to be written. These chords had to be rolled slightly with my modern concave bow, standardized and refined with superb craftsmanship by the eighteenth-century French bow-maker François Xavier Tourte. The modern-style concave bow hugs the strings less easily than the Baroque bow, but it provides a stronger sound and greater variety of articulation. The modern violin and bow together, a muscular duo, fill any concert hall with far greater ease than the twosome of Bach's era.

But might not an eighteenth-century violinist transported into the present think the modern violin and bow loud and vulgar? Perhaps, but I, pondering the possibility of reverting to the musical tools of Bach's time, had another problem. I'd already heard the epic symphonies of Beethoven, the heart-wrenching song cycles of Schubert and Schumann, Stravinsky's audacious *Rite of Spring,* and the revolutionary Bartók string quartets. I would always want to play Bach in an appropriate style, but inevitably filtered through my own musical timeline. The sweet and elegant caresses of a Baroque violin appealed to me well enough, but I often wondered whether Bach wasn't the most modern of composers disguised in three-hundred-year-old clothing, or even a composer for all times and tastes. Schumann and Mendelssohn provided piano accompaniments for Bach's solo violin works, both Brahms and Busoni transcribed the Chaconne for piano, and Alban Berg wove a Bach chorale into his violin concerto. Bach's works have been adapted for instruments as wildly diverse as the lush modern orchestra, the unlikely solo marimba, and the swinging jazz band. Bach seems a man filled with almost too much emotion and substance for his carefully delineated Baroque world. I decided to serve his music with my modern violin and bow.

One summer the cellist Pablo Casals arrived in Marlboro. Casals, born in Catalonia in 1876, achieved recognition only slowly, because despite his supreme instrumental command, he insisted on reverentially serving music rather than shallow virtuosity. "Freedom with order," he admonished us. "Variety!" he cried out after we played a section of a Bach orchestral suite rather blandly. Then he moved his jaw back and forth in thought and continued. "Variety, yes . . . music, nature . . . No two leaves are ever the same on a tree, eh? . . . And no two notes are ever the same in a phrase." In the mouth of any other musician this might sound trite, but uttered by Casals, it was gospel, in that the words merely reinforced the miracle of his music-making.

Casals eschewed a beautiful sound for its own sake. Indeed, his tone possessed an almost raspy undercurrent. A Casals phrase had an unerring sense of form and variety. Every note seemed to occupy its essential, preordained place. At different times and for different political reasons, Casals refused to set foot in Spain and later in Britain and the United States. One could sense that same integrity and unassailable resolve in the nobility of his playing.

Casals gave several master classes at Marlboro that summer, and I volunteered to play. I had played for him once before, in New York City after winning the Leventritt Award. Sascha Schneider, second violinist of the Budapest String Quartet, organizer of the Casals Festival, and judge at the Leventritt that year, had fallen in love with my playing and arranged the meeting. The trouble was that, as any number of his amours, friends, and colleagues knew all too well, Sascha fell in and out of love rapidly and unpredictably. I was overwhelmed standing before the great Casals, a small, balding man who sat like Buddha in his hotel room, smoking a pipe. I did not play particularly well, and Casals had little to say, but Sascha more than made up for his reticence. The door to Casals's room had hardly closed when Sascha released a flood of invective. "*Gonif*. How could you play like that? You played nicely. Nicely is terrible." Sascha was right. I had been nervous in front of Casals and therefore cautious. It was counterintuitive to play out when nervousness begged me to play safe.

My performance for Casals at the master class was much improved over my private appearance before the great cellist. Sascha's tirade had served as shock therapy. A master class is just that — a class given by a master. But in front of an audience, anything from grandiose philosophizing to obsessive nitpicking can take place. For some who played for him that day, Casals taught by demonstrating on the cello. For others he offered a few new ideas. But for me he took a different tack. Casals listened to the entire Adagio from Bach's G Minor Sonata in the Marlboro dining room, filled with an audience of musicians and music lovers who hung on his every word, his every grunt. In his eighties, he had by this time acquired an international reputation as both artist and humanitarian. I finished the last chord and waited for him to say something.

He sat in silent contemplation for a moment and then took the pipe out of his mouth. "Good. Very good," he said, nodding his head. I was relieved. Sascha was in the audience. Another short silence followed, and then Casals continued. "Let me tell you a story. Many years ago, the Cortot-Thibaud-Casals Trio played a concert in Budapest. Afterward we asked the presenter to recommend a good place to eat. He insisted that we go to one restaurant in particular, not for the food but to hear a great Gypsy violinist who was playing there. When we entered the restaurant, the Gypsy immediately recognized us and motioned for his band to stop playing. The three of us had hardly been seated when he approached our table, bowed formally, and began to play the same Adagio that you have just played for me. It was the freest rendition of Bach I have ever heard, and also the best. Being a Gypsy, he had none of the inhibitions that we classically trained musicians suffer from. He did not know how one should or should not play Bach, and so he simply played freely and from the heart. And that is what you must do. You play intelligently and with spirit. Now let yourself go."

I do not remember what followed, but this advice was more than enough. It was "Freedom with order" said yet another way. My enduring task would be to seek out these two ingredients in the right proportion.

When I returned to Cleveland and Szell for the next season, I soon became aware of another remarkable musical treasure residing in Cleveland — the pianist, scholar, and writer Arthur Loesser. Arthur was the brother of the musical theater composer Frank Loesser, who had a reputation for being difficult. (Their friends dubbed Frank the evil of two Loessers.) One of Cleveland's most anticipated musical events was Arthur Loesser's yearly performance of Bach's *Well-Tempered Clavier.* Already advanced in years, he would shuffle, slightly stooped, to the piano bench and greet members of the audience whom he recognized from the stage. "Hello," "Nice to see you," "Glad you could come," he called out politely, as if he were playing privately for us in his living room rather than in a formal concert hall. Loesser was a learned scholar. His book *Men, Women, and Pianos* is still read and talked about fifty years after publication. Yet Loesser's *Well-Tempered* was much more than scholarly. His playing was elegant and supple.

I stood applauding with the rest of the audience at the end of one of those memorable performances and wondered whether Loesser might listen to me, and indeed, when I asked, he agreed. Not long after, I played Bach's D Minor Partita for him in his living room. When I finished, Loesser asked me whether I knew how to dance the partita's five movements. It had never even occurred to me that a record of the actual dance steps still existed. Almost as a non sequitur, Loesser began telling me about the severe economic and social disruptions caused by the Thirty Years' War at the time of Bach's birth and how Germany experienced a period of reconstruction that lasted one hundred years, covering his entire life. He explained that many German courts and cities imported French and Italian culture during that time, and that Bach would have encountered French language, music, dance, and theater when he was a student. Loesser went on to say that most of Bach's titled dance music — minuets, gavottes, passepieds, courantes, sarabandes, gigues, and loures — were fashioned after the dances of the French court.

"Now, let me show you how to dance the D Minor Partita," he said. He took off his glasses and let them dangle from a silken cord around his neck; then, smiling sweetly, the elderly Loesser danced the serious Allemande, the lively Courante, the sensuously graceful Sarabande, the high-jinks Gigue, and finally the lusty Chaconne around his living room. He moved by steps, transferring his weight from one foot to another, and by springs. Occasionally he bent both knees and called out, "Plié," or he bent both knees, moved one foot to a new place, transferred the weight of his body onto that foot, and straightened both legs while rising onto the leading foot. Basically, it was an elegant bend and rise, the bend occurring with the last pulse of a measure and the rise coinciding with the first pulse of the following measure. He called out breathlessly, "Sauté," and sprang onto one foot, and then "Pas glissé," sliding his foot to its new place rather than simply moving it there. The slow, sustained effort of the glissé was especially stylish to see. Loesser surprised me by adding turns and even pirouettes, his arms and hands gracefully changing position in carefully controlled circular motions that were coordinated with those of his legs. When he finally came to a stop, he looked at me, eyes glistening, and said, quite out of breath by now, "This is the noble style of French court dancing, and you must make us want to dance while playing your D Minor Partita."

When I returned to my apartment an hour later, the visual image of the elderly, frail Arthur Loesser joyously bending and springing and gliding and turning remained indelibly etched in my mind. I picked up my fiddle and played the beginning of the D Minor Partita with Loesser dancing before my eyes. The Allemande seemed to have wings on it. I sampled all the other movements with similar results. Loesser was clearly on to something. If only I could capture the feeling of dance, perhaps the actual steps were relatively unimportant. A sense of motion in music, of ebb and flow, of bending and springing, was the essential thing to hold on to.

At the end of the 1961–1962 Cleveland Orchestra season, my final paycheck was unusually large. The pay stub listed my weekly salary and one more item — a round-trip fare from New York City to Geneva and back. True to his word, Szell had financed my trip to Switzerland, where Joseph Szigeti lived. That summer I cut short my stay at Marlboro — the closest thing to musical paradise — in order to study with someone who was more than a great violinist. Szigeti's playing engaged my mind as it pulled at my heart. Everything he touched — concertos by Brahms, Beethoven, Mozart, Mendelssohn, Prokofiev, and Berg, the great sonata literature, modest salon pieces like Hubay's "The Zephyr," and, of course, Bach — reflected his interlocking qualities of intelligence and sensitivity. In my last year at Curtis, several of us had made the trip to Radnor, Pennsylvania, to hear what must have been one of Szigeti's last performances before retiring from the concert stage. His bow shook and his vibrato was slow enough to provoke muffled laughs as he began. And yet, by sheer will and sense of purpose, Szigeti made his vision of the music triumph over his failing body. The laughter stuck in our throats as he played. Who else could boast of such magic?

I flew to Geneva, took the train to a station just short of Montreux, and climbed the hill to Baugy sur Clarens, where Szigeti lived. His house overlooked Lake Geneva, shimmering in the late afternoon sun under a backdrop of jagged mountains — les Dents du Midi (the Teeth of Noon). Everything seemed exotic in the canton of Vaud. People spoke another language (French); the local wines had a different character; seductive fruit tarts the likes of which I had never seen posed glamorously in the bakery window; and Mr. and Mrs. Rutz, the gardener and his wife, with whom Szigeti had arranged for me to stay, often served food outside the realm of my experience. "Why do you keep rabbits?" I asked M. Rutz. "Have you never eaten rabbit?" he exclaimed in astonishment. He reached into the cage and in one fluid motion twisted a rabbit's neck and handed its limp form to his wife. That night we had rabbit stew.

But surely the most interesting thing about this little corner of Switzerland was Szigeti. Arriving for my lessons, I would often hear him playing Bach for himself, the sound emanating from somewhere inside his house — probably the music studio, where I would soon be playing for him. Rather than ring the doorbell, I stood transfixed under his window, listening to a rambunctious gigue or a fugue whose principal voices rose effortlessly to the surface through a maze of two-, three-, and even four-note chords as if he were a storyteller skillfully reciting the intertwining dialogue of several characters. Szigeti's playing had faltered enough for him to have given up concertizing entirely the year before. But inexplicably, his command of Bach, the composer who most often exposed a musician's weaknesses, remained virile and bold; and when the music softened, his sound, unlike the generic solidity of many violinists', became longing and plaintive — qualities that quite undid me.

When Szigeti finished playing, I slipped away from the window like a thief and rang the doorbell. His halting footsteps approached, the door opened, and he greeted me forlornly, in a voice reminiscent of the very sound I had just heard. A litany of complaints poured forth: he had not slept well, his fingers hurt him, and his digestive system was again not in order. Szigeti's ailments came as a shock. Gods did not suffer from aches and pains. But aches and pains were forgotten when the lesson began. The violin was a talking instrument in Szigeti's mind. "Parlando, parlando," he called out during Béla Bartók's First Rhapsody. "You are speaking, and there is a rise and fall to the words and stresses on certain syllables that must be emphasized." For every Hungarian raised with his native language and music, those stresses or leanings must have been as natural as mother's milk, but they were foreign to me. A whole world of history and culture might reside in a single note. As I played, Szigeti, perhaps not trusting my memory, would often write down the things he considered most important directly on my music. At the end of a languid section of the rhapsody interrupted by two biting notes, Szigeti scrawled the word *Impatient.* An angry cluster of three notes followed the two impatient ones. Szigeti listened to me play them and then tried to describe their essence: "The notes are like a brushstroke of color." I tried again. He shook his head. "It must sound more urgent." Yet again. "No, no." Szigeti thought for a moment. "Somebody has just offended you and your reaction is 'Get out!'" That did the trick.

Szigeti had first heard the radical Bartók in 1903 in Budapest, but it was not, he wrote, "until the twenties that his Second Sonata and some transcriptions I had made of piano pieces of his, as well as his Rhapsody No. 1 (which he dedicated to me as a token of friendship), brought us into ever-deepening contact." Szigeti and Bartók had performed the rhapsody many times together, and Szigeti passed on suggestions that had come directly from the horse's mouth. They made me feel lightheaded. It was the same sensation I experienced in Marlboro when Galimir spoke of his friend Alban Berg and their conversations or Marcel Moyse about working with Debussy. I was only once removed from the giants of music themselves.

Toward the end of the summer, Szigeti informed me that he was about to take his customary two-week vacation in the high mountains and asked whether I would like to accompany him. I accepted eagerly. A few days later we traveled several hours by train and then by small cable car up to the high reaches of Riederalp, a small village nestled alongside the Aletsch Glacier, supposedly the largest in all of Europe. Before the age of cable cars, Szigeti had made the trip by mule.

During our stay, I ate most meals with Szigeti, took daily walks with him, and had several lessons a week. Being young and a late sleeper, I was invariably the last one down to the breakfast room. There, handsomely laid out before me, was a basket filled to the brim with fresh croissants, a plate full of individually curled pieces of butter, a pot of jam, a pitcher of hot milk, and a canister of coffee. I had never been to Europe before and considered this an odd breakfast. No eggs, no bacon, no toast? The first day, I looked around the empty room uncertainly and then resolved to take the situation in hand. I ate all the croissants, the entire pot of jam, and every single squiggle of butter, then drank all the hot milk and finished it off with the entire canister of coffee. A strange breakfast, I thought, but filling. At lunch, Szigeti leaned forward and lowered his voice: "I hear from the staff that you have quite an appetite." I had no idea what he was talking about. "And that you drink the hot milk first and only then the coffee." How else were you supposed to drink milk and coffee? Szigeti smiled indulgently at this authentic American barbarian. "Here in Europe, we like to mix the coffee and hot milk together."

The two weeks, filled with music and stimulating conversation, passed quickly. Szigeti was about to celebrate his seventieth birthday. He spoke of the great musicians he had known and heard in the early twentieth century — the violinists Joachim, Ysaÿe, Kreisler, Elman, Heifetz, the composers Busoni and Bartók, and his own teacher, Jenö Hubay. Occasionally he talked about the more recent past — the Nazis, anti-Semitism, art, and the state of music. But Szigeti often returned to something of far less significance that rankled him in the present. Over our daily late-afternoon coffee, he tapped on the newspaper in which he had just read about another mountain-climbing accident. "Can you imagine the idiot who risks his life for the stupid thrill of . . . what? Adventure? Danger? Two people dead, one severely injured." He angrily threw another cube of sugar into his coffee and stirred vigorously. I nodded with as much solemnity as I could muster. Szigeti did not know that I climbed every weekend with a Swiss guide, gradually increasing the level of difficulty of the climbs we tackled. It was exhilarating, challenging, and only marginally dangerous. And if I did lose my grip on some rockface and fall several hundred feet, there would be no worry about injuring my delicate violin fingers — I'd simply be dead. When Szigeti questioned me about my mysterious weekend disappearances, I used sightseeing in beautiful Switzerland as my cover.

My climbing adventures served as a diversion, but lessons remained the core of my Swiss stay. Despite the varied repertoire we covered, two composers, Bartók and Bach, seemed always to take center stage. In Bartók's Second Concerto, Szigeti used the word *étage* — French for level or floor — to describe the intrinsic differences in the sound of the violin's four strings and how I might use them in the service of four phrases that appeared one after another in various registers. The idea was innovative and highly effective. Was Bartók himself whispering in Szigeti's ear?

I had a similar but undoubtedly irrational feeling that Bach also spoke to Szigeti. Bach died in 1750; Szigeti was born in 1892. It was fanciful to think that these two men, separated by 142 years, were connected. Yet something of substance must have been handed down from one generation of fine musicians to the next — ever changing with the styles of the day but nonetheless retaining some essential nuggets of Bach's intent. Once, passing Szigeti's hotel room, I heard him play the Chaconne with the sort of freedom that could come only from someone completely at home in Bach's idiom. How else could he have dared to indulge in such lavish tempo changes and still keep the work alive and the individual variations flowing organically from one to another? Szigeti was playing for no one but himself, yet it was a performance to be remembered, and one that defied the presumed constraints I as a young musician felt obligated to obey. Szigeti, the radical every artist must be, forcefully brought home Casals's mantra, freedom with order — those two indispensable pillars in every note of music, in every note of Bach.

On the plane back to the United States at summer's end, I wondered once again where my future lay as a violinist. I was as eager as ever to pursue a solo career, increasingly tired of being lost in the midst of an orchestra, and ever more passionate about chamber music. One thing seemed clear, however. Joseph Szigeti was a template for the musician I would like to become: inquisitive, innovative, sensitive, feeling, informed. It had been a good summer, and I planned to thank Szell profusely when the next orchestra season got under way. It would also be a difficult year. I would have to juggle playing in the orchestra with the intense preparation needed for the 1963 Queen Elizabeth Competition in Brussels. Szell had agreed to let me out of the orchestra for the competition, and Szigeti had worked with me on much of the required repertoire.

But what was the point of thinking about the future just now? I far preferred burying my head in the book about mountain climbing I had just bought at the Geneva airport. Given that Bach walked two hundred miles in order to visit the celebrated composer and organist Dietrich Buxtehude, it was not hard to imagine that he would have also enjoyed hiking in the Swiss Alps. The thought tickled me. For a moment, I imagined myself as Bach's climbing partner. Only Szigeti must never know.

CHAPTER 8

A Flying Leap

I F I PLAYED WELL at the Queen Elizabeth Competition next spring, *if* I won a prize, and *if* anyone in the music business cared to take notice, then I just might be a step or two nearer to my life-long dream of a solo career. But if that goal was truly so important to me, why was I spending so much time playing chamber music? Except for unaccompanied Bach, most music I played was with other musicians. The question was, with which musicians and in what setting did I most want to play? With one hundred other members of an orchestra? With an orchestra as soloist? With a pianist in the vast and stunning virtuoso repertoire? Or with small groups of players in endlessly varied music? Even during Cleveland's busy orchestra season, several of us stole away in our spare time to play chamber music together for the sheer joy of it, and every summer I did the same with some of the world's best musicians at the Marlboro Music Festival.

But chamber music was just an avocation, I told myself. It was something to do, albeit with great pleasure, when I wasn't trying to be the next Mischa, Jascha, Toscha, or Sascha, and to that goal I worked late into the night month after month on the repertoire required for the competition. When I was ready to depart, George Szell wished me well and insisted that I be sure to sample the *moules marinières,* the marinated mussels, for which Brussels was famous, and Gerald Warburg once again generously lent me his Spanish Strad. At the airport, a customs official asked me the name and value of my violin. His eyes widened when I told him, and for a brief moment he hesitated. Then he pressed a button on the wall. Several officials appeared from out of nowhere and gathered speechlessly around the instrument. Stradivari's reputation had spread so far and wide that even laymen knew his name. Finally one of the officials haltingly ventured a question: "Does it . . . does it have a serial number?" I picked up the violin and squinted through an f-hole with mock solemnity until I could read the label — *Antonius Stradivarius, feciebat 1727* — and looked the gentleman straight in the eye. "Why, yes, it does. Number 1727."

Queen Elizabeth, born Elizabeth von Wittelsbach, a duchess in Bavaria, married Crown Prince Albert of Belgium around 1900 and was herself a good violinist. She had inherited a passion for music from her father, a military man turned eminent ophthalmologist and a pioneer of cataract operations. When Eugène Ysaÿe, who had just reached the pinnacle of an exceptional career as the most famous virtuoso of the day, was appointed royal music director in 1912, he and the queen became fast friends.

Ysaÿe had by then developed a grand vision for an international violin competition in which young virtuosos would be required to play wide-ranging programs that demanded technical and artistic maturity and that included contemporary music. He envisioned including an unpublished work that the contestants would study in confinement, without help from any outside source. Ysaÿe died in 1931, and in 1937 Queen Elizabeth presented the first competition in his honor, with an international jury of exceptionally high standing. David Oistrakh won the first prize.

Since its foundation, the Queen Elizabeth Competition has been considered the world over to be one of the most prestigious and difficult in existence. Despite Ysaÿe's noble intentions, such an event inevitably turns the conventional function of music on its head. Normally one plays *for* music lovers. Here it is *against* other violinists in hopes of winning a top prize. The locals might view the whole proceeding as a high-class horse race and even bet on their favorites, but the contestants are in deadly earnest. Too much work has gone into the Queen Elizabeth, and too many hopes ride on its outcome. A prize means recognition and publicity. Yet competition winners are seldom assured a glittering concert career as a victory trophy. Indeed, some have accepted their prize and disappeared into oblivion. For most, competitions serve as one in a series of vaguely defined steps that might lead to concerts, a manager, and a name.

Before the 1963 competition began, dozens of terrifyingly proficient violinists from around the world gathered backstage at the queen's Music Chapel, part of the conservatory she had founded, to draw their first-round entry numbers. Two days later, I waited for my turn to play before a distinguished panel of judges and an audience from all over Belgium. Under the glare of the dressing room lights, I sat facing my open violin case and silently communed with the photo gallery of violinists that accompanied me everywhere. Perhaps they would help me summon up the courage and composure to do well.

When I made the finals as one of twelve contestants to be sequestered in the Music Chapel and was given one week to learn and play a concerto composed specifically for the occasion, the stakes were high. There was nothing to do but work, eat, and sleep. The eight, ten, and sometimes even twelve hours of daily practice we needed to master the new concerto and maintain the rest of our required repertoire were broken up only by breakfast, lunch, and dinner. There were consequences to this unholy state of affairs. Excessive hours of daily practice brought on muscle spasms, tendonitis, insomnia, anxiety attacks, loss of appetite, heart palpitations, and skin eruptions. I myself could proudly claim three of those seven afflictions.

Contestants sought relief from the competition's stress in any way possible — with gallows humor, practical jokes, and constant speculation about our standing among the judges. We ate at one large table. The four Americans sat across from the four Russians; the two Japanese — one trained in Russia, one in the United States — joined their counterparts on each side; and the Israeli and the Syrian sat at opposite ends. Charles Castleman, Paul Rosenthal, Donald Weilerstein, and I, representing the United States, spoke no Russian, and the Russians spoke no English. The cold war was in full swing, and we eyed each other curiously at first and then attempted unsuccessfully to communicate in several languages. In frustration, someone said "Oy vay," and Yiddish instantly became the lingua franca of the chapel. There were moments of levity and even camaraderie in our royal prison, since we were forbidden to communicate with outsiders in case we gleaned some of the new concerto's secrets, but as the final performance approached, the stress level rose exponentially. The Israeli, Yossi Zivoni, who occupied the room next to mine, suffered sleepless nights filled with worry. The Russian Dmitri Snitkovsky looked across the lunch table at Zivoni's bloodshot eyes and could not resist singing, to the tune of Lalo's *Symphonie Espagnol*, "Schlafen sie gut, Zivoni" — Sleep well, Zivoni.

Finally the momentous day arrived, and one by one we were led from the chapel to the concert hall, like prisoners to their execution. Waiting my turn to play, I stood in the shadows of the wings assaulted by nerves and irrationally feeling unprepared. Had those hundreds of hours of work been for naught? Then a curious thing happened as I walked out onto the stage of the Palais des Beaux Arts before a glittering array of judges, a packed house, and Queen Elizabeth of Belgium herself: my nerves fell away, and I played my best. The sudden transformation from negative to positive had happened so often that you would think by now I could simply forgo the preperformance anxiety, the terrible abyss in the pit of my stomach, the panicky hyperventilating, but it seemed that the two extremes of severe doubt and high-flying confidence were Siamese twins, and if a Dr. Freud could succeed in banishing my insecurities, he might throw the baby out with the bathwater and leave me a solid but lackluster fiddler. No — whatever impression I had made in Brussels and would make in my future professional life would depend on those nerves as an engine of communication, as the spark that jumped across the footlights and captured the listeners' attention.

When all the contestants had finished playing, the judges retired to a private room for discussion, and after a seeming eternity they emerged to announce the results. Two Russians, Alexis

Michlin and Dmitri Snitkovsky, had captured the first two prizes and I the third. I received the news with a mixture of regret and elation. A first prize would naturally have garnered the most attention, but the next prizes were also impressive. As bronze medalist, I would perform many times with orchestras and in recital throughout Belgium during the coming months.

The queen shook each of the contestants' hands onstage and posed for a group picture with us, and all at once the planning, the dreaming, the arduous labor, were over and done with. The next morning I woke up feeling relieved. Now I could go on with my life.

When I returned to Cleveland, Szell and my friends in the orchestra congratulated me enthusiastically, but there was little time to savor my great adventure. Szell had granted me a brief leave of absence for the competition, but now once again I was his assistant concertmaster, his chattel, with the sole function of providing a small detail in the grand orchestral mosaic he envisioned. Sitting in my chair directly under his nose, Brussels, the queen, and her competition seemed like an exotic dream. It would be nice to play those solo concerts later in the year, but I looked forward to another summer of chamber music at Marlboro even more, and to orchestra life even less. Szell and his magnificent ensemble had thrilled me too many times, provided too many golden opportunities for me not to be extremely grateful, but what good was the artistry that Szigeti urged me to cultivate, or for that matter the magical tone of Warburg's Strad, if it was neutralized by two dozen other fiddlers playing in a phalanx of sound engineered by a conductor waving his arms at us?

I cherish memories of the orchestra, but to this day, over forty years after leaving, I still have occasional dreams about Szell, and none of them are good. I'm late for a performance, I've lost my music, I can't find my concert clothes, and, worst of all, A. Beverly Barksdale, the orchestra manager, has somehow hoodwinked me with his courtly southern manner into signing another multiyear contract. When I confront Barksdale and tell him that there has been a terrible misunderstanding, he merely shrugs his shoulders and points to my signature on the contract, condemning me to servitude to a harsh and unforgiving taskmaster — George Szell.

But there was no conductor, Szell or otherwise, dictating the agenda when I sat down with friends on a free night to play chamber music. There was no conductor — or we were all conductors. Each of us was in charge of our distinct voice in the group's music-making. We were the masters of our own ship. And despite the very exacting demands of ensemble playing, it was also possible to answer the call of my old mentors, Casals and Szigeti, to strive for that elusive thing called artistry.

John Dalley, Michael Tree, David Soyer, and I had played together dozens of times in various combinations both in music school and at Marlboro. The day finally arrived when we were caught up in a collective gravitational field governed by our admiration for each other's playing and a great love for the string quartet literature. When I returned to Marlboro in 1963, the four of us began to talk seriously about playing quartets together, and in 1964 we founded the Guarneri String Quartet.

Before the quartet could perform a note, however, the three of us who played both violin and its close relative, the deeper-voiced viola, had to decide which instrument we would play in the group. The viola, a few inches longer than a violin and descending five notes lower, is a stretch that most violinists can manage. After a lifetime with the violin's silvery tone, the viola's dark and mellow qualities made me feel as if I were slipping into a new costume and an entirely different stage role. Michael, John, and I, full-time violinists, had all enjoyed playing the viola occasionally since our school days. It was not going to be an easy decision.

One night I dreamed that I was in my vegetable garden holding two packets of seeds. One said "violin," the other "viola." The dream garden looked like the real one I had grown every year since childhood. I stood next to my pole beans and debated which seeds to plant. The violins and violas would grow like beans, hanging from vines under the warm sun until fully grown and ripe, when they would be picked. I asked a woman standing next to me which to choose. "Look," she said impatiently, "you're the musician, not me. You decide." In the end, the entire group decided. John and I would be the quartet's violinists and Michael its violist.

As students at the Curtis Institute of Music, Michael, John, and I had gone to movies, shared banana splits, and indulged in sophomoric pranks together, and we had all quickly become friends with David at Marlboro. Yet this guaranteed very little. Quartet careers most often founder on personality clashes rather than artistic disagreements. A quartet that constantly rehearses, travels, and plays together does not necessarily stay together. We had no inkling of our fate as we sat down to read through our first string quartet on a late summer day in Marlboro. The seeds of our communal garden were now planted, and only time would tell if and how they would grow. A pessimist would give us no more than a year. A cockeyed optimist, who knows — half a century?

CHAPTER 9

The Dating Game

CHAMBER MUSIC WAS originally performed in intimate sur-
roundings — in actual chambers, we might presume — but in
modern times a string quartet plays for an audience of two thousand rather than twenty. My Pressenda's sound was certainly robust enough, but at the Guarneri Quartet's very first rehearsals I
began to wonder about its basic qualities. It is often said that
the difficulty in playing Mozart's music stems from its disarming
simplicity, but I prefer the theory that attributes its thorny as-
pects to Mozart's genius in presenting complex ideas under the
guise of so-called simplicity. The Pressenda's strong but relatively uncomplicated sound seemed ill at ease with the aching
sadness, the defiant outbursts, the ever-changing rise and fall of
Mozart's D Minor Quartet. I was driving a car that was fast on
the straightaway but clumsy in the curves. For this new career of
mine, replete with quartet masterpieces, I needed a violin with a

whole palette of magical sounds hovering between extremes of loud and soft, a violin that could be alluringly breathy, sternly assertive, sweet, and melancholy, a violin that could touch a listener and make his or her heart beat faster.

I blithely assumed that a few visits to violin shops would quickly produce a satisfactory violin, as if it were nothing more than a high-quality delicatessen item, but finding a fine violin proved more difficult than I had expected. I wanted an instrument that matched my musical personality, but exactly what was the shape and scope of that personality? Every violin brought a set of new traits and new possibilities. As a bachelor living in New York City, I found the language of courtship surprisingly similar to that of my violin search. Was I not looking for a deep relationship — a bride, if you will? The instrument dealers served as dating services, introducing me to prospective mates — presenting violins out of glass-fronted armoires and from massive vaults. Some violins I took out and returned immediately — one-night stands. Some violins I kept for a week or so before losing interest — infatuations, you might say. And occasionally an instrument struck my fancy enough for me to spend several weeks with it — a heated but short-lived affair. When I put a violin under my chin and drew the bow across its strings, I listened expectantly to the sound produced by wood, varnish, and horsehair and hoped for something I could not as yet describe but that would reach out to me when I heard it. I waited and hoped for nothing less than to fall in love.

A Carlo Testori with an unusually dark and rich sound came my way, but there was a disturbing nasal element to its otherwise pleasing tone, which dampened my enthusiasm. A gorgeous Carlo Bergonzi (a pupil of Stradivari's) attracted me briefly, but its sweet sound was rather muted, and the instrument was dangerously expensive. Eventually my head was turned by a beautiful blond, narrow-waisted, eighteenth-century Sanctus Seraphin. It was the violin's answer to a fashion model — slender, high-arched, shapely.

Seraphin, who intended to study painting but turned to violinmaking instead, went to Venice from Udine in 1717 and lived and worked there until his death, in 1755. He took Nicolas Amati's and Jacob Stainer's violins as models and made instruments that were the polar opposite of Pressenda's. The Seraphin's grain, both top and bottom, was much finer and tighter, the scroll more delicately carved, and the violin's textured sweetness more seductive. What's more, it seemed to blend well with the quartet's other instruments. At the shop of Erwin Hertel and Son in the Carnegie Hall building, where Mr. Hertel, Sr., regularly took care of my violin and bows, I traded my Pressenda for the more expensive Seraphin. (The Pressenda had hardly appreciated in my five years of ownership, for the rare-instrument market had yet to take off. A fine violin, like a house, was still seen as something to use rather than something to invest in.)

Recently I received a call from Don Robertson's instrument shop in Albuquerque, New Mexico. They wanted to verify that the Pressenda in their possession had once belonged to me. Don's son, a bass player with the Philadelphia Orchestra, brought the violin to a room in the Curtis Institute of Music, where I had just finished teaching, and opened the case. It had been almost forty years since I had laid eyes on the instrument, yet like the face of an old friend I had not seen for ages, it was instantly recognizable. I picked up the violin and played a few notes. Out came that same woody, robust sound, as if no time at all had passed. The violin was easier to play than I remembered, and its palette of colors was much more varied. This car could take any curve handily. I wondered whether the passage of time had improved its steering mechanism or merely my ability to drive it, and I also wondered whether I would have exchanged violins so readily back in 1964 if I had known then what I know now.

In the first concerts of the Guarneri Quartet, the Seraphin's sound had a cutting edge that seemed to promise carrying power, but what I heard under the ear was not necessarily what went out into a hall. Learning exactly how to produce the robust sound that flowed so easily from the Pressenda would take time. One violin responds to brute force, another to gentle coaxing. What's more, the Seraphin was a bit of a prima donna. One day it would sing with a clear and bell-like voice, then the next it would clam up as if it had come down with a cold. I chalked up its unpredictable nature to changes of weather. All violins seem to thrive best in a particular combination of temperature and humidity; dry, cold weather often threw the Seraphin into a state of mild tonal dysfunction. Thus, if the Seraphin had a good day, I had one as well, and if I had a good day, then the Guarneri Quartet at the very least had a 25 percent chance of having a better one.

The violin's best days inspired me in 1966 to undertake the recording of two unaccompanied Bach works, the G Minor Sonata and the D Minor Partita. Although the Guarneri Quartet was a full-time occupation, all of us managed to find time for individual musical interests. It was a way to stay fresh and be connected to a larger musical world. Occasionally I played other chamber music, recitals, and concertos with orchestras, but while those occasions came and went without rhyme or reason, Bach remained a stubborn constant in my life. If I succeeded in playing the sonatas and partitas flawlessly, my technique in general would inevitably improve. If I began to grasp their overall design, my horizons for all music would broaden. And if I opened my ears to the intertwining of independent voices, I would come that much nearer to hearing the way a composer does. The violin's principal role in life was presumably to sing, even if that meant throwing in an occasional chord or two for spice, but Bach drew the instrument into the active world of harmony. Treating fiddlers as he did keyboard players made it incumbent on us to hear and micromanage several voices at once. We (rather than I) were performing Bach.

But this makes it sound as if Bach were some kind of vitamin supplement for health and longevity. Behind the conventional forms of the individual movements lurked contradictions, surprises, and inspiration. A serious fugue might unexpectedly turn playful. A seemingly playful dance often revealed an underbelly of darkness and melancholy. The more brilliant movements — presto, gigue, preludium — rushed forward with dizzying energy and an exuberance that defied the image of Bach as a dour kappelmeister. Bach's music could be devout, intellectual, complex, but also imaginative, playful, melancholy, daring.

It is generally true that practice makes perfect, but recording Bach was no ordinary project. My rendition would be added to those made by an almost endless list of violinists. For such an ambitious undertaking I wished to play perfectly — an ominously unrealistic goal. The nearer the recording date came, the worse I seemed to sound. The ghost of J. S. Bach had rattled me. To make matters worse, I had the bad luck of having to fly home after a concert not long before the session. Marooned for five hours between planes at Denver's Stapleton Airport and desperate to put what I hoped would be the finishing touch on the Bach works, I marched up to a United Airlines representative, explained that I was a violinist, and asked if she knew of a place where I might practice in the airport. Suspicion and alarm spread across her face. She shook her head adamantly. No, it would not be possible to practice in the airport. One employee after another greeted me with the same bureaucratic intractability, leaving me to scour the airport on my own in the slim hope of finding some suitable nook or cranny. Fifteen minutes later I came across a set of dimly lit stairs at the farthest reaches of the building. I climbed to the top, opened a plain, unmarked door, and found myself on the roof of the terminal. The day was unseasonably mild, and the foothills of the Rocky Mountains spread out breathtakingly before me. I had stumbled onto the mother of all practice spots.

I recorded the Bach sonata and partita for TownHall Records in the Robert Fine Recording Studio, formerly the grand ballroom of Manhattan's Great Northern Hotel. The Great Northern was too fine a hotel for me ever to have stayed in it as a student. Living in New York City, I knew its lobby only as a shortcut from Fifty-seventh to Fifty-sixth Street. The ballroom, replete with large pillars and crystal chandeliers, turned out to be a very lively acoustic space. I arrived for the first day of recording excited but edgy. I had never made a solo record before.

In the middle of the empty ballroom stood a single music stand with a microphone hanging directly in front of it. The engineer was installed in a small soundproof room, huddled and oddly out of place between the ballroom's massive pillars. His disembodied voice leaped out of the small black speaker placed next to me. "Could I hear some loud and soft passages of the Bach, please?" I launched into the Chaconne's opening chords and took courage from the Seraphin's sound. Thank God, it was having a good day. While the engineer made some final adjustments, I stood in the ballroom alone with my thoughts. If only I could harness the cherished beliefs of Pablo Casals, Isaac Stern, and Arthur Loesser — play with the abandon of a Gypsy, the intellect of an architect, and the spirit of a dancer — and then emerge with a conception that was truly my own rather than a hodgepodge of other people's ideas. The loudspeaker broke my reverie. "Bach D Minor Partita. Take one."

All the elements needed for a good performance seemed to be in place — a well-prepared violinist, lively acoustics, and a stylish concert space. The one missing ingredient was an audience. Granted, I inevitably practiced alone, but a performance was supposed to be for live, feeling people, not for a microphone hanging coldly and impassively above me. One by one, I recorded the Allemande, the Courante, the Sarabande, and the Gigue, but without listeners, my playing felt bloodless. The only ears in the ballroom besides mine were those belonging to the engineer in the sound booth. Facing the microphone, I began the partita's last movement, the Chaconne. Out of the corner of my eye, I could see the engineer through the sound booth's window. His head was tilted at an odd angle. He was reading something. When I squinted, I could see more clearly: he was reading a newspaper. It was the *New York Times*. He was reading the sports section.

The recording session ground to a halt. I would not, could not, perform for three pillars, two chandeliers, and a man reading the sports section. I called Lincoln Mayorga, the owner of TownHall

Records and the producer of the Bach record, from a pay phone in the lobby and complained churlishly. "Take it easy. Just take it easy," he said, trying to calm me down. Lincoln, an excellent pianist, had no trouble understanding the problem. "I will have a listener for you tomorrow morning — a real music lover. I promise."

The next day Nancy, Lincoln's mother, greeted me in the Great Northern ballroom: "Good morning. I'd like to introduce myself. I'm your audience." Nancy, whom I had known since Lincoln and I, age twelve, met in junior high school orchestra, was a passionate music lover. Lincoln had indeed lived up to his word. Nancy pulled a chair over to the far wall while Lincoln discreetly removed all traces of newspaper from the sound booth, and the recording session soon began. For me, the presence of even a single listener changed everything. The pianist Arthur Rubinstein once remarked that he never played for an entire audience but rather for a single individual in that audience — preferably a beautiful woman, he would add with a quick smile. Though my listener was in her sixties, she was unquestionably an attractive woman. The cold microphone and the indifferent engineer receded into the distance and I played for Nancy — Nancy, who listened intently, whose expressions changed with the music, who clapped enthusiastically when I was done.

I heard the finished master a month later. Much of it pleased me, but not all. Why hadn't I taken more time at the end of the adagio? Why hadn't I played the fugue's four-note chords more assertively? And why hadn't I been more reflective in that special place in the Chaconne? As a listener, those things were crystal-clear to me; as a player, there was so much to attend to that the most obvious things sometimes slipped by undetected. But by and large I was satisfied. On February 6, 7, and 8, 1966, this recording was what could be expected from this violinist with this music and this violin.

Composer, musician, instrument — the three essential ingredients in every piece of music! In the case of Bach, the composer was the most stable element in the recipe. His exalted music knew no need of alteration. I, the player, however, would always be a work in progress, forever trying to live up to my potential as I strove to be Bach's worthy servant. The violin itself was a more fluid element. I would not change Bach, I could not change who I was, but I was free to change violins at any time. My Seraphin sparkled on the finished record. Still, the microphone does not hear like a human ear. The grand ballroom, for all its lively acoustics, had none of the characteristics of a true concert hall.

As the Guarneri Quartet's career grew, so did our audiences. In Nuremberg, Germany, we played for upwards of four thousand people. The Seraphin struggled in the cavernous space. By the end of the quartet's second season, I could not avoid seeing the violin's ingratiating qualities as components of its weakness. What good were those seductive sounds if people in rows H to Z could not hear them? Our relationship was definitely on the rocks. I began frequenting fiddle shops again — Jacques Français, Rembert Wurlitzer, and Erwin Hertel in New York City, Hans Weisshaar in Los Angeles, Walter Hamma in Stuttgart, Charles Beare in London. The shops began to feel like singles bars where violins and violinists met in the hopes of hitting it off. Wherever the Guarneris played, I looked at violins.

While the frustrating dating game continued, I felt little compunction about letting friends know of my bachelor status. There are thousands of violinists scattered throughout the world, and though our fraternity may seem unmanageably large, gossip travels fast. I soon learned through the grapevine that Veda Reynolds, the assistant concertmaster of the Philadelphia Orchestra, wanted to sell her Lorenzo Guadagnini. If the Seraphin was a flashy model, Veda's Guadagnini was a ravishing beauty. Its varnish was a mixture of yellow, orange, and gold with an overlay of deep red patches. The violin's upper bouts sloped downward like shoulders in sweet resignation. The Guadagnini, made in 1743, was listed in a book of the fifty most beautiful violins in the world. After I played only a very few notes, it was evident that its beauty was much more than skin deep. The violin was firm, attractive, and quite bright in sound yet sensitive to fine shadings of tone, and I knew instantly that if Veda and I could come to an agreement about price, I would buy it. But when we did shake hands on what was a very reasonable sum, I felt a twinge of regret. The Seraphin spoke with a more eloquent voice than the Guadagnini's. Was I trading up or only sideways? The next day I put the Seraphin up for sale at Erwin Hertel's shop.

The Guadagnini served me well, not only in hundreds of quartet and solo concerts but also in dozens of recordings. I could easily have played this robust and appealing violin for the rest of my life, yet I could never find it in me to love the instrument fully. When I think back on the Guadagnini, its broad outline and glamorous varnish appear glowingly before my eyes. Perhaps I fell in love with its looks and hoped the rest would follow.

Not long before the Guadagnini and I parted company, the violin suffered a fluke accident that attests to both the dangers lurking at every corner and the astonishing sturdiness of stringed instruments. I had planned a week-long hike in the Rocky Mountains with two friends, the composer Michael Riesman and the pianist Anton Kuerti, who were both attending the Aspen Music Festival. I arrived in Aspen thinking that I would leave my instrument in one of their apartments, but the festival had just finished and both Michael and Anton were vacating their places. Short of canceling our trip, there was nothing to do but take the fiddle along with us and leave it well covered in the trunk of the car.

The main highway became two lanes, then a dirt road, and finally petered out to nothing as we passed the ghost town of Marble, named for its once thriving marble quarry. It was time for us to start hiking, but the idea of leaving my rare old violin entombed in a car trunk under the sweltering sun unsettled me. No need to worry, my friends insisted. They swaddled the violin case in heavy blankets and for good measure parked the car under the shade of a large tree. We left the car and began our journey, which would take us past Capitol Peak and up to the top of 14,000-foot Snowmass Mountain. Every night I crawled into my sleeping bag and gazed up at the star-studded sky — a moment for large thoughts about the mystery of the universe and our insignificance in the grand scheme of things. But worries about my violin, huddled far away in its own sleeping bag of blankets, often pushed the meaning of life aside. What if my Guadagnini was severely damaged by heat, or even stolen?

Anton, Michael, and I finally retraced our steps to the parked car. To my relief, there it stood under the tree, in one piece and with the trunk seemingly intact. But when we approached I smelled something odd, and when we opened the trunk we discovered, to my horror, that the blankets were soaked in gasoline. Because we had parked at an unusually steep angle in order to fit the car under the shade tree, gasoline had leaked out of the tank's safety valve directly onto the violin case. Numb with shock, I unwrapped the sopping wet blankets to find the case cover, the music inside, and the violin itself covered in gasoline. I lifted the poor reeking creature out of its case and wondered whether it had played its very last tune. But when I played the Guadagnini, it sounded the same as it always had, and when I cleaned it as best I could with water from a gurgling brook nearby, the smell abated somewhat. On the trip back, Anton and Michael repeatedly asked whether it wasn't time to stop and give my violin a tuneup or a change of oil, or to check its antifreeze, but the jokes were not funny.

As soon as I returned to New York, I took the violin to Erwin Hertel and, without divulging what had taken place, asked him to check it for any damage, to clean, polish, and adjust it, and to give me a detailed report on its health. Two days later Hertel called: "The Guad's in great condition. No cracks, no openings. Looks as gorgeous as ever. Pick it up whenever you want." The violin had just joined the ranks of an amazingly large survivors' club — a group of fiddles that have stories to tell: Sascha Jacobsen's Red Diamond Stradivarius floating out to sea, Erick Friedman's Stradivarius half crushed under the back wheels of his car, Bronislaw Huberman's Guarnerius stolen from Carnegie Hall, and all of them returning from the dead to play again another day. I invariably think of that event in the Rocky Mountains whenever I perform Beethoven's last string quartet, op. 135. To this day reddish traces of gasoline still stain my music for this piece. How unwise I was, and how durable is the seemingly fragile little instrument we violinists play.

The next violin that entered my life required no dating service. On a visit to Rembert Wurlitzer's shop, I was greeted by the violinmaker Fernando Sacconi with the news that he had just re-varnished a Guarneri del Gesù that was now for sale. I tried to explain that there was no way a violinist of my modest means could afford a del Gesù, whose maker was ranked alongside Stradivari as one of the two most revered violinmakers in the world. The going price for a del Gesù in the early 1970s was easily $100,000. An "affordable Guarneri del Gesù" was an oxymoron as far as I was concerned.

But Sacconi brushed me off. "See how lustrous the new varnish is, yet worn in the usual places as if violinists' hands had rubbed over it for two hundred years," he said proudly. The elderly Sacconi was as excited as a schoolboy about his success in simulating age. "This took a great deal of time and, if I might say so, a certain amount of skill." He had created a mottled effect to approximate the wear and tear that the original varnish would have shown over centuries, leaving the wood more exposed in some places while adding a touch of thicker, redder varnish in the corners and at the edges, where it might have stubbornly remained. Then Sacconi's face darkened and he pointed to the f-holes, which had been recut to arch at their tops and bottoms in gothic hyperbole — an act driven by a greedy if futile effort to make the violin appear to be from del Gesù's most sought-after late period, the last three or four years of his life, rather than 1739, its probable birth date, a mere five years before his death. Sacconi smiled sadly and shook his head. "I don't know who did this or when, but he has ruined some of the natural beauty of del Gesù's work. Look at this scroll. How beautiful. How daring!" The scroll — usually a model of precision — looked as if it had been made on the heels of a drunken binge. Its concentric circles wobbled; its opposing ears appeared slightly askew.

"Play, play," Sacconi urged.

I picked up the violin reluctantly. Guarneris were going for ten times the price of my Guadagnini. I would have to trade the Guad plus my firstborn for such an instrument. Nevertheless, I drew the bow across the Guarneri's strings. If the classic Stradivari sound was silvery, the del Gesù's was a rich, dark molasses, with a signature growl emanating from its lowest tones.

"The violin is marvelous, Mr. Sacconi," I blurted, "but it's simply out of my price range."

Sacconi, looking like an aging Italian movie star, smiled. "Well, perhaps not." He leaned back and told me in his accented English some of the violin's story, the rest of which I picked up from Charles Beare months later. Legend had it that the instrument had once been painted black and hung on a wall, but was then recognized as something special and revarnished cheaply around 1900 by a French instrument firm. Along the way someone misguidedly altered its f-holes. From there the violin made its way to the London shop of Arthur Beare, who judged it to be the work of John Lott, an Englishman well known for his skillful copies of del Gesù. For years the instrument languished in pieces in his vault, until Arthur and his son, Charles, now a partner in the firm, decided to examine it again. This time there was no question in their minds. The violin was a genuine Guarneri del Gesù.

Because of the violin's altered condition, Sacconi assured me, the price would be a fraction of what a del Gesù ordinarily went for. As tempting as the offer seemed, I worried about the toll that revarnishing had taken on the instrument. Cremonese varnish was justly famous for its beauty and for the golden sound it helped produce. Brown and amber varnishes of earlier times were gradually abandoned for golden yellow, orange, and finally the deep red colors associated with many of the great Cremonese instruments. The varnish, applied in layers with a brush, became soft and elastic when dry. In 1692, Christopher Morley offered a recipe for "Italian varnish" in his book *Collectana Chinictea Lydensia*: "Take 8 ozs. turpentine and boil on a fire till it evaporates down to 1 oz.; powder when cold, and dissolve in warm oil of turpentine. Filter through a cloth before use." It was indisputably Italian varnish, but for what — a violin, an oil painting, or furniture? Mr. Morley did not say. The varnish's composition was said at one time to be common knowledge among both Cremonese and Venetian instrument-makers, but by the mid-eighteenth century shortcuts in the process had allowed the old recipe to languish and then disappear entirely. J. B. Guadagnini, son of Lorenzo, was purported to be one of the last to use the old method. What was known openly by the old masters became the stuff of myth in more modern times.

The secrets of Cremonese varnish did not overly concern me. I was a violinist, after all, not a violinmaker. But the violin I held in my hands had been through a varnish striptease (take it off, put it back on, take it off, put it back on again), and I needed to know what effect, if any, this had had on its sound. Sacconi assured me that traces of the del Gesù's original varnish still remained in the wood's pores — the "ground," as he put it — and that this was crucial to the sound it produced. True, most old violins through wear and tear retained little of their original varnish. It made sense to suppose that what remained hidden from view contributed at least in part to the vaunted Cremonese sound.

Samuel Zygmuntowicz, a renowned and distinguished violinmaker, recently explained varnish in terms I could understand. "A violin sounds alive, free, but somewhat raw in an unfinished state. It's like toast without butter," he explained. Then Sam tried another metaphor on me. "You know how soft a dress shirt feels when it's laundered right and how uncomfortably stiff it is when too much starch is added. Same with varnish." In his view, an excellent soft varnish protected a violin from the elements and left it free to ring out, while a poor one only stifled its intrinsic sound.

On the basis of the Guarneri del Gesù's legendary reputation alone, I wanted to believe Sacconi. No fewer than five members of the Guarneri family — Andrea Guarneri (1626–1698); his two sons, Peter Guarneri of Mantua (1655–1720) and Joseph Guarneri filius Andrea (1666–1740); and Joseph's two sons, Peter Guarneri of Mantua (1695–1762) and Joseph Guarneri del Gesù (1698–1744) — made outstanding string instruments over a period of almost 150 years. But Guarneri del Gesù was the artist craftsman in the family, standing far above the others. His were the instruments coveted by international concert violinists, sometimes even above Stradivari's, for their boldness of design, individuality of style, and dark and powerful tone. (And his was the all-too-brief and difficult life that engendered never-proven gossip about the murder of a fellow violinmaker, ending in imprisonment.) Even the designation "del Gesù," stemming from the cross and the initials *IHS* that appeared on his violin labels, caused speculation about whether *IHS* was the abbreviation of the Greek spelling of Jesus or the abbreviation for the Latin *Jesus Hominum Salvator,* Jesus, Savior of Man.

In a room reserved exclusively for trying out instruments, I played the violin for the better part of an hour, reveling in its somewhat rough-hewn sound. The del Gesù purred when I played lightly and growled more full-throatedly when I dug aggressively into the strings, an approach that would have smothered the more refined sound of Stradivarius violins I had played. During the next weeks I played the Guarneri at home, in the quartet, and for friends, and although the consequences of its poor condition were never fully answered in my mind, it mattered less and less as time went on. I had fallen in love. Soon after I traded my Guadagnini plus cash for the del Gesù and walked out of Wurlitzer's shop feeling like both a king and a shrewd businessman. I now owned a great violin and had made a 50 percent profit on the Guadagnini in just two short years.

A crystal ball would have muted my good cheer. For all its fine attributes, the Guarneri would eventually reveal an Achilles' heel and the Guadagnini would increase well over fiftyfold in value during the ensuing years. But even if I had seen the future, it might not have made a difference. I was smitten.

The Guarneri Quartet had the splendid good fortune to perform and record with Arthur Rubinstein at about this time. At eighty-two, Rubinstein was at the twilight of a great career, while we in the quartet were only beginning an uncertain one. There was much to learn from this celebrated pianist up close. A Rubinstein performance was fluid but not excessive, grand but never strident, and as natural and artful as the way he spun out one delicious story after another at dinner. Rubinstein sat at the piano, head tilted back, jaw slightly dropped, and played with a smile of sheer pleasure spread across his face. From the set and movement of his body alone, one could see just how comfortable he was with music and with his instrument. There were never any angular or harsh movements as his hands came down on the keyboard, and this was reflected in the glowing sound he produced. A pianist sits and plays in a more or less natural position, whereas a violinist must be something of a contortionist in the way his or her arms wrap around the instrument. Rubinstein's relationship to the piano set me thinking about how I used my own arms, hands, neck, and shoulders in playing.

But I looked for more. What ingredients actually went into the making of Rubinstein's spectacular life in music? It was not an idle question. I wanted a distinguished career as well. Didn't every musician? And here before my very eyes, in our countless rehearsals, in remarkable concerts in London, Paris, and New York City, and in the recording over several years of ten different works for piano and strings, was the supreme example of success in Arthur Rubinstein. His great artistry notwithstanding, success came to him as the natural byproduct of a radiant personality, through the ease with which he dealt with people and the sheer joy with which he seemed to live his life. The entire Rubinstein package proved irresistible to those who hired him, who worked with him, who listened raptly to him on the great concert stages of the world, and, of course, to the Guarneri String Quartet. But had he no bad moods? Did he not experience jealousy? Was he not afflicted occasionally with melancholy or self-doubt? Rubinstein was almost too good to be true.

At the end of the many full days spent with him, I went to bed inspired, intrigued, and a bit mystified. There seemed to be no dissonances to disturb the grand C-major chord of Rubinstein's life. I hoped to glean something from this larger-than-life figure — artist, raconteur, gourmand, wine and cigar connoisseur, art lover and collector — that might guide me in my own future. But what? The only art in my price range was reproductions, the Cuban cigars Rubinstein smoked were illegal in the United States, I could hardly spell *cabernet sauvignon,* much less tell how it differed from other wines, and there was no competing with the stories he told, which drew on three quarters of a century of rubbing shoulders with virtuosos, composers, managers, and audiences.

One night I dreamed that I drove past a large mountain of garbage on the way to Harpur College in Binghamton, New York, where the Guarneri Quartet played and taught. Oddly enough, a barely discernible metal trash can stood perched on the very top. I wondered why it was there and what could be in it. Finally curiosity got the better of me. I stepped out of the car and began climbing up the garbage mountain. To my surprise, it proved much higher and steeper than I thought. At last, winded, I reached the summit and stood before the can, whose contents were concealed by a tight-fitting lid. I hesitated for just a moment, anxious about what might lurk inside, but then I gingerly lifted the lid off. There, hunkered down at the bottom of the can and dressed in an elegant three-piece blue suit, was Arthur Rubinstein, who grinned sheepishly up at me and shrugged his shoulders apologetically.

Not long after, Jean and Tom Kirsch, old friends of mine, invited me to lunch at their home in Palo Alto, California. Jean and Tom, who are Jungian psychoanalysts, invited two other Jungians to the table. One, the now hundred-year-old Joe Henderson, had been a patient of Carl Jung's in Zurich in 1929. Since all present were music lovers, talk quickly turned to the Guarneri Quartet's work with Rubinstein. I suddenly remembered my dream. The lunch mood was relaxed and I recounted it, oblivious for the moment of the fact that the interpretation of dreams is a Jungian's bread and butter. Up the garbage mountain I went, off came the lid, and finally I told of Rubinstein's sheepish grin. There was a brief silence when I finished, and then all four Jungians burst out laughing. "Climbing the garbage mountain to success," one of them intoned solemnly, which provoked another round of laughter. It was my turn to grin sheepishly.

In the years that followed, there was no discernible mountain of garbage for me to climb in my career. The Guarneri Quartet played a hundred concerts a year, made recordings, and traveled all over the world. And I loved my violin, whose troubled past and ambrosial sound both intrigued and inspired me. The del Gesù sang out in everything from late Beethoven to unaccompanied Bach, but doubts occasionally nagged at me. Was this my dream violin, the one I had always heard in my inner ear, the one with a sound that would reach to the very last row of a great hall, or was this "affordable del Gesù," if not an oxymoron, then merely the wishful thinking of a violinist with limited means? Time would tell.

CHAPTER 10

True Love

EACH TIME THE Guarneri Quartet played in Buffalo, New York, Mischa Schneider came to hear us, not only as a faithful friend and an enthusiastic admirer but also as an honest critic of our playing. I loved Mischa, the Budapest String Quartet's cellist. He was quite the opposite of his brother Sascha, who was the Budapest's second violinist. Mischa was thoughtful, loving, and somewhat reserved; Sascha, as I knew from firsthand experience, was volatile, emotional, and often excessive. Yet the two of them certainly had traits in common. They clearly looked like brothers. Both were short, compact, and broad-faced, both were remarkable musicians, and both spoke English with a Russian accent thick enough to parody. Only in getting to know them well did I notice that their accents occasionally parted company. Mischa, unlike Sascha, had a tendency to mix up his *v*'s and *w*'s. Therefore, a "white vest" might come out of his mouth as a "vite west."

After one of our Buffalo concerts, early in 1972, Mischa, look-ing thoughtful, spoke to me backstage: "Your wiolin is veek." The comment was sadly true, I had come to realize. My del Gesù might purr and even growl in small halls, but recently we had played in Carnegie for some three thousand listeners. To my ears the violin had indeed sounded "veek." "Maybe I can do zumzing," Mischa volunteered.

Several weeks later, he rang to tell me that the Budapest's first violinist, Joseph Roisman, who had recently retired, was thinking of selling his violin. "He iss vaitink for your coll." I had never met Roisman, only admired his artistry from afar.

"Steinhardt," Roisman said on the phone (he always addressed me by my last name), "come to Washington, try the violin, and then we'll talk."

I took mental inventory of my Budapest String Quartet en-counters as the train from New York pulled out of Pennsylvania Station and headed south. I had heard the quartet first on my par-ents' records of the Schumann Piano Quintet with pianist Clifford Curzon and the complete Beethoven string quartet cycle, and then later in several live performances. As a music student, I sat in the balcony of the Metropolitan Museum's Grace Rainey Rogers Au-ditorium and watched the Budapest emerge from the wings. Its members were more or less the same height and walked almost perfectly equidistant from one another, as if thirty-five years of ensemble playing had gradually whittled them down to a uniform, carefully calibrated set of musicians. But when they sat down and began to play, a different picture instantly arose. True, the group's precision was remarkable. A seemingly effortless sheen pervaded its sound, yet each musician managed to play with his personal and individual style untamed. Team players who insist on exhibiting star qualities might work to advantage on the basketball court, but that these men brought it off in a string quartet was remarkable.

Roisman, a small, slender man with a domed forehead and thinning hair, had caught my attention in particular. Unlike the violist, Boris Kroyt, and the cellist, Mischa Schneider, who swayed, and Sascha Schneider, who gyrated, Roisman sat relatively still in his chair and played with a gliding and compelling elegance. His sound, which floated easily up to the balcony where I sat, was refined and somewhat husky. Did it come from the violin or the violinist?

Roisman greeted me at the door with a pipe in his mouth. Pola, his wife, made tea for us, and then he handed me the violin. It looked like no other violin I'd ever seen — extremely broad, patterned flatly at the top and bottom like a cello, and with unusually large f-holes, a deep, burnished brown-gold top, and a back whose wildly swirling grain almost made me dizzy. I gingerly took the instrument and played it for Roisman and his wife in their living room. That unmistakably rich and throaty sound I had heard in Roisman's hands for so many years poured forth. I played on and on, bewitched.

"Steinhardt," Roisman said, seeing how affected I was, "I will sell the violin to you someday, but not just yet. I still enjoy playing quartets for fun with my friends. Give me a little time."

I left Roisman's apartment without the violin but beside myself with excitement. In the not too distant future, I would be playing a miraculous-sounding instrument. The meeting with Roisman gave me pause, however. How did he feel watching and listening to me, a veritable stranger, playing his beloved violin? And what was it like to contemplate giving up his partner in music-making for the past thirty years? The thought dampened my ebullient mood for only a moment and then was gone. I was, after all, a young man, more concerned with my own future than with Roisman's past. The idea of any sort of ending — of career, of health, of life itself — was too distant, too theoretical for me to consider seriously. Today, now that I approach Roisman's age, those issues are slowly shifting to center stage. How will *I* feel when my playing career is over and I must hand my violin over to its next owner?

Several months after my visit, Mischa called to tell me that Roisman had died suddenly, on October 10, 1974, and that Pola, following the wishes of her late husband, would sell me the violin. Again Pola served me tea in the Roismans' apartment, which now felt strangely barren. Death had in an instant stolen Pola's husband from her and snatched his silken playing from the ears and hearts of music lovers. As we chatted, I could see Roisman's violin case resting on the sofa. Roisman was in his coffin, and the violin, now temporarily masterless, in its own. When tea came to an end, Pola retrieved the violin case with tears in her eyes and handed it to me. It contained the violin, a fine Albert Nürnberger bow, and papers of authenticity. Not daring just yet to look too closely at these treasures, I closed the case, hugged Pola, and prepared to leave. She held on to me. "I'm sure Joe would want you to have this as well," she said, handing me a dozen or so pipes housed neatly in a rack. I do not smoke, but I left the apartment feeling that something of Roisman's spirit was accompanying me.

Returning home, I eagerly threw open the case and took a close look at the instrument. The violin was relatively flat and unusually wide; the corners were stubby, the f-holes almost too massive, the purfling, or thin sandwich of veneer, inlaid carelessly, and the swirling maple back emblazoned with an indelicate knothole. Yet the overall impression it gave was one of almost haphazard beauty and boldness. I began to play. Legally I was now the violin's owner, practically speaking its guardian, but on hearing the sound that filled my living room — a sound that literally gave me goose bumps — I felt even more deeply connected to this inanimate object. I played whatever came into my head for moments on end and then focused on each of the violin's four strings. The E string was piercing and silvery, the A creamy with a bit of grit, the D rich and dark, and the G powerful and husky. Inevitably, I compared this as yet unnamed violin to my del Gesù. That instrument might purr and growl, but the one under my chin growled and roared. The lower register had a somewhat rough rumble that reminded me oddly of a teenager's hot rod. This was the characteristic and prized sound of the great late del Gesù. Looking through one of the violin's f-holes, I could barely make out the label's inscription, covered in dust and rosin: *Guarneri del Gesù, fecit Cremona anno 1741.* The violin's uncharacteristically large f-holes were certainly reminiscent of his late style, and so was its slightly misshapen scroll. Yet Roisman had cautioned me when we met that the label was not authentic and that honestly he wasn't sure what the violin was, only that it made a remarkable sound.

When I began to read the certificates of authenticity that Pola Roisman had enclosed, it appeared that some of the experts had already spoken. Emil Hauser, the Budapest String Quartet's original first violinist, had had the violin appraised in 1926 by Otto Möckel in Berlin as a Guarneri del Gesù, in 1932 by Rembert Wurlitzer in New York City as an Angelo Bergonzi, and in 1946 by Jay Freeman as a Nicolo Bergonzi. When Hauser retired from the

Budapest, he sold it to Roisman, his replacement, but as what was anybody's guess.

With such confusion, there was nothing left but to take the violin to another round of experts. I chose two of the reigning rare-instrument authorities, first Charles Beare in London and then Jacques Français in New York City. Charles told me that the violin, except for its scroll, was unquestionably the work of the Cremonese master Lorenzo Storioni and that the instrument, probably made in the 1780s, was originally a small viola, so small that either Storioni himself or a later violinmaker decided to cut it down to violin size. Charles pointed to the oversized f-holes, which made sense in this context, to the artfully shortened length, which managed to retain the original edging and purfling, and to the place where the wood must have been removed from the center to draw the sides closer together. He admired the violin's appearance and craftsmanship but questioned whether its unusually broad shape could produce a beautiful sound. As I played the violin, sampling each register, I could see Charles's eyes widen and his face flush. When I finished, he graciously apologized for his mischaracterization and pronounced the violin's sound uncommonly beautiful.

Several weeks later, Jacques Français served up an identical opinion but in addition made me an offer I ultimately could not refuse. Jacques explained that he had a del Gesù without its original scroll and that in his opinion I had a del Gesù scroll without . . . Here he stopped in midsentence. "Excuse me, *mon ami*." Jacques disappeared into the back of his shop and emerged moments later with a small Storioni viola scroll, which matched my instrument astonishingly well in both color and proportion. He contended that this was very possibly the violin's original scroll, separated for profit years earlier by an unscrupulous dealer working in what amounted to a violin chop shop. Scroll and violin, about to be rejoined in harmony, would be the story of Tristan and Isolde retold.

Mercifully, the violin's identity crisis had been definitively resolved. Lorenzo Storioni was born in Cremona on November 10, 1744, just three weeks after Guarneri del Gesù died, and he died on January 10, 1816, at the age of seventy-one, in apparent poverty despite the great acclaim he had achieved. Storioni's instruments had none of the elegance and refinement of the earlier Cremonese masters'. Instead, his was a bold and sweeping style devoid of ornate details, yet highly artistic and harmonious. Storioni's models varied freely, but he returned again and again to Guarneri del Gesù for his inspiration. The fact that my violin bore a resemblance to and sounded quite like a del Gesù was a testament to his influence.

The Storioni still had an important hurdle to jump — the Guarneri Quartet itself. We could be tough on anyone bringing a new voice — an intruder, really — into the mix of sound we had labored long and hard to produce. A violin with a particularly nasal tone might cause someone to comment, "Sounds like it has the flu," or, if the violin was unusually bright and piercing, "Stop. Stop. You're rattling my fillings." To my relief, taking the Storioni to its first rehearsal with the group, akin to introducing a new fiancée to the immediate family, turned out to be a success. John, Michael, and David already knew and admired the violin from the many times they had listened to the glorious sound produced by the Budapest Quartet. When we sat down to play, the Storioni blended beautifully with Michael's Dominicus Busan viola and David's Andrea Guarneri cello, both lustrous and deep-toned old

Italian instruments. John and I, the two violinists sitting side by side, had the most obvious need to match sounds. John's violin, made by Nicolas Lupot, considered to be the Stradivarius of French makers, had a relatively bright and penetrating sound, which enabled him to be easily heard sitting several feet back from me in the quartet. Stationed further forward and often playing in a higher, more brilliant register, I could afford the luxury of a rounder, darker sound. Yet John and I were able to blend and balance our individual voices when the music called for it. For all their vaunted uniqueness, violins sound like the violinists who play them, and sound itself comes as much from the mind and heart of a player as from wood and catgut.

The Storioni's first Guarneri Quartet concert took place in Ann Arbor, Michigan. My old friend the violinist Charles Avsharian came backstage afterward to say hello. "Is that Joe Roisman's fiddle you're playing on?" he asked.

I smiled. "Word seems to travel fast."

Charlie looked at me blankly. "What word?"

I assumed he was play-acting. "The word that I just bought Roisman's fiddle."

Charlie shook his head. "I had no idea. Only, as I sat in the audience listening to you play, I thought to myself that that dark and smoky sound could come out of only one violin in the world — Roisman's."

In the next months one concert followed another, and with it came the inevitable travel. Lorenzo accompanied me everywhere — in cars, trains, planes, subways, taxis, and strange hotels. This should have come as no surprise to the violin, for it was only resuming the concert violinist's life it had known for so many years in the Budapest Quartet. Occasionally I worried about the

Storioni. One of my violins had already been unceremoniously bathed in gasoline, but I had heard far worse tales. A violin was fragile enough to break and small enough to lose or be stolen in a careless instant. Naturally, I made sure that the violin was insured for its full value, but how could money possibly replace something I had spent most of my life looking for? I avoided any situation where the violin could conceivably be bumped or squeezed; it almost never left my sight while I traveled, and when I left my hotel room, I always placed it behind the drapes or sofa on the presumption that a thief in a hurry furtively grabs the first things he can see and then flees.

Despite those precautions, my fears came true one day in the New York City subway system. I tripped and fell as I ran for a train, and my violin case flew from my hands and crashed onto the platform. A case is designed to protect an instrument from garden-variety knocks and bumps, but from the sheer force of my fall, I knew something bad had happened. I opened the case to find a crack in the top of my violin. Staring at the wounded instrument, I wished for the impossible. I wished to turn the clock back so that I could walk, not run, to the subway car whose doors were about to close. How could I have been so foolish! But time stubbornly refused to reverse itself, the crack gaped at me cruelly, and when I regained a semblance of composure, my thoughts turned practical. The violin would have to be repaired, and of course it would have to be repaired by an expert.

The name that immediately came to mind was René Morel, master luthier. As a young man, René had first worked with Rembert Wurlitzer, then with Jacques Français, and recently he had gone into business for himself. He repaired and cleaned my violin as needed and adjusted the sound post occasionally in order to get the optimal sound out of the instrument. I would play, he would listen intently, and then with an S-shaped tool that he inserted through an f-hole, he would move the sound post a mere fraction. This slender piece of cigarette-shaped maple that connects the violin's top and bottom plates is crucial for its sound. A millimeter of movement in any direction makes a world of difference in both volume and quality. The process of playing, listening, and adjusting was repeated over and over until René suddenly exclaimed, "Aha!" and pointed to his forearm triumphantly. "You see. You see. Goose bumps! The sound is perfect. You have given me goose bumps." Unquestionably, René's extensive knowledge of string instruments drew many of the world's great players to his shop to buy and sell their violins, to receive expert repairs, and to undergo his renowned goose-bumps test.

I slept very badly the night of my accident, replaying over and over again the subway fall and wondering how the violin's sound might be affected. Early the next morning I called René, who was good enough to see me immediately. First he examined the violin carefully, and then he looked up at my stricken face. "This is not as serious as you might think. Naturally it would have been better not to have happened, but you will hardly see the crack when it is repaired. The area will be stronger than before, and the violin's upper register will probably be more brilliant than ever." He explained that he would thoroughly clean the crack, apply a thin layer of glue, and then seal it with clamps. Afterward he would strengthen the area inside the violin with small wooden cleats.

I was skeptical. I thought that René might be humoring me out of kindness, especially when he allowed me into the work area several days later to see the violin lying on a bench, open — its maple back, ribs, blocks, and lining exposed and its spruce top off to the side, smothered in clamps. Seeing my violin for the first time in such a compromised position made me apprehensive. This was open-heart surgery, with Dr. Morel the head surgeon and the attending luthiers his assistants. But when René handed the violin back to me a few days later, all traces of the crack had vanished, and an entire upper octave range of sound rang out more brilliantly than before. All the things René prophesied had miraculously come to pass.

Mozart once wrote to his father about how the Augsburg piano-maker Stein dealt with cracks: "His pianos are really built to last. He guarantees that the soundboard will not break or crack. Once he has made a soundboard he exposes it to the fresh air, rain, snow, the heat of the sun, and God knows what else, so that it will crack. Then he glues in wedges, making it as strong and firm as possible. He is glad if it does crack, for that way he is assured that nothing further will happen to it. Often he cuts into the soundboard himself, then glues it again, making it all the stronger."

I breathed a sigh of relief. If there was a god of accidents, René had somehow foiled him. For all intents and purposes he had managed to accomplish my fantasy — he had turned back the clock, as if the subway incident had never taken place.

Old instruments almost inevitably sustain damage of one kind or another in the course of their lives, but this accident shook me. For months afterward I traveled overcautiously, seeing potential accidents at every turn, and I began to have unpleasant dreams. I dreamed that the entire Guarneri Quartet, destined for a concert, managed to crowd into a single taxi with all our instruments except mine. Try as he might, the taxi driver could not find a way to squeeze my violin into the tight mass of bodies and instruments already jammed into his vehicle. But this driver was resourceful. He strapped my violin case to the front bumper, climbed behind the steering wheel, and began to lurch in and out of traffic, braking violently in order to miss the cars in front of him — often by mere inches. I was terrified for the violin's sake, and to make matters worse, my colleagues took an incomprehensibly light view of the situation. They made jokes during the roller-coaster trip about my violin's new, improved condition as a flatter experimental model.

As time passed, though, I gradually grew comfortable again with the idea of carrying around a veritable fortune in what amounted to a suitcase. I developed a subconscious vigilance about where I placed the violin in restaurants, trains, planes, or the supermarket. My violin and bow might be worth a fabulous sum in today's marketplace, but they were still my indispensable work tools.

Along with this familiarity came a familiarity with the Storioni's capabilities and moods. I grew to know that I could dig in freely in its lower register, that I must skate more lightly over the upper strings, that the instrument was brilliant in the bone-dry dead of winter and froggy-sounding in oppressively hot and humid summer weather. The violin that for the past fifty years had been in the Budapest String Quartet now assumed a similar role in the Guarneri Quartet. It continued to play the first violin part, resting patiently on my lap during rehearsal discussions, which were sometimes heated, only this time in English rather than Hungarian or Russian; and it continued to sing for people in that distinctive voice that I now knew so well. I often wondered whom I should thank for the heavenly sound that rose out of this little wooden box I now owned — its maker, Storioni, its former owner,

Roisman, or the great cellist and now matchmaker extraordinaire Mischa Schneider, who had remarked, "Your wiolin is veek." (Matchmaker indeed! I first met my wife, Dorothea von Haeften, in Mischa's home.)

The violinist Ivry Gitlis once said that he didn't own his Stradivarius, it owned him, and that he was only passing through its life. I could not say how many people had passed through all two hundred years of the Storioni's life, but I did know of those who had inhabited it during the past hundred. Roisman had told me that according to Emil Hauser, the violin's previous owner, the instrument had once been in the possession of no less than Joseph Joachim, the great Hungarian violinist. I eagerly passed on this tantalizing bit of information to Jacques Français when he first appraised the violin. "Boolsheet," he said. "If all zee violins claiming to be Joacheem's were really heez, *mon ami,* he would have owned thousands." Still, I wanted to believe the story. It made the violin more glamorous, and besides, why would Hauser fabricate such a tale? Roisman was his friend and colleague. Adding Joachim's name to Hauser's, Roisman's, and my own, four people are known to have passed through the Storioni's life in modern times, leaving an entire century unaccounted for. How many other custodians has it had, and who were they? That remains Lorenzo's secret.

CHAPTER 11

Chaconne

I consider Johann Sebastian Bach the greatest man who ever lived, along with Abraham Lincoln and Franklin Delano Roosevelt. — FATS WALLER

I believe that Bach's solo works for violin are perhaps the greatest example in any art form of a master's ability to move with freedom and assurance, even in chains.

— LUDWIG VAN BEETHOVEN

To me the Chaconne is one of the most beautiful, incredible compositions. On one staff, and for a small instrument, this man pours out a world full of the most profound thoughts and powerful emotion. — JOHANNES BRAHMS

NOT LONG AFTER becoming Lorenzo Storioni's guardian, I was asked to play Bach's Chaconne at a benefit concert in New York City's Town Hall. Here was a chance to hear the Storioni in solo repertoire that I knew well on many different violins. I had studied the Chaconne on a student violin, played it on a Pressenda, recorded it on a Sanctus Seraphin, performed it recently in recital on a del Gesù, and now would play it again with my new Cremonese friend — a violin variously described as dark, smoky, husky, melting, creamy, silvery; a violin that Charlie Avsharian was able to pick out of thousands he must have heard at one time or another.

The Storioni's character was wilder and rougher than my Guarneri's had been, and from the Chaconne's authoritative opening chords, I immediately felt as if I had just shed an uncomfortably tight skin. This was both good and bad. If I was not careful, the Chaconne would sound coarse, but if I altered the speed and pressure of the bow slightly, the notes would turn luminous. This violin set new restrictions and created new possibilities for the Chaconne. My role was to serve as a mediator between instrument and music even as I tried to develop my own ideas — an interaction more commonly known as practicing. As I got to know the violin, the courtship process dipped below the conscious level, and adjustments took place almost without my realizing it. Inevitably, I began to focus more on the Chaconne itself.

Every one of my violins rendered the Chaconne differently, but the principal agent of change rested in me rather than the instrument. As an adolescent, I often considered music a vehicle for my own personal glory and the violin a mere servant. I shudder to think of my teenage rendition of the Chaconne. Blame it and the acne that afflicted my face at about the same time on hormones. But ego glorification eventually gave way to raw, unfettered emotion, which in turn yielded to some level of thoughtfulness. Much later, I began to worry that my rendition of the Chaconne was in danger of being smothered by another brand of excess — too much thought.

This time I worked from a facsimile of the composition's original autograph manuscript in Bach's own hand, something I had never considered before, either with Bach or any other composer. I found the manuscript's notation uncramped and surprisingly easy to read. Each staff ended with the note or chord of the next line, and "Turn immediately; turn quickly" was inscribed in Italian at the bottom of each right-hand page, suggesting that Bach intended it to be used in performance.

The title page read:

SEI SOLO

Ã

VIOLINO

SENZA

BASSO

ACCOMPAGNATO.

LIBRO PRIMO.

DA

JOH. SEB. BACH

AO. 1720.

"Six Solos for Violin Without Bass accompaniment. Volume One. By Joh. Seb. Bach, year 1720." It was a simple statement of fact, yet "Without Bass accompaniment" caught my eye. The Baroque era usually called on at least one bass instrument to support the solo voice with some kind of harmonic foundation. Apparently an unaccompanied work was unusual enough for Bach to have felt the need to spell out this aspect unequivocally on the title page. "Volume One" also piqued my curiosity. What might Volume Two be? I found the answer eventually on the title page of Bach's Cello Suites: "Vol. 2 / Violoncello Solo." Then there was the year, 1720.

Bach was the kapellmeister for Prince Leopold of Anhalt-Cöthen from 1717 to 1723. More than likely these violin works were composed during his time there, but it was tempting to speculate that 1720 might only be the year in which Bach presented this almost spotless manuscript to a fellow violinist for performance. Of the few Bach manuscripts I had seen in facsimile, this was by far the most beautiful, its undulating waves of notes hinting at motion and something rhapsodic in the music's character.

Aside from the sheer pleasure of reading Bach's own writing, I felt the manuscript copy would allow me to receive the music directly from its source without interpretation or alteration. Since the first edition of Bach's sonatas and partitas appeared in 1802, literally dozens have followed, edited by Ferdinand David, Arnold Rosé, Joseph Joachim, Lucien Capet, Leopold Auer, Jenö Hubay, Carl Flesch, and Ivan Galamian, to name just a very few. Editors occasionally took it upon themselves to "correct" a note here and there that they presumed to be the absent-minded slip of Bach's mind or pen, and since whole movements, if not entire works, might go by without a single indication of how loudly or softly passages should be played, the music was in some sense an empty container begging to be filled with a coherent scheme of rising and falling dynamics by a Joachim or Hubay. Once the interpreter's personal story line, as it were, had been developed, he or she had to deal with the question of bowings. Should Bach's bowings — that is, his indication of notes to be played separately or grouped together on a single bow stroke — be taken as gospel coming from someone who was himself a highly skilled violinist, or were they merely polite suggestions meant as a player's point of departure? And finally there was the never-ending matter of fingerings. The G above middle C might sound simple and sweet played on the D string, more assertive and rich up high on the G string. Which was best? For every violinist, faced with hundreds of such choices, there was a different answer.

I had nothing against these editions, which featured the artists' personal views based on a lifetime of study. In my formative years I leaned heavily and gratefully on the opinions of these wise old musicians each time a teacher assigned me Bach, but while Ivan Galamian undoubtedly had a valid point of view, he presented scripture through the filter of his own experience. At this point I desired no such middleman. For better or worse, I wanted to receive Bach's wisdom, his quirky bowings, his sparsely notated dynamics, directly with my own eyes and ears.

I decided to read through the first four movements of the D Minor Partita — the Allemanda, the Corrente, the Sarabanda, and the Gigue — in order to get my bearings before tackling the fifth and final movement, the Ciaconna. (Bach employed Italian for the entire manuscript.) The work could easily have ended with the brilliant and upbeat Gigue. The first four movements were a more or less standard format for Bach's dance-based suites. Why then did he add another movement, which is easily as long as all the others combined? I shuttled back and forth between the various movements to see if I could find any common elements. Sure enough, each movement began with a bass line resembling that of the Chaconne's initial four-bar phrase. This in no way explained the need for the towering Chaconne on the heels of these four beautiful if modest movements, but at least the connection between them gave me assurance that some kind of glue might be holding everything together.

I had stalled long enough. It was time to start work on the Chaconne itself. In my childhood I found Bach baffling; in my adolescence his work seemed turgid. Now, as an adult, the Chaconne's power and mystery presented me with an intriguing challenge. By definition, a chaconne generally consists of a repetitive chord progression as well as a basso ostinato, or repeating bass line. There were in fact sixty-four such phrases in Bach's version, each independently pleasing but deeply moving when linked together.

As far as I could see, my first task was to figure out how best to combine these ever-changing variations cohesively. I had not forgotten Isaac Stern's advice in violin camp years ago: think of the Chaconne's variations as occurring in groups, so that the evolution of thought and feeling unfolds convincingly. At the outset my course seemed relatively clear, since the early variations all came as matched pairs in which the second of each could be treated as a simple response to the first. But every now and again a lone variation would appear, begging me to direct it somewhere. These orphans vexed me. Did each belong with the next or the previous pair, or did they stand alone to freshen the palate between courses? The basso ostinato also perplexed me. This recurring bass line was supposed to do just that — to repeat endlessly without significant alteration and to serve as the work's distinctive theme. Yet Bach refused to stick consistently to the bass template he fashioned for the beginning and chose rather to draw from several quite distinctive and different ones.

Another characteristic trait of a chaconne is a regularly repeating harmonic structure. Here again I could easily recognize not one but three or four different patterns. It was as if Bach had begun a card game with hard-and-fast rules that he then changed at whim again and again during play. Even the most easily identifiable element of a chaconne, a dance-related emphasis on the second of the bar's three beats, appeared only sporadically. If I were to dance the Chaconne, where and how would I place my feet when the stress was not on the second beat?

In previous encounters with the Chaconne, I had mostly busied myself with the daunting task of mastering the many awkward hand positions and building enough endurance to play fifteen minutes of uninterrupted and difficult music. Those hurdles still remained, but analytical thinking was relatively new to me. Unhappily, it brought few answers, only more questions. Perhaps Toscha Seidel had had a point when he had admonished me in that very first lesson on the Chaconne, "Just play it from the heart."

I decided to put past considerations aside for the moment and try to look at the bigger picture. The Chaconne was divided into three large sections. The dark and brooding outer sections flanked a hymnlike inner one that evoked peace, gratitude, and optimism. Was it far-fetched to think that Bach, a devout Christian, might have offered the Chaconne as an expression of the Holy Trinity, its bedrock spiritual principle? The first section, in D minor, would represent the Father; the next, in D major, the Son; and the final section, in D minor, the Holy Spirit. This line of thought intrigued me, even though I was on shaky footing as a secular Jew with only the flimsiest knowledge of Christianity. The more I looked, however, the more "threes" I found. The Chaconne's basic building block was a three-beat bar, the initial theme appeared three times — at the beginning, the middle, and the end — and then there were those evocative three-note groups that appeared over and over again. Was the Chaconne some kind of message in a bottle destined for (dare I think it?) God?

There were other threes that I considered. According to Pythagorean theory, the triangle is the basic building block of the universe. Might that not somehow relate to the Chaconne's three main sections — its very own triangle of building blocks? I pondered such other groupings as past, present, and future; morning, noon, and evening; youth, maturity, and old age. And perhaps there were numbers besides three that held the Chaconne together. For example, why had Bach settled on sixty-four variations, rather than, say, fifty-nine, or twenty-three? If all sixty-four had been four bars in length, they would add up to two hundred and fifty-six bars. Curiously enough, Bach chose to introduce an extra bar in the last variation, raising the number to two hundred and fifty-seven. I could make a case that an extension of the last phrase by one bar in such a long work served to dramatize its ending, but Bach just as easily might have kept the four-bar unit and put a *fermata,* or hold, on the last note. Was there something special about the number 257?

Bach certainly knew the numerical value of the letters in his name (that is, $B = 2$, $A = 1$, $C = 3$, and $H = 8$) and often used their sum, 14, as a kind of musical signature. And if you took the number of bars in the Chaconne, 257, and added its digits together, the total was Bach's name again: $2 + 5 + 7 = 14$. If so, the master's skill was such that he could create a work of high art and play games at the same time.

The wigged Bach gazing solemnly out of music books, the master whose life I was required to read about in music school, had seemed in those days merely a wooden figure of history. I had learned about where Bach lived, his immediate and extended musical family, where and whom he worked for, and the cultural and historical crosscurrents of his day, but these facts had failed to bring him to life. As the Town Hall concert approached, however, historical facts acquired a new allure for me. A careful reexamination might just lift the two-dimensional Bach off the printed page and breathe life into him and, by extension, into the Chaconne.

I read several biographies in hopes of gleaning something significant. I learned that Bach was involved in litigation because of a scrap with a student bassoonist, that he spent a brief stint in jail for having the cheek to request a move from Weimar to Cöthen, and that the greater Bach family was so intertwined in the musical life of northern Germany that when a Bach left his post as organist, the music director demanded that he be replaced by another Bach — any Bach, but only a Bach. I read Bach's detailed report on the condition of a church organ he was hired to assess, and looked over a receipt for a significant amount of wine he ordered for his household. These snippets of information put only a little flesh on the man's bones.

I turned to the first critical biography: *Johann Sebastian Bach,* by Philipp von Spitta. To my delight, I quickly found something specifically about the Chaconne.

> The hearer must regard the Chaconne as some phenomenon of the elements, which transports and enraptures him with its indescribable majesty, and at the same time bewilders and confuses him . . . Consider that all this was written for a single violin! And what scenes this small instrument opens to our view! From the grave majesty of the opening through the anxious restlessness of the second theme to the demi-semi quavers which rush up and down like very demons, and which are veiled by the weird form of the third subject — from those tremu-

lous arpeggios that hang almost motionless, like veiling clouds
above a gloomy ravine, till a strong wind drives and rolls them
together and scourges them down among the tree tops, which
groan and toss as they whirl their leaves into the air — to the
devotional beauty of the movement in D major where the evening sun sets in the peaceful valley . . . This chaconne is a triumph of spirit over matter such as even he never repeated in a
more brilliant manner.

I closed the book gently and glanced at the Bach facsimile
perched on my music stand. Fine for Spitta to talk about gloomy
ravines, anxious restlessness, and devotional beauty, but I could
not see how these expressions, poetic as they might be, would
help me play the Chaconne. Even if I could agree on words to describe variation 1 as noble, variation 7 as reflective, 13 melancholy, 18 brilliant, 34 prayerful, 64 triumphant, would they offer
anything more than a blanket assessment devoid of detail? As I
had so often been told, the devil is in the details — ever evolving,
ever changing.

The tantalizing scraps of information I uncovered — religious, numerical, historical, and other — held the promise of being signposts along the Chaconne highway, yet each proved disappointing in the end. The Chaconne as an expression of no less
than the Holy Trinity gave me pause. What could be more inspiring than to think about Bach, the devout Lutheran, offering this
work as a testament of his faith? But when I stood before the music on my stand and tried to translate the concept into something musically meaningful, it remained stubbornly theoretical
rather than useful. Far easier was to string variations together and
have them go from loud to soft or soft to loud according to some

instinctive process. For example, the opening three- and four-note chords were a noble and grand kind of proclamation, and as the paired variations gradually became more transparent, they begged to become correspondingly quieter. The variations were like building blocks that looked better or worse depending on how you grouped them. I could not tell why a certain arrangement felt right, only that it did, and since Bach offered not a single dynamic in the entire Chaconne, I was forced to rely on practical and vaguely aesthetic considerations in creating an overall plan. Something was missing.

I decided to call Ralph Berkowitz. Ralph, my senior by a good thirty-five years, was a pianist who had studied at the Curtis Institute during its earliest days and gone on to a rich professional life touring with, among other luminaries, the cellist Gregor Piatigorsky. I had had the pleasure of playing with Ralph, but what often struck me in both rehearsals and conversation was how eloquently he spoke about music. Without a doubt you would have to call him a scholar, but in no way was he the dry, learned theorist buried in some remote library corner. One of his keenest interests was J. S. Bach, and I placed the call with the hope that he might provide some insight into the Chaconne.

He listened to my litany of complaints: references to Bach the man and his thoughts about music were skimpy, writings on the Chaconne were vague or fanciful, I myself had run out of new ideas. There was a moment's silence on the other end of the line, and then Ralph asked in his lazy, singsong voice, "What if you learned that Bach was mean to his wife or kind to his children? And Arnold, what if you came across a letter in which Bach described exactly how the Chaconne should be played? Let's say he wanted a certain passage in the Chaconne to be fast or slow or to sound like leaves blowing in the wind or like a beautiful sunset. It would be of very little use to you."

Ralph warmed to his subject. "Read Spitta if you want, although I myself never found anything satisfactory in nineteenth-century purple prose. One can write about Bach from an emotional point of view, but I like to *see* what the guy was thinking. His music itself is incontrovertible, like a court of law. Did you know that Brahms and his friend Joachim exchanged puzzles — double and triple counterpoint inversions? On one level these guys were playing with notes, and so did Bach. As you know, Bach's name in letters is fourteen. Backwards it's forty-one. A tune in one of his chorales adds up to fourteen, another three add up to forty-one. But those were *his* games, *his* preoccupation with numbers. Any meaningful instructions *you* need on how to play the Chaconne are all in the notes themselves."

Another silence followed, this time on my end of the line. Ralph's advice was of such a basic nature — like telling a reader that he must look at the words in order to understand *War and Peace* — that I felt a twinge of disappointment.

Ralph spoke again, at the same slow pace, as if he had just been napping. "Tell you what, Arnold. I'm going to send you something I cooked up a while ago that might be useful. By the way, did you hear what the waiter said to the four Jewish women sitting in a restaurant? 'Ladies, is anything all right?'"

I had already forgotten about the telephone call when a manila envelope arrived in the mail several days later. In it I found two large sheets of music paper pasted together. Ralph had written, "For my dear Arnold in admiration and with all affection" on the blank outer page, but unfolded, it was covered with writing, music notes, and symbols. At first glance it looked like some kind of map for buried treasure. Formal and stylish block letters on the top left page announced, "An analysis of Bach's Chaconne for my dear friend Joe Gingold by Ralph Berkowitz." Directly underneath it continued, "A Précis of Bach's Chaconne — made for the birthday — October 28, 1979 — of his dear friend Joseph Gingold by Ralph Berkowitz." What followed was an analysis in which Ralph had laid out the Chaconne's three main sections, the exact order of eight- and four-bar variations, the eight devices Bach used for harmonic progression or linear basses, the variations grouped with identifying devices in their corresponding main sections, and unusual points of interest along the way, such as "6 chromatic notes rising in bass," "Bass somewhat allied but harmonies differ considerably," "Double canon at the 4th on a tonic pedal-point." Ralph added one final thought at the bottom of the right-hand page: "Throughout the work there are freedoms subtly varying these formulas which attest to the astonishing invention of Bach's creativity."

I stared at the paper in my hands. It was in effect a plan for the Chaconne, not unlike an architect's blueprint. Assuming that Ralph had gotten it right, would this not have been the basic structure that Bach envisioned as his creation came to life? And if so, had I not stumbled onto some sort of Rosetta Stone here? I took both Ralph's précis and my music to the dining room table, where I had room to spread them out side by side. Then I proceeded to transcribe as best I could Ralph's birthday present to my old mentor Joe Gingold onto my music. It was the first time I had ever worked on the Chaconne without my violin, but even stranger was the feeling that I was superimposing Ralph's analysis directly onto a copy of Bach's actual manuscript. This was the moment when Bach might have risen from his grave and shouted, "Who are you to tell me what I was thinking when I wrote my masterpiece? What chutzpah, what unmitigated gall!" But the great Bach said nothing, and eventually I put the music back on the stand and picked up my violin and bow.

Ralph's précis afforded the luxury of an overarching view of the Chaconne, as if I had suddenly donned magic glasses. I worked through the sixty-four variations once again with a new-found sense of power. Every piece of music from "Mary Had a Little Lamb" to Beethoven's Ninth Symphony has a blueprint of some sort. If I hoped to do justice even to Mary and her little lamb, wasn't it incumbent on me to examine what those two did, how they did it, and in what order? For the next few days I played the Chaconne over and over, taking note of things Ralph had pointed out — a bass line that unexpectedly rose rather than fell, a small harmonic alteration, a double canon.

Around the time that Ralph's précis arrived, my wife, Dorothea, and I were in the process of building a vacation house in upstate New York. The materials we chose — ponderosa pine, Douglas fir, and metal roofing — were utilitarian and inexpensive, in keeping with our tastes and budget. One night I dreamed that I arrived at the building site to find that the modest house under construction had become unrecognizably grand. Unbeknown to us, our architect had ordered the finest artisans to erect fluted columns inside the main room and then paint them in rich shades of red and ocher. Workmen were rushing about in a flurry of activity, and to my alarm I could see that our little dream house was rapidly turning into a mansion. How could this possibly have gone so wrong? But all at once work ceased and I could see the results clearly. The columns were beautiful, the whole house wonderfully pleasing. The architect was also content. He stood in the middle of the living room and played the violin as a way of acknowledging to me, to my wife, and to the workers that his masterpiece was complete. Perhaps not coincidentally, he played Bach's Chaconne, and what amazed me was how well he did it without ever having studied the violin.

The dream underscored my embrace of Ralph's structural road map as a secret weapon, but the delicious feeling of power it provided lasted only briefly. No matter how all-seeing I might feel with my blueprint of the cathedral-like Chaconne in hand, the strings of notes that made up each individual variation demanded that I breathe life into them. There was more to a cathedral than its grand design.

Ralph's gift prompted me to pose a question to an architect friend, Tom Casey, who works at Taliesen, Frank Lloyd Wright's school of architecture. Would giving the same architectural plan to ten different builders result in exactly the same building ten times?

Tom shook his head emphatically. "No, not at all — especially if the builders were in different regions or even different countries. They would be dependent on the materials at hand and their personal tastes. You would certainly recognize the structural similarities of the buildings, but their feel would be very different."

Ten violinists, ten violins, ten Chaconnes, I thought to myself. Only then did I let the cat out of the bag about Ralph's précis.

Tom leaned back in his chair. "Do you know what Frank Lloyd

Wright had on the wall at Taliesin? It was a quote from the ancient Chinese philosopher Lao-tzu, I believe from the Book of Tea:

> The reality of a building
> Does not consist in the roof and wall
> But in the space within
> To be lived in!"

What would Lao-tzu, or for that matter Frank Lloyd Wright, have had to say about the Chaconne? Would they have stressed the work's structure, its details, or that intangible space emanating from within? With the Chaconne performance imminent, these were the essential questions that Bach, Storioni, and Steinhardt, the fiddled, the fiddle, and the fiddler, would have to face head on in order to come up with a meaningful rendition. The Chaconne expected no less from them at Town Hall.

CHAPTER 12

A Most Heavenly Music

THE TOWN HALL PERFORMANCE went well enough, but what most impressed me was my latest dance partner, Lorenzo Storioni, who had shown me dazzling new steps to the Chaconne. I was ecstatic to have this dream violin at last. But there was a second instrument onstage with me always, one easy to take for granted. Of course my ten fingers moved nimbly. Why shouldn't they? I worked hard almost every day of the year to keep them strong and fleet. Now and then I heard stories about musicians having physical problems, but these didn't concern me. In my forties, I was still invincible. Somebody else's body might crumble, but not mine.

I can't remember when I first noticed it, but gradually, almost imperceptibly at first, the last finger of my left hand became weak. Certain passages that I had once played in my sleep were becoming harder to bring off. When I began the Chaconne, for example, my little finger seemed reluctant to come down on the string for those first declamatory chords. I changed some of my hand positions to avoid having to use that finger too much, but it continued to lose strength. I was angry. How could a vital piece of my machinery, something I had taken for granted all my life, betray me like this?

I turned to the experts. They would be able to fix this. But to my surprise, the doctors' verdicts differed: one said I was suffering from tendonitis, another that it was arthritis of the neck, a third that I might have a tumor. It reminded me in an odd way of the rare-instrument experts — violin doctors, if you will — who had attributed my violins over the years to different makers. Some doctors were friendly, some in a rush to get to the next patient, some cruelly abrupt: "Your arm hurts? Don't use it." "Your hand weak? Time to teach!"

Anguished, I was grateful to the friends and colleagues who called. Isaac Stern offered his counsel and a list of doctors. Sascha Schneider recommended that I sometimes play second violin in the Guarneri Quartet to ease my burden. At the Casals Festival in Puerto Rico, where the Guarneri and the violinist Henryk Szeryng were both appearing, Szeryng, having heard of my problems, generously offered to help. I was touched that a violinist of his stature, someone I knew only casually, would take the time. One afternoon he invited me to his hotel suite, where, dressed in a silken gown, he had just finished an interview with an awed young reporter. Szeryng's double violin case lay open, revealing two of the world's greatest instruments, his Stradivarius and Guarneri del Gesù, nestled side by side. He greeted me warmly and then turned back to the young man. "I must introduce you to my two great loves before you go," Szeryng proclaimed, extending his hand toward the violins, as if he had just unveiled the *Mona Lisa*.

Szeryng was a flawless and elegant violinist. Furthermore, he spoke at least a dozen languages fluently. People in Spain told me that he was able to adjust his Spanish accent according to region. Unquestionably, he was a highly gifted and brilliant man.

But there was also a screw loose somewhere in him. Szeryng ushered the journalist to the door, turned, and pinned me with his gaze. "Arnold Steinhardt," he said loudly, as if I were in another room. Easily ten seconds of silence followed. I shifted uncomfortably on my feet. Then he repeated my name, much slower, and continued. "Arnold . . . Steinhardt. I will show you a series of exercises that I've gathered from my travels. They will solve all your problems and change your life. Come out onto the balcony with me and we shall do them together."

My heart sank. Doctors were unable to come up with a definitive diagnosis or course of treatment, yet Szeryng, without asking a single question about my condition, blithely offered a magic cure.

He led me onto his balcony, overlooking a semicircle of beach covered with sunbathers, and proceeded to demonstrate a series of bizarre calisthenics that looked like a circus clown's parody of an exercise routine. "Lift both arms high and stretch your right leg behind you," he commanded.

Reluctantly, I obeyed. How could one refuse the great Henryk Szeryng? Out of the corner of my eye I could see dozens of heads on the beach turn in our direction. Almost everybody associated with the Casals Festival — orchestra members, soloists, music lovers — was gawking at a balcony of the Caribe Hilton Hotel where Henryk Szeryng in a silk gown and Arnold Steinhardt wearing slacks and a Hawaiian shirt were performing a strange, ritualistic dance.

Szeryng's was not the only well-intentioned advice I received that proved ineffective. Musicians, after all, are not doctors. Still, the outpouring of sympathy comforted me. In a world where we were all competing for a finite number of places on the concert stage, I gained the feeling that the people of our close-knit community supported one another generously. Musicians with a wide range of physical problems, many of them strangers, called to give me the names of the best doctors and to tell me how they had dealt with the threat of never playing again. Some were quite open about their maladies; others divulged them to me in strict confidence, out of fear that they would lose work if the news got around. Some were violinists, but violists, cellists, pianists, flutists, and bassoonists were also among the afflicted.

My round of doctors and tests continued for months on end. In each waiting room my hopes would rise. *This* doctor would provide the magic bullet, *this* test would reveal what all others had missed. But when no definitive diagnosis presented itself, I left the doctors' offices feeling uncertain and increasingly frustrated. I longed for resolution. *Let my arm be healed or tell me I cannot ever play again, but do not condemn me to this purgatory.*

Finally the moment I had long hoped for arrived: a medical verdict had been reached. The weakness in my hand was apparently caused by a pinched nerve in my elbow. If the condition grew much worse, an operation was recommended — one that would have some chance of success.

Some chance? Those were not odds that I warmed to. I decided to tough it out. If my little finger refused to work, I would only use the others. If my hand got weaker, I would practice harder.

But my condition did gradually worsen, and playing well became increasingly difficult. I felt as if I were dying. The violin, that sweet giant core of my life, was in danger of being taken away from me. The violin had been my great gift, my living. Without it, what would I be? Music should have given me solace in my hour of need, but it was, ironically, too painful to listen to — above all, violin music. I lectured myself: life would go on without the violin. I was a musician at heart, not a violinist. I could teach, write, perhaps try conducting. But my soul rebelled. I had begun the violin at an age when I was learning to tie my shoelaces, to speak in complete sentences, to ride my tricycle in the back yard. What deep roots that fiddle had grown in me!

I confided my difficulties to my friend and fellow violinist Shmuel Ashkenasi. We took up our violins in my living room and began comparing playing positions. Shmuel and I examined closely how we moved the fingers of our left hand. What if I held the violin higher or moved my elbow slightly to the right or flattened my fingers? A slight change in old habits might yield surprising results.

But nothing seemed to make a difference, and soon Shmuel and I moved away from such technical shop talk. Just what did the fiddle mean to each of us? When things were going well, the violin was our best friend; when its difficulties overwhelmed us, it could be a wicked adversary; but to live without the violin was something we could only theorize about.

The menacing presence of my unresolved hand problem stuck in my throat as we put our fiddles away. Suddenly I blurted out my fear that I was nothing without the violin.

Shmuel remained lost in thought for a moment and then said something I can never forget: "If you think you are nothing without the violin, then you are also nothing *with* the violin."

The rock-hard truth of this statement struck me full-force. My unwillingness to imagine life without the violin was at the very core of my despair.

That night I dreamed that Shmuel and I were standing with our violins before two quaking aspen trees. While the leaves shimmered in the wind, we were somehow able to read them as musical notes. Side by side, we played a most heavenly music together.

I awoke from the dream refreshed and hopeful for the first time in weeks. The dream's optimism blocked my downward spiral into depression and unlocked a door I could not or would not open on my own in full consciousness. I *would* be able to move on and make music — a different kind, perhaps, but satisfying nonetheless. I had only to trust myself to read the leaves. Shmuel and my other close friends would provide comfort and help me to do just that.

My hand became even weaker as the days and weeks slipped by, and I decided to risk an operation. The idea of a doctor cutting through my skin, flesh, and muscle with razor-sharp surgical steel and then sewing me up again made me squeamish: what if the surgeon's hand slipped and severed a nerve or maimed a tendon? But if I hoped to play again, I had to submit to this unholy act. To my surprise, I felt a glacial calm when the orderly wheeled me into the operating room on a hospital gurney. It was that old performance phenomenon of preconcert nerves transforming themselves into optimism — only on this occasion I wasn't the performer; the surgeon would be the one onstage. Small wonder that he would be working in what is called the operating theater. Something else kept me relatively at ease: the quaking aspen dream hovered in my memory as a touchstone. No matter what happened, I would be all right.

I awoke from the operation with my painfully swollen left arm imprisoned in a cast. I would not be able to touch the violin for at least six weeks. At first being released from the burden of practicing felt as if I had been let out of school, but within days that sense of release was replaced by a void that made me uncomfortable. I had practiced the violin almost every day of my life. As an undisciplined and rebellious child, I dreaded having to practice. But by now, in middle age, practice had become as ingrained as brushing my teeth. What was life without the tactile feel of the violin and bow in my hands, the pleasure of improving a musical phrase by repetition, and the sheer thrill of making music?

Still, nature abhors a vacuum. Having no choice, I tentatively explored the violinless universe. Nothing could take its place, of course — not learning a foreign language, not collecting fine wines — but what remained of my life gently began to encroach on those times I would normally have held the violin and bow in my hands. Like a former smoker who forever longs for a cigarette, I never stopped missing this dear friend — this addiction, if you will — but as time passed I knew that the aspen dream had guided me wisely.

When the cast came off, the operation was pronounced a success — in theory. But in practice (forgive the pun), only time would tell. Five weeks later, Dr. Michael Charness, my astute and devoted neurologist, allowed me to begin playing for just two minutes a day. Opening the violin case, I looked at the Storioni, winsome in its velvet nest, for the first time in almost two months. Might the violin have forgotten how to sing its song? I picked it up gingerly and played a few tentative notes, then a simple scale. My fingers were able to move, to fall more or less on the right places. I drew the bow across the strings. The violin's sound emerged shyly at first and then with gathering confidence. Enough! Two minutes were up. Tomorrow Dr. Charness had granted me permission to play for three minutes, and the next day, if all went well, for four. The glacial pace of my comeback was of little importance. I could play the violin again! Slowly I gathered up the life I had so feared losing.

The act of moving one's arms, hands, and fingers over and over again in a very specific way, perhaps hundreds of thousands of times in a given year, is a risky business. It was now my turn to accept calls from musicians in trouble and to assure them that most likely there would be a path to their recovery. Often I looked at those who seemed to have no physical problems whatsoever and thought that they were somehow the poorer for it. A humbled survivor, I had been given an enormous gift. I knew that to be someone with the violin, I must also be someone without.

CHAPTER 13

The Dance of Life and Death

ONCE AGAIN I was a live, breathing fiddle player, but the scars I bore from that uncertain time were more than the six-inch one down the inner side of my left arm. Never again would I take my calling for granted. The illusion of any permanence in my life had shattered forever. I might die in my sleep, choke on a pit, or be run over by a trolley. Every phrase, every concert, might be the last, and therefore I played as if it really were.

I decided to update my will. My wife and I met with our lawyer in his office and went through the basics — assets, debts, and taxes. The lawyer had a disquieting habit of prefacing remarks with "If, God forbid, you should die . . .": "If, God forbid, you should die, Mr. Steinhardt, whom would you designate as your beneficiary?" or "If, God forbid, you should die, Mrs. Steinhardt, the United States government will tax your estate in the amount of so many dollars."

But what if I *did* die? Never mind the will. Would there be a funeral service? And if so, who would attend, and what would they say about me? There would have to be music, of course. Funeral services always have music, above all musicians' funerals. I had played at dozens of them. What music would I want at my own funeral? It would obviously have to include the violin. I would roll over in my grave if a brass quintet played. But exactly what? Perhaps something touching yet not too sad. It was bad enough that we all had to die, but deathly serious music on top of it? No, that wouldn't do. Ah, the slow movement of Mozart's Divertimento in B Flat, K. 287, for Two Horns and Strings. That was certainly music of ethereal beauty. Would my lawyer be willing to stipulate the divertimento in my will? And also the names of the musicians I wanted in the group? I wouldn't want a shoddy performance. Also, I hated slow movements that were treacly and long-winded. Perhaps I should suggest a metronome mark — one more thing to put in the will. I could control the entire musical portion of my funeral service from six feet under.

Then the best solution of all occurred to me. Let Joseph Szigeti, the violinist who arguably had moved and influenced me more than any other, play for my funeral. Szigeti had recorded the divertimento in a version for solo violin and chamber orchestra conducted by Max Goberman. The slow movement remained in its original string quartet setting, with Szigeti playing the first violin part. How nobly he had played, and yet with such feeling! And when the movement unexpectedly turned to a minor key, it made me want to weep along with Szigeti, who seemed to be crying on the violin. There *was* sadness to this music — an almost unbearable sadness — but also a feeling of limpid serenity, and a little flourish of a cadenza that dissolved into the movement's end. It was an ending that gently faded away to almost nothing, as if Mozart were bidding us goodbye. Mozart, an outstanding violinist, had boasted to his father after he himself had performed the first violin part, "Last night I played like the greatest violinist in all of Europe." Unfortunately, no record existed of Mozart's performance, but Szigeti's was all I could ever ask for. Let the producer of my funeral service play this transcendent music for my friends. If, God forbid, I should die, let something beautiful happen when I leave the world.

I mentioned the idea of having Szigeti play at my funeral to Dorothea. She smiled. If I died before her, she agreed to honor my wish, but it seemed distant and theoretical. I was, after all, a healthy middle-aged man recovered from my surgery and could reasonably look forward to a long life.

Then the unimaginable did happen. My friend Petra Shattuck, having gone for her usual morning jog and then to work, complained to her colleagues of a severe headache, lapsed quickly into a coma, and died several days later of a cerebral hemorrhage. Petra, forty-six, left her husband, John, and their three children, Jessica, Rebecca, and Peter, to fend for themselves, suddenly and unexpectedly. In his profound grief, John nonetheless managed to plan a moving service for Petra at Harvard's Memorial Church. He asked me to play. I could think of only one work that was suitable — Bach's Chaconne.

Perhaps cathedrals are grand in order to hold the powerful emotions that grip us, lofty so that we can more easily reach out to our mysterious universe and its creator, and artful and personal in detail to enable us to slip into the recesses of our own souls. *Grand, lofty,* and *personal* are words that also describe the Chaconne, but what, if any, was the reason for this mighty cathedral of a work? Bach's employer, Prince Leopold of Anhalt-Cöthen, was a sickly man who found the spa at Carlsbad beneficial for his health. Since the accepted course of treatment took months, there was no reason not to indulge in his favorite pastime while he took the baths — making music. Prince Leopold's kapellmeister, Bach, made the long trip with him. There were several such visits to Carlsbad, but the one in 1720 was marked by tragedy. Bach returned home with the prince to find that his wife, Maria Barbara, had died, at the age of thirty-five, and was already buried in the cold ground. It is hard to imagine what his shock and grief must have been and how he managed alone with seven children.

The six sonatas and partitas for solo violin were published later that year. Some people are of the opinion that the Chaconne was added to the D Minor Partita at the last moment as Bach's profound and immediate statement of grief and mourning. Helga Thoene, a German musicologist, has put forth the intriguing theory that the Chaconne is filled with many references to death and sorrow borrowed from some of Bach's own sacred works. Therefore, anyone living in Bach's time who was familiar with those works would recognize and be affected by the implications of the musical quotations as the Chaconne was being performed.

I wanted to believe this theory, yet the hard-nosed skeptic in me resisted. True, many snippets from Bach's sacred tunes interlock quite neatly with the Chaconne, but with a bit of clever juggling, wouldn't I be able to fit in "Happy Birthday" or "Take the A Train" just as easily? Thoene believes that the Christmas ditty "Vom Himmel Hoch da Komm' Ich Her" ("From Heav'n Above I Come to Earth") and "Christ Lag in Todesbanden" ("Christ Lay in the Bonds of Death"), a reworking of an Easter hymn by Martin

Luther, both appear as mystery guests in the Chaconne. Her ideas set me thinking as I prepared for Petra's service. Yes, there were sixty-four variations; yes, the chaconne was an old dance form; and yes, I was obliged to think of the work structurally in order to present it coherently. But even as I hewed to discipline I ached from the loss of my friend. One moment Petra was here, interconnected in a thousand ways to the people who knew her; the next moment she was gone, erased from the earth, with nothing left but a gaping void that swallowed every one of my confused emotions.

In the days leading up to the service, I derived at least a measure of solace from the Chaconne itself. It seemed in step with my bewilderment and aching heart, in step with the loss of a loved one. Inconsolable grief, prayer, and a rising spirit were the Chaconne's true building blocks. Whether or not Bach intended it as a memorial to his wife, I hoped to present this dance in the same rising spirit to Petra some 250 years after Maria Barbara's death.

Although the Shattucks had eventually moved from New York City, where we first met, to Washington, D.C., our two families had remained close through the years. I had often stayed with Petra and John when I performed at the Kennedy Center. Petra prepared the attic room for me, where I could practice in privacy. The attic had one drawback, however: the ceiling was so low that if I wanted to play standing up, I had to open the skylight in order to accommodate my ascending bow. It was a Shattuck joke that John and Petra could tell I was practicing when they came home from work by seeing the sliver of wood emerge again and again from the rooftop.

Shortly before the service for Petra took place, I dreamed that she brought Johann Sebastian Bach up to her attic to meet me.

Bach was not wearing his flowing wig and was dressed in contemporary clothes, but his identity was immediately clear. What good fortune for me! Here was a golden opportunity to get at the Chaconne's essence from the master himself. I opened the skylight so I could play for him, but Bach, seemingly uninterested, waved my violin away. I tried for the next best thing — to ask him about the connection between Maria Barbara and the Chaconne — but unexpectedly he grabbed both my arms and began to dance with me around the cramped attic space. Bach danced slowly and mournfully, all the while instructing me on the proper steps. Intermittently he whispered such things as "Bend, spring, land" into my ear. He was an accomplished dancer. He steered me gracefully around the bed, the table, and the chair where Petra sat quietly. As we danced I became aware that he was humming to himself: *Rim . . . , rim, bim, bim . . . , rim, bim, bim . . .* I knew that rhythm. It was the Chaconne. Bach was teaching me how to dance his Chaconne.

I awoke from my dream. The idea of dancing with Bach was daffy, yet Bach had moved with such grace and ill-concealed melancholy that the attic scene felt credible. He had had ample opportunity to see minuets, gavottes, passepieds, courantes, sarabandes, gigues, and loures, which were frequently danced at courts in cities where he lived. Although he composed only three chaconnes — the one for solo violin, the Passacaglia for Organ in C Minor, and the concluding piece of Cantata 150 in B Minor, "Meine Tage in den Leiden," for chorus — it was entirely possible that he knew how to dance the chaconne adroitly.

I could not imagine what the original court dances might have been like, much less their effect on Bach. Were they bawdy? Sensual? Reserved? Stylish? A chance encounter with a passage from

Pomey's long-forgotten French and Latin dictionary, published in Lyons in 1671, gave me an inkling of their character. The dictionary described the dancing of a sarabande:

> At first he danced with a totally charming grace, with a serious and circumspect air, with an equal and slow cadence, and with such a noble, beautiful, free and easy carriage that he had all the majesty of a king, and inspired as much respect as he gave pleasure.
>
> Then standing taller and more assertively, and raising his arms to half-height and keeping them partly extended, he performed the most beautiful steps ever invented for the dance.
>
> Sometimes he would glide imperceptibly, with no apparent movement of his feet and legs, and seemed to glide rather than step. Sometimes, with the most beautiful timing in the world, he would remain suspended, immobile, and half leaning to the side with one foot in the air; and then, compensating for the cadence that had gone by, with another more precipitous unit he would almost fly, so rapid was his motion.
>
> Sometimes he would advance with little skips, sometimes he would drop back with long steps that, although carefully planned, seemed to be done spontaneously, so well had he cloaked his art in skillful nonchalance.
>
> Sometimes, for the pleasure of everyone present, he would turn to the right, and sometimes he would turn to the left; and when he reached the very middle of the empty floor, he would pirouette so quickly that the eye could not follow.
>
> Now and then he would let a whole rhythmic unit go by, moving no more than a statue, and then, setting off like an arrow, he would be at the other end of the room before anyone had time to realize that he had departed.
>
> But all this was nothing compared to what was observed when this gallant began to express the motions of his soul

through the motions of his body, and reveal them in his face, his eyes, his steps, and all his actions.

Sometimes he would cast languid and passionate glances throughout a slow and languid cadence; and then, as though weary of being obliging, he would avert his eyes, as if he wished to hide his passions; and, with a more precipitous motion, would snatch away the gift he had tendered.

Now and then he would express anger and spite with an impetuous and turbulent cadence; and then, evoking a sweeter passion by more moderate motions, he would sigh, swoon, let his eyes wander languidly; and certain sinuous movements of the arms and body, nonchalant, disjointed and passionate, made him appear so admirable and so charming that throughout this enchanting dance he won as many hearts as he attracted spectators.

The description was breathtaking, but one phrase in particular caught my attention: "[He] began to express the motions of his soul through the motions of his body." In my dream Bach had danced with elegance and grace, yet the movements had hinted at the profound sadness that must have cloaked his soul. The shadow of Maria Barbara's death hung over him.

At Petra's service, people rose one by one to speak about her as wife, mother, friend, lawyer, expert on Native American law, and champion of the poor and dispossessed. Many cried, and many groped for words to explain why she had been unreasonably, cruelly, and irrevocably taken from us. Then I played the Chaconne. There was no applause when I finished. One does not applaud after a sermon — by rights, a sermon that should have been given by the Lutheran pastor Johann Sebastian Bach, who unfortunately could not be with us that day.

Years later I decided to make a trip to Cöthen in order to

visit the city where Bach had lived, to see the palace where he had made music with Prince Leopold, and to play the Chaconne at Maria Barbara's grave. Over lunch I told the pianist Gary Graffman and his wife, Naomi, of my plans. Naomi, looking amused, suggested that I think of organizing a concert tour of gravesites around the world. I could play for Paganini, who was buried in Parma, for Beethoven in Vienna, for Stravinsky outside Venice, and of course for all their wives and mistresses. The possibilities were endless.

Perhaps it was a foolish idea, but I couldn't shake it. On a warm and sunny morning at summer's end, I played the Chaconne for Maria Barbara Bach, who was buried in a lovely park on the outskirts of the old city. Dorothea, the violinist Benjamin Bergmann, who accompanied us to Cöthen, a journalist and photographer from the local newspaper who had gotten wind of the unusual concert, and a couple passing by with their dog were the only listeners. Maria Barbara, of course, did not respond to my performance — though at the very least she might have commented on the Chaconne. To the best of my knowledge, no one had ever played the Chaconne for her before.

I cannot speak for the others at the grave that morning, but the performance affected me. Musicians, actors, jugglers, trapeze artists — we are all cautioned early on not to be moved by our own hard-won craft, for fear of losing it in a whirlwind of emotion. But the quality of my playing was not at issue. As the Chaconne progressed, I felt the tragedy of Maria Barbara's death and the aching in Bach's heart as no music history book could ever convey. I imagined Bach, his grief-stricken and bewildered children, and their circle of friends listening to the Chaconne at Maria

Barbara's funeral service — quite possibly played by Bach himself. The atmosphere might have been similar to the service at which John, his children, and their friends reluctantly bid their beloved Petra goodbye. They too must have struggled to make sense of what had happened and wondered how to grope their way through a thicket of chaotic emotions as they listened to the Chaconne — a dance of both life and death.

CHAPTER 14

Dance Fever

PEOPLE TEND TO THINK that musicians get to see the world as a fringe benefit of touring. They don't realize that managers usually arrange concert tours with maximum profit in mind, meaning minimal time in between for relaxation. "You were in Rome and didn't see the Sistine Chapel? Shame on you!" My mother, an inveterate sightseer, had a point. It would have been nice to crane my neck upward at God's famously outstretched hand reaching across the chapel's ceiling like a constellation in Michelangelo's night sky. I tried explaining to her that I had traveled all morning to get to Rome, checked into my hotel, stolen a quick nap, practiced, played the concert that evening, and left for another city early the next morning. Unmoved, Mother shrugged her shoulders. "People save up for a lifetime to see the Sistine Chapel," she said.

Mother was both right and wrong. I should have seen the Sistine Chapel, but I couldn't. The rare opportunity to visit tourist attractions came as an unexpected gift. Over the years I had managed to squeeze in between concerts such unrelated items as Mount Rushmore, a Gypsy band in Budapest, a Stanford University football game, the Watts Towers in Los Angeles, a ballet in Riga, Latvia, koalas in an Adelaide zoo, and the Bilbao Art Museum. As stimulating as those places and events were, they remained merely anecdotes waiting to be trotted out when the subject of a musician's life on the road arose.

Once, on a South American Guarneri Quartet tour, I was taken to see the tango danced to live music in a smoke-filled Buenos Aires nightclub. In this case the experience set off an unexpected chain of events. I watched a man and a woman with arms and legs seductively entwined glide across the dance floor. Occasionally they separated almost violently from their stylized embraces and then came together again just as abruptly. It was hard to know whether they were fighting or having sex with their clothes on, but I blushed as if I'd stumbled onto lovers in bed. The music was equally provocative. Violins wailed their ardent song while the accordionlike bandoneons, the emblematic sound of the tango, snapped back at them. *Life is hard,* they berated the violins — those fools with sappy, sentimental notions of love.

At the end of our South American tour, I finally had the opportunity to be a tourist for ten days before returning home. I decided to hike the Inca Trail and visit the legendary ruins of Machu Picchu. From Buenos Aires, I first flew to Lima, Peru, traversing the continent's waistline. En route the plane crossed the towering Andes, whose craggy peaks threatened to scrape the undersides of our wings. The Inca Trail and Machu Picchu, embedded far below me in the vast mountain range, passed by within a matter of seconds. That same trip on foot over a trail that had endured for five hundred years would take me four days of hiking, at the end of which I would finally see the lost and once secret city.

The prospect of this adventure as high-altitude hiker, camera-laden tourist, and seeker of something vaguely spiritual made me exceedingly happy. I hummed to myself bits and pieces of tangos as the plane landed in Lima. In fact, I could not get the sounds and images I had just seen and heard on the other side of the continent out of my head. The male dancer's movements, mannered and domineering, the female's, sensuous and submissive — apparently the fruit of the tango's origins in the bars, gambling houses, and brothels of Buenos Aires' poorest slums — flitted before my eyes, and the vocalist's emotion-laden sound welled up in my chest and throat as a tactile memory.

Before continuing the journey, first to Cuzco and then to the Inca Trail, I had pressing if mundane matters to take care of in Lima. The Guarneri String Quartet was scheduled to record Schubert's *Death and the Maiden* Quartet in New York City one week after I returned from Peru. Schubert's music demanded that a violinist be both poet and thinker — a goal as lofty as the mighty Andes themselves — but the poet and thinker demanded an athlete's body. As much as I loved the idea of abandoning myself exclusively to the climb, I would have to practice daily on the way to Machu Picchu.

Thinking of myself as an athlete didn't come naturally. The sedentary life I led tended to make me flabby, a condition I became unpleasantly aware of when I began training for the Andes adventure. For the past two weeks I had climbed diligently up and down the fire stairs of every South American hotel I checked into, in preparation for the hiking and high mountain passes to come.

Five floors gave me no problem, but at ten I breathed heavily, and by the twentieth floor I was completely winded, gasping for air in a stairwell of the São Paulo Hilton. Obviously I was no athlete, and yet I *was* — at least insofar as those very specific muscles needed to run fleetly up and down the fingerboard went. Without practice on the Inca Trail, Schubert's *Death and the Maiden* would become *Death of a Violinist.*

Fiddling on the trail presented a problem, however. Taking a rare violin into the wild would be like driving a Rolls-Royce into a war zone: unthinkable. My beloved Storioni suddenly acquired the status of a pet that had to be provided for before its master could go on vacation. As far as I knew, Peru had no violin kennels, but there was a solution at hand: my wife, who was to join me for the hike to Machu Picchu, brought from New York the cheapest practice violin she could lay her hands on, and I left my Storioni in the apartment of a friend's friend in Lima.

With my violin safely stored in a stranger's closet, we flew to Cuzco, elevation 11,000 feet, and remained there for several days in order to become acclimatized to the altitude. Then we traveled for several hours by truck to the Inca Trail and set out on the hike. I rapturously embraced the Andes — if one can embrace anything of that overpowering size and impact — and marveled at the Peruvian villagers we encountered. Their traditional clothing seemed almost too colorful, too festive for everyday wear. As the days progressed, our guide and translator, Teresa, told us about the Inca people, the ruins we passed, and Machu Picchu — the five-hundred-year-old city we would see on the fourth day of hiking.

Along the trail, one of the ten porters assigned to our party carried my violin strapped to the top of a cooking stove. At the first campsite, he carefully separated the fiddle case from the stove and handed it to me. I took out the violin to play while the evening meal was being prepared. The sun, which had beaten down on us while we hiked, sank early, disappearing behind the massive Andean peaks, and with its departure came a shocking drop in temperature. I was obliged to play smothered in my parka, woolen cap, and gloves cut off at the fingers. At first I practiced only scales, to thaw my hands in the bone-chilling night air; then the passages of Schubert that persistently gave me trouble; and finally some of the tangos I had just heard, which continued to chase each other in my head. I played the most famous ones, which were easy to remember: G. H. Matos Rodriguez's "La Cumparsita" ("The Masked One"), Jacob Gade's "Jalousie," and "El Choclo."

The mountain peaks, ghostly outlines in the gathering darkness, were impassive witnesses to my fiddling. Dorothea, our son, Alexander, and Maru and Paolo, two friends from Mexico City, occasionally looked my way and smiled as they unpacked and prepared for our first night in a tent. The porters, dressed in traitional Peruvian clothes, caps, and the skimpiest of sandals (their standard hiking gear), stood in a group at a distance, silently regarding me. Some of them did not even speak Spanish, only their native Quechua. Had they ever heard tangos before, or was I Tango Mary, bringing a new dance disease to the Peruvian highlands for the first time? Music has always traveled that way — from mouth to mouth, instrument to instrument, stopping abruptly in one place from lack of interest, spreading like wildfire elsewhere when it catches people's fancy.

The next morning our party arose early and prepared for what was to be the most challenging day of the trip. We would have to traverse the highest of three passes, Abra de Huarmhuañusca, or

Dead Woman's Pass, en route to Machu Picchu. My pace slowed and became unsure as we approached 14,000 feet. If only those hotel stairs I had run up and down had been at high altitude! My violin, however, had no such problem. The porters, who had left camp after us, were already far ahead. I could see my fiddle case, again fastened to the stove, which in turn was strapped to a porter's back, weaving monotonously back and forth on the trail's endless switchbacks above us. Then the violin disappeared without fanfare over the pass.

When we trudged wearily into our campsite that evening, the tents were neatly in place, the smell of cooking meat wafted seductively through the crisp air, and my violin awaited me. A group of strangers stood off to one side, eyeing us expectantly. Teresa spoke with them and then informed me that they were all waiting for the violinist. I was flabbergasted. How on earth could they have known? It seems the porters had spread the word along the Inca Trail that there was a fiddler among us.

Teresa nodded in the direction of one man in particular. "He wants you to teach him how to play the violin," she said.

I laughed. "Be serious, Teresa."

She told me that he played several folk instruments but not the violin and that he had come a long way to meet me. The man began speaking animatedly in Spanish. Occasionally he punctuated his remarks by mimicking the gestures of a violinist. Teresa turned to me. "He's wild to have a violin lesson. Show him at least how to hold it."

The man, no more than twenty-five, had an open, eager face. He grinned broadly at me. Ordinarily I might have declined, but his enthusiasm was unexpected and touching. I retrieved my violin from the tent.

By now quite a crowd had gathered: my family and friends, the prospective student and his friends, several porters, and Teresa. I put the violin under the young man's chin and the bow in his other hand and explained how to hold them. Teresa translated into Spanish. Again and again I corrected his hand positions, until they had a semblance of naturalness, and then I tried to explain how to draw the bow across the strings. Several false starts brought forth squawks from the violin and groans from his friends, but then the bow fell onto the sweet spot between fingerboard and bridge that the Suzuki violin method calls "the Kreisler Highway" in honor of the great violinist Fritz Kreisler. A quite respectable sound sprang out of the violin.

The young man's face registered surprise. Then he threw back his head and burst out laughing for sheer joy. His friends nodded their heads and murmured in appreciation.

I showed him where to put his left-hand fingers, one by one, on the string. Again he drew the bow. A few shaky but recognizable notes emerged, and we hooted and whistled in appreciation. Flushed with success, the young man handed the violin back to me and smiled expectantly. Apparently he wanted a professional demonstration.

I wondered what to play for this uncommon collection of people. Bach seemed too severe, Paganini too difficult. The dancehall tangos that continued to stalk me as I trudged along the Inca Trail seemed like a good idea, but I did not know any of them well enough. Fortunately, the tango had infiltrated my own world of music long ago. Igor Stravinsky wrote tangos. So did Isaac Albéniz and even the violinist Mischa Elman. In the end I played Albéniz's deliciously lilting tango for an unusually quiet and attentive standing-room-only audience (no chairs at the campsite), against a backdrop of oversized mountains that gradually faded to a bare outline in the growing darkness.

Day three on the Inca Trail began very early, like days one and two. We had much ground to cover if we were to reach Machu Picchu the next afternoon. Teresa told us how in 1911 the American explorer Hiram Bingham had first stumbled onto the Inca ruins of Machu Picchu, strangled in a tangle of trees and dense undergrowth. Three days out of Cuzco and camping alongside the Urubamba River, Bingham asked a local farmer about Inca ruins in the area. The farmer told him that there were excellent ones on top of the opposite mountain. After a long climb in humid afternoon heat, Bingham caught sight of a magnificent flight of stone terraces that led to what lay above — a maze of buildings and temples sprawled like a dream across a mountain saddle, with the domed Huayna Picchu looming over it like a massive watchtower. The Spanish conquistadors had no idea that this remote and mysterious city in the jungle even existed, and for that matter, neither did the average Inca citizen.

As we scrambled along the unnervingly precipitous high-altitude trail, I thought about Machu Picchu and the previous evening's serendipitous student-teacher concert. The event had had a faintly missionary feel to it, as if I were spreading the gospel to the natives. Perhaps I might win more violin converts the next day amid the ruins.

Then I thought about the tango. In a hundred years it had gone from South America to Europe and back, from bordellos to salons to concert halls, from sea level in Buenos Aires to this improbable Andes outpost. I thought about those countless souls who had fled the desperate poverty of Europe during the last quarter of the nineteenth century in search of a better life in the New

World. Many must have worked from dawn to dusk in dreadful conditions and then drowned their loneliness at night with cheap bordello wine and barroom liquor. I had read that the first tangos, welling up out of a mix of desire and desperation, were coarse, seductive, and forbidden fruit to the more affluent. They were immensely popular, though, and the tango soon became fashionable in Parisian society, in England, and then throughout Europe and the Western Hemisphere. What I had heard in that Buenos Aires dancehall was a tango evolved even further, now garbed in tuxedo and tight-fitting evening gown. Still, I could hear the gritty urgency in the singer's voice and feel the tango's siren call of yearning, sensuality, lust, love, and violence.

One of the most famous tangos, "El Choclo" ("The Corncob"), was initially a phallic reference, but tangos expressed far more than sheer lust. In "La Cumparsita,"

> The masked parade
> of endless miseries marches
> around the sick man
> who will soon die from grief,
> this is why he lies sobbing in his bed
> afflicted, remembering the past
> that makes him suffer so.

> He left his dear old mother,
> Who felt abandoned.
> And crazy with passion, blind with love
> He ran to his lover who was pretty,
> an enchanting seductress, a flower.
> She mocked his love until she tired
> and left him for another.

> Today, all alone and abandoned,
> Sorrowful about his luck,
> he anxiously awaits death,
> which will soon come.
> And, between the sad frailty
> that slowly invades his heart,
> He feels the raw sensations of his wickedness.

Misery. Sorrow. Suffering. Abandonment. Death. The lyrics of "La Cumparsita" were an inventory of human misery. I could think of no other dance form that dwelled so obsessively on the soul's darkness, and yet the tango's history had a familiar ring to it. The chaconne, a lilting dance in three-four rather than the tango's two-four or four-four time, most likely also originated in the Americas, also was banned as indecent, and also evolved into something more civilized. One of the earliest mentions of the chaconne appeared in a list of dances in a long poem by Mateo Rosas de Oquendo, *Satíra hecha a las cosas que pasan en Perú, año de 1598.* The chaconne may have first been danced on the very Peruvian soil where I now stood, before being taken back to Spain by the conquistadors.

Two kinds of dances were in vogue in Spain at the end of the sixteenth century: the *danza,* a formal, stylized dance of gliding and bending motions, and the *baile,* a wild, sensual, and uninhibited dance that used the entire body, including the face and eyes. There were many *bailes,* including the *zarabanda,* which had the double distinction of being, depending on whom you asked, the most popular and the most objectionable. But without a doubt the wildest, most provocative, and most popular *baile* was the *zarabanda*'s cousin, the *chacona,* which appeared at the beginning of the seventeenth century. As early as 1599, Fray Juan de la Cerda complained about the indecent customs of dancing girls and the obscene effect caused by movements of the eyes and neck, tossing of hair, and facial expressions. The invention of the *chacona* was frequently attributed to the devil.

On April 8, 1615, Spain passed a law banning the *chacona* and other dances from theaters. It had no real effect. The *chacona* evoked a way of life so exuberant and carefree that it could entice — so the lyrics often went — even monks and nuns to dance. This *vida bona* (good life) is reflected in the words of every *chacona* refrain:

> Vida, vida, vida bona,
> Let's go to chacona.
> Vida, vida, vidita vida.

None of the chaconnes I had ever played or heard required the performer to shout lustily, "*Vida, vida, vida bona,* Let's go to chacona." Yet all chaconnes, including those by the Englishman Henry Purcell, the Italian Tomaso Vitali, the Germans Heinrich Biber, Johann Sebastian Bach, and Max Reger, the Hungarian Béla Bartók, the American John Corigliano, and the Finnish Esa-Pekka Salonen, drew on the same five-hundred-year-old source.

That night in camp I played my scales and my Schubert, but I decided to forgo the usual tangos for one of the chaconnes that had stealthily worked its way into my mind. Unprepared, I limped as best I could through Bach's Chaconne. Again the porters stared unblinkingly at me and seemed to listen. Did the Chaconne stir up some ancient ancestral memory? (*Ah, listen. He's playing our beloved ur-song. But why does the gringo know it?*) The previous night I had played missionary, bringing the violin to the infidels, but this night I began to wonder: What do you call someone who brings a dance back to its source five centuries later, as I was doing tonight?

Day four began more or less like all the others: up early, onto the Inca Trail, hiking, ruins, lunch. Teresa announced that we would reach Machu Picchu by midafternoon. The arduous journey, the glowing descriptions, the photographs of a city perched in its aerie like an improbable artist's fantasy, had gradually swelled my expectations, but with our arrival imminent, I began to fear that in reality the ruins would turn out to be smaller than life, or sullied by tourism, or, worst of all, merely "interesting."

Suddenly we came to a standstill. The porters unloaded our belongings off to the side and stood next to one another in front of a rock outcropping like soldiers at attention. Machu Picchu was close by, and they would accompany us no further. Our group, now winnowed down to five, said goodbye to Teresa and the porters. Soon we came to a stone gate. Through it, Machu Picchu came into view, hundreds of feet below. *Ruins* seemed the wrong word to describe the dozens and dozens of stone buildings spread out majestically over a mountain saddle now scrubbed free of the encroaching jungle. Huayna Picchu rose up primally behind the city, almost as a physical response to the saddle's falling sides — one gentle, one dizzyingly precipitous. We had arrived late in the afternoon. The tourist buses were gone, and Machu Picchu was in essence ours to explore alone. A single structure, the Watchman's Hut, adorned with a new thatched roof, stood as an example of how most of the roofless buildings might have once looked. We descended a long staircase and lost ourselves in a maze of squares, caves, stone baths, sacred temples, and exquisite carvings.

The young priest Cristóbal de Molina witnessed the Inca wor-

ship of the sun during the first months after the Spanish occupation of Cuzco, only a few miles from Machu Picchu. There were
eight days of sacrifices, thanks given to the sun for the past harvest and prayers for the crops to come, and then the Inca king,
presiding from a rich throne, opened the chanting. Molina wrote
that "as soon as the sunrise began they started to chant in splendid harmony and unison. While chanting each of them shook his
foot, . . . and as the sun continued to rise they chanted higher . . .
When the sun was about to set in the evening the Indians showed
great sadness at its departure, in their chants and expressions.
They allowed their voices to die away on purpose. And as the sun
was sinking completely and disappearing from sight they made a
great act of reverence, raising their hands and worshipping it in
the deepest humility." The ceremony took place in Cuzco, but it is
likely that similar ones took place in the sun temples of Machu
Picchu. Without any basis in fact, I imagined priests celebrating the harvest in the Sacred Plaza, each shaking a foot while all
chanted in their Inca language: *Vida, vida, vida bona,* Let's go to
chacona.

Later that night, seated in hot springs to soothe the aching
muscles in my legs, I thought about our adventure and the coinci-
dences of history. Machu Picchu may have come to life at the same
time and place as the chaconne, and the violin was born at the
very moment when the chaconne was first danced. Machu Picchu,
built out of stone, had withstood a ravenous jungle, enormous
earthquakes, and the vandalism of time, but the violin's fragile
wooden form and the chaconne's evanescent song had proved no
less durable. And if the chaconne has been such an impressive
survivor, who is to deny that the tango, four hundred years the
chaconne's junior, will have an equally long life?

On the plane back to New York City, it occurred to me that I might cajole some of my composer friends to write tangos for me. A few days later I called my brother, Victor, the jazz pianist and film score composer Dave Grusin, and the pianist and composer Lincoln Mayorga. To my surprise and delight, all three agreed to write me one.

Victor delivered a tango so slow and deeply mournful that it made me want to weep. Dave's "Tango Parque Central," in contrast, was intense and high-spirited on both ends, throbbing and improvisatory in the middle. Lincoln, perplexingly, presented me with a "Rumba" (without the *h*).

"I asked for a tango, Linc. Why a rhumba?" I inquired.

Lincoln waved his hand dismissively. "Everybody's playing tangos these days. I'm sick and tired of them." His "Rumba" had a lazy, sultry, yet almost nonchalant lilt that recalled Xavier Cougat's Latin American rhythms of the 1940s.

All three works turned out to be gems, but independently, Dave, Victor, and Lincoln each decided to compose an entire dance suite around them. Perhaps the spirit of Bach, the greatest of all dance masters, would hover over my composer friends, and I had every reason to believe that the violin would serve them well after almost five centuries of use as a dance instrument. What would they demand of it? Wit, humor, joy, coquetry, sadness, anguish, passion, love? The violin could do that.

CHAPTER 15

Cremona

Ye, who to wed the sweetest wife would try,
Observe how men a sweet Cremona buy!
New violins, they seek not for the trade,
But one, on which some good musician play'd:
Strings never try'd some harshness will produce;
The fiddle's harmony improves by use.
— Anonymous, *Annual Register of the Year 1787*

IF YOU HAD ASKED ME several years ago where Cremona was, I
would have been able to tell you rather sheepishly only that the
most renowned violinmaking city in the world was located somewhere in Italy. Geographic fogginess dissolved on my first day in
Emilio Reggio — a place famous for, among other things, its sub-
lime Parmesan cheese. On the morning of the concert I was to
give there, I glanced at a map of northern Italy posted in the hotel
lobby. Milan was the first name I spotted. A short train ride had
just brought me from there. Nearby was Parma, where Paganini

is buried, and, a stone's throw away, Florence. But sandwiched in among these cities, Cremona suddenly popped out at me. Cremona! The place where many of the greatest violins came from, the place where my beloved Storioni was made!

Lorenzo Storioni had probably made my violin in Cremona in the 1780s or '90s. I wondered how the city had eluded me all these years. It would be nice to show my Lorenzo around, to visit some of his old haunts, if any were left, and maybe even to play him for his fellow citizens. I looked at my tour schedule in the hope of finding a free day, but one concert tightly followed another. The next day I would be playing in another city, even another country.

I was disappointed, and oddly enough, I felt a twinge of guilt. After owning the Storioni for so many years and having played it so many times in Italy, I should have had enough sense of history to have made the trip to violin Mecca. Now, though, the idea of taking my Storioni back to its birthplace refused to die. The violin had circled the globe almost endlessly under the chin of Joseph Roisman in the Budapest String Quartet's forty-year career, but had it ever once been to the renowned city of its origin? When the general of the French armies passed through Cremona in 1795, he asked for a violin of Amati and a viola of Stradivari, thinking that there would be an abundance of them in their native town. None were for sale. My violin, made more or less at the same time, had most probably been commissioned by a well-heeled client from outside Cremona, and was likely to have left town as soon as it was completed.

I remembered that the violinmaker Francis Kuttner, an old friend, now lived part of the year in Cremona. I wasted no time in calling him, and he was tickled by the idea of the prodigal son's return. Francis had gone to the violinmaking school in Cremona years earlier and fallen in love with the place. It was not just the fiddle culture that attracted him. Something about the city's scale, the people he rubbed shoulders with, the wine he drank, and the food he ate added up to a general atmosphere that drew him back for regular visits. He eventually settled in San Francisco, but Cremona seemed to be his spiritual home. I told him that I was willing to play the Storioni in the town square until the carabinieri dragged me away, but he laughed and said that wouldn't be necessary. Cremona boasted four hundred violin-makers — one hundred and fifty professionals, the rest students. He said that he could easily arrange a proper concert.

On a hot and sunny summer day, Dorothea, her brother Jan, and I flew to Milan, rented a car, and headed south. In little more than an hour, signs for Cremona began to appear. Fertile-looking farmland nourished by the Po, Adda, Serio, and Oglio rivers spread out across the wide plain. I tried to imagine the connection between rich harvests and the great stringed-instrument center that arose here. As we approached the city, an enormous tower appeared in the distance. It was Il Torrazzo, an engineering miracle and reputedly the largest brick belltower in the world. Francis had advised us to use it as a guide to the town's center and to our hotel nearby.

A violin case waited for me behind the hotel desk, with a card taped to it inscribed "Benvenuto. Call me. Francis." I dropped my luggage in the corner of our room and eagerly opened the case. Two new violins lay head to foot beside each other like babies in a crib. Their varnish was an attractive orange-red, but Francis had expertly antiqued one of them to simulate a hundred years of wear by violinists' shoulders and arms. Both were Guarneri del Gesù models in their outline, arching and with the gothic f-hole style that Francis called his "samurai" f-holes. Inscribed on the label inside each instrument was *Francis Kuttner, Cremonensium discipulus, San Francisco, 2003.* The violins had in at least some part been made in San Francisco, but their proportions were those of the great Cremonese tradition.

These violins were a late entry in my plans. While talking with Francis weeks earlier, it had suddenly occurred to me that the Cremona concert would be far more interesting if my old violin, the conquering hero returning home, shared the stage with a new Cremonese-inspired violin just starting its career. Francis had obliged with these two instruments. They had in common a full and rather dark sound, but I took an instant liking to the non-antiqued one, which seemed warmer and more brilliant — perhaps because it reminded me of my Storioni. While Dorothea unpacked, I played the violins over and over. My initial impression remained. Both had healthy and appealing sounds, yet one left me indifferent while the other beckoned me to continue.

Francis had boasted about the beauty of Cremona's main piazza. When we met him there for an *aperitivo,* we saw that the massive yet whimsical Torrazzo loomed over the square as if in a fairy tale. An enormous astronomical clock with fanciful signs of the zodiac adorned one side. To the tower's right stood the Duomo, the great cathedral, replete with towers, arches, figures of saints, lions, and a Madonna with child. Francis, tall and slender with movie-star good looks, greeted us warmly and ordered a sweet, orange-colored, mildly alcoholic drink all around. We sat at an open-air café under a series of arches facing the belltower and the great cathedral across the piazza, with the imposing octagonal baptistry to our far right. All of these structures were built more or less in the twelfth century, the period of Cremona's highest splendor as a city-state. Lorenzo Storioni and all his illustrious colleagues lived within walking distance of this square, the city's beating heart — the Amati family in the parish of San Faustino, the Guarneri and Stradivari families in San Mateo. Perhaps they sat right here after work, immersed in shoptalk while they quaffed their favorite local brew.

Eventually the subject turned to Francis's own violins. It took him, on average, two hundred hours to complete one instrument. Therefore, four hundred hours of work had gone into the two violins in my hotel room. The violin of my choice had a spruce top made from wood that had grown near Bolzano, Italy, near the Austrian border, a bottom of maple from Yugoslavia, and a scroll of maple that grew in upstate New York, not far from where I spend my summers. As we talked, people constantly stopped to say hello. Patricia and her husband, Francesco, arrived. An attractive woman in her fifties, Patricia sometimes served as Francis's assistant, one of a dizzying list of jobs she juggled — translator, guide, public relations agent, and writer. Francesco was a stocky man with curly salt-and-pepper hair whom everyone called Ceco. When I asked about his work, he said, "I am about to start a La Dolce Vita school," smiling through crooked teeth. "Everyone is born knowing how to live the good life, but most of us forget. I am going to retrain people who have lost their way."

Ceco, sporting a T-shirt with an ad for a brand of violin strings, consulted briefly with Francis. They decided that dinner would be at their favorite local hangout, Mellini's. En route Francis acted as tour guide. He showed us the old violinmaking center of town, torn down in the thirties to make way for a shopping mall. The exact place where Stradivari's workshop stood was now occupied by a McDonald's. In Italy as elsewhere, business is business, and yet even the average Italian knows who Stradivari was. To this day, if a man achieves great wealth, it is common to call him "rich like Stradivari." We came to Via Guarneri del Gesù, a street where, ironically, the great violinmaker never lived. Then Francis pointed out a place where Lorenzo Storioni had worked. My violin was passing within feet of where it could have been made two centuries before.

Francis might not have known the workshop's location save for Duane Rosengard, a double bass player in the Philadelphia Orchestra and an expert on the Cremonese makers. He had painstakingly researched Cremona's archives for clues to the lives of the great makers. Duane had once given me copies of Storioni's birth record, stating his day of birth to be November 10, 1744, and two census reports from 1776 and 1802 acknowledging him as a resident. Duane had succeeded in prying open a piece of the past.

Francis, Dorothea, Jan, and I entered Mellini's, a small, cozy restaurant with a sixties décor. To my surprise, Ceco handed us the menus. His friend Romano, the manager, was out sick, and Ceco, now wearing a T-shirt with a quotation in Italian by Oscar Wilde, was our waiter. We were served pasta al dente with sea urchins, veal done in the oven, rabbit, sausage, and *lardo* — quite literally lard, with not a trace of meat on it. Alongside these treasures came a refreshing white wine from Friuli in the north, a sparkling red from the Apennine Mountains not far away, and a full-bodied red from the Naples area. Francis and the Italians knew their wines and talked about them the way Americans might talk about Coke and Pepsi. When the meal finally came to an end, we raised our glasses to Ceco, the deliverer of splendid bounty, who bowed in mock formality. Then Dorothea, Jan, and I walked back to our hotel, extremely pleased with our first day in Cremona.

The next morning we again met in the piazza, this time for an espresso, and then headed toward the town hall to see the Hall of the Violins. The instruments in this collection hung separately in glass cases like small animals in winter hibernation. Francis led us to a Stradivarius, Il Cremonese, once owned by Joseph Joachim. Although very little original varnish usually remains on old instruments, this one, made in 1715, had escaped the ravages of time. Francis pointed out how much varnish still clung to parts of its top, back, and ribs.

Francis introduced us to Andrea Mosconi, the instrument curator, a gray-haired, spry-looking man in his sixties who was also a violinist and violinmaker. He escorted us into the Stradivari wing, where we saw the master's violins, bows, the truncated neck of a guitar, and finally his work tools laid out in glass cases. Mosconi showed us Stradivari's wooden calipers, paper templates for scrolls and f-holes, stylishly carved bridges, and dozens of wooden violin forms that looked almost alive. We know that Stradivari worked assiduously to the age of ninety-three and that he had two sons, Francesco and Omobono, who followed in his footsteps. But almost nothing is known about his ancestors, where he came from, and why he became a violinmaker. A tantalizing exception is the description of Stradivari offered by the Torinese violinist and composer Gaetano Pugnani, who knew him from childhood: "He was tall and thin, his head always covered by a white cap made of wool in winter and cotton in summer, and with an apron of pure white leather which he put over his clothes when he worked, but as he worked constantly, his outfit never changed." These words were enough to inspire the Cremonese painter Alessandro Rinaldi. His 1886 rendition of "Antonio Stradivari in His Workshop" now hangs in the town hall.

As we moved through the exhibit, Francis and Mosconi kept up a running conversation in Italian, some of it not entirely serious, for Andrea more than once smiled at me, pointed to Francis, and said, "Charlie Chaplin, eh?" Storioni's name kept popping up. It seemed that Mosconi was dying to see my violin, especially since the museum had no example of Storioni's work. A violinist can never appreciate an instrument quite the way a violinmaker does. I opened the case and drew it out for him to scrutinize. He studied its front, back, and scroll intently for telltale signs of the master's distinctive style. What exactly was he looking at — the outer pattern, the arching of top and bottom, the consistency of varnish, or the somewhat gnarled scroll that reminded me of late Van Gogh? Mosconi smiled and handed the Storioni back to me.

It was quite impossible not to like the man. On an impulse, I told Mosconi a story: After a performance, I learned from a member of the audience that the violinist Ruggiero Ricci had recently played in the same hall. Before his concert began, Ricci announced from the stage that his wife wanted him to dispose of one of his violins. He told the audience that he would play the first before intermission, the second after, and let them decide which one to keep. (I had heard that Ricci loved Storioni violins and had collected them avidly over the years.) When the concert finished and the applause died down, he stepped to the front of the stage and asked the audience which violin he should get rid of. Someone called out from the back, "Get rid of your wife!"

There was a time lag while Francis translated my story into Italian, and then Mosconi grinned mightily. Our friendship was sealed. Mosconi said he would try to get the mayor's approval for me to play some of the instruments the next day. (Imagine New York City's mayor granting me similar access to rare instruments in the Metropolitan Museum of Art!) Mosconi shook hands with us. "Arrivedurci," he said. "Arrivedurci," answered Francis. *Arrivedurci?* Wasn't it *arrivederci?* Even I knew the word for goodbye in Italian. Francis explained that Mosconi loved Laurel and Hardy movies and that the actor who dubbed Stan Laurel's voice in Italian always said *arrivedurci* to Oliver Hardy when they parted. So I also bid Mosconi a fond *arrivedurci.*

Near the town hall, a band on the street made up of two guitars, a bass, and a violin was playing Django Reinhardt's lilting "Djangology." If I were to spirit Il Cremonese out of the great Hall of Violins and hand it to the young violinist, he could have played "Djangology" on it with equal success. The country violinist Mark O'Connor once invited me to his summer fiddle camp, where violinists of all types — jazz, bluegrass, country and western, blues, rock, Texas style, old-time, classical, and Cape Breton — gathered to teach and play. Amazingly, we all played on the same standard violin, with its seventy-two essential and unchanging parts. During an informal jam session, Claude "Fiddler" Williams, a ninety-two-year-old jazz violinist who once played in Count Basie's band, shuffled into the room to listen. Claude didn't have his violin with him, but it was obvious he was itching to fiddle. I handed him mine on the condition that he play one of my favorites, "Lime House Blues." In an instant he was swinging irresistibly on my ancient Cremonese violin, a violin that hours earlier had very soberly rendered a Bach solo sonata. And if roles had been reversed, Claude's violin would play Bach just fine. You could count on those seventy-two essential and unchanging parts.

The back room of Francis's apartment was his workshop. Two walls were littered with wood sections piled one on another. Lengths of quarter-cut maple with violin bridges perched decoratively on top leaned against one of the walls. In one corner stood a larger piece of wood with the outline of a cello drawn on it. Against a third wall were his tools — saws, planes, chisels, rasps, scrapers, gauges, and so on. We stood in a violinmaker's workshop for the ages — almost as unchanged by time as the violin itself.

After lunch I rushed back to the hotel to practice. That night's concert in San Vitale, a decommissioned church dating back to the fifteenth century, was for violin alone. There would be no piano to share the burden. What's more, I would have to get acquainted with Francis's violin in a hurry. I spent the afternoon learning where to dig into the string, where to let the bow glide, where to place my fingers on an unfamiliar fingerboard — a host of nuanced motions that were ever so slightly different on my violin. By dinnertime the instrument and I had reached some kind of comfort level together.

Francis and I arrived at San Vitale one hour before the concert and found Ceco standing in front looking unhappy. The doors should have been open already, but they were not. It was six P.M. and the sun still beat down fiercely. While Ceco went looking for someone to open the hall, Francis suggested we seek refuge from the heat in the furniture shop next door. By chance he knew the owner, who cut wood for him occasionally. Introductions were made. The man, an expert woodworker, was curious about my

Storioni. Francis showed him first the front and then the back, pointing to its wild grain. *"Oppio?"* Francis asked. The man shook his head vigorously. *"Poppio!"* he said firmly. Francis turned to me. "He thinks it's poplar, not maple." The woodworker moved purposefully to the next room. Suddenly we heard the whine of a bandsaw. In a moment he returned with a slab of poplar he had just cut. The woodworker motioned us to follow him outside into his back yard, where he turned on a water faucet, wet the wood to simulate the luster of varnish, and then moved it back and forth in the light so its grain seemed to dance. Then he beckoned for my violin. Francis pointed out the slab's open grain, not at all unlike some swirling patterns of my violin. "He has a point," Francis admitted. "Many instruments have poplar backs, especially violas and cellos, and yours started its life as a viola."

Ceco returned to tell us the doors of San Vitale were now open and the former church was rapidly filling with people. Adorned with vaulted ceilings, it was small, intimate, and welcoming. At concert time I stood before a surprisingly full house of listeners who had come as both music lovers and a welcoming committee. "Homage to Lorenzo Storioni," announced the printed program. I hesitated a second before putting the violin under my chin. Let the violin savor this sentimental moment of return after its two-hundred-year odyssey. The Storioni played music of Francesco Geminiani and J. S. Bach, the Kuttner played Paul Hindemith, Fritz Kreisler, Mark O'Connor, and Kurt Coble. Lorenzo sounded unusually good that evening, as if sensing the occasion's significance. He roared, he sang, he emoted. Francis's violin also sounded vibrant and appealing, no small accomplishment following on the heels of Cremona's "last great maker." The violin spoke in a somewhat younger and simpler voice but nevertheless one that had an alluring character all its own.

When the concert finished, Francis joined me onstage to accept enthusiastic applause on behalf of our violins. Then the mayor of Cremona, Dr. Paolo Bodini, a practicing doctor half the day and mayor for the rest, mounted the stage. He thanked me for the performance, Francis for his violin, and both of us for the celebration of Cremona's great violin tradition. Then he granted me permission to play the museum's violins. Had the performance also been an audition? Had Mosconi talked to the mayor about me? Or was it Ceco, now sporting a T-shirt with violins and the word *Cremona* on it? Ceco had gone to grade school with Dr. Bodini, and Patricia had said that Dr. Bodini was the mayor but Ceco was Dr. Fix-it . . .

After the concert we were invited to dinner at a large farmhouse just outside Cremona, where a single immense table was set for twenty-five people. The invited guests included friends and at least six or eight violinmakers. Large plates filled with mounds of cheese arrived, along with an assortment of other dishes and wine. By popular demand, Ceco got up and did his Benito Mussolini imitation, to great applause. The violinmaker seated to my left informed me matter-of-factly that Mussolini had been a violinist and owned an Amati instrument. His violin had recently sold for twice the market value because of its infamous pedigree. This news secretly pleased me. For years I had been collecting names of unlikely people who played the violin: Albert Einstein, Paul Klee, Casanova, Thomas Jefferson, Charlie Chaplin, Louis Farrakhan. Mussolini was a prize for my collection.

This was not the typical after-concert dinner reception in which the performer is showcased for his brilliance and artistry. Yes, I was congratulated for my efforts. Clearly, though, the Storioni and the Kuttner, and more broadly the violin itself as a miraculous instrument, were the stars that night.

On our last day in Cremona, Andrea Mosconi selected a glass case at the Hall of the Violins, opened it with a key, gingerly lifted the violin inside off the semitransparent line that held it in suspension, and handed it to me. The violin was Joachim's Il Cremonese, one of ten violins that Stradivari made in 1715. In the flesh, the workmanship and condition were even more breathtaking than when seen through its glass prison. The violin's outline, its f-holes, and its scroll were exquisitely carved — a collection of curved lines done with unwavering confidence and conviction — and yet the overall impression was one of ravishing beauty rather than cold perfection. Il Cremonese looked surprisingly new. After three hundred years of playing and handling, most of Stradivari's lustrous red-orange varnish remained.

I drew the bow across Il Cremonese's strings, and a sound like sunshine emerged — golden, warm, full, soothing, sweet. A host of different components in the violin's voice merged into something I could only call luminous. Young wine, waiting to be transformed by the workings of time, often tastes of the grape from which it is made. Francis's new violin reminded me of a youthful wine in that I could hear its wood. That "woodiness" was pleasing, to be sure, but the Stradivari's sound was streaming sunlight itself. How could this happen? Was it Stradivari's choice of wood, his recipe for varnish, the way he shaped the sounding box, or the constant playing by fiddlers who slowly but inexorably altered the wood's molecular structure? Bound to a fixed point in time, I could not know what Il Cremonese had sounded like in Joachim's hands or what the violin's progress would be in the next hundred years. I decided to play Fritz Kreisler's "Cavatina." Its near-swooning lyricism would show off Il Cremonese's radiant qualities. "The sound of that violin is extraordinarily beautiful," murmured my brother-in-law, Jan.

Mosconi carefully put the violin back in its glass house, locked it, and moved on to another. Out came an Andrea Amati made in 1566. The violin was one of twenty-four commissioned by the court of Charles IX of France and one of only four that have survived. Mosconi handed the violin to me. On the back, sizable traces of the coat of arms of Charles IX and his mother, Catherine de Médicis, were visible; and on the ribs I could still see part of the motto "Pietate et Justicia." The refined purfling and delicate edges complemented the instrument's formal elegance.

A violin inevitably picks up nicks, scratches, and cracks over centuries. I have seen instruments banged, dropped, sat on, and even crushed. The Amati I now held in my hands, however, thumbed its nose at age. I could see no cracks, top or back, the edging showed little wear, and the violin's beautiful orange-brown varnish shimmered. A violin remains stubbornly mute about its own history, but this much is known about the Amati. It was kept, along with its twenty-three mates, in the Chapel Royal, Versailles, until 1790. Then, on October 6 and 7 of that year, the instruments were taken out of the chapel and destroyed by the mob during the French Revolution. This violin was one of the few that miraculously survived.

The Amati had the added distinction of being one of the earliest known examples of an instrument at the dawn of its own history. The first documented violins appeared sometime around 1530. The violin that emerged was a hollow box, from thirteen to fourteen inches in length; at the widest part eight and a half inches, and at the narrowest four and a half. It was about two and a half inches deep at the deepest part, and weighed about eight and a half ounces. In only twenty or thirty years from that murky beginning, Amati was making beautiful, and beautiful-sounding, violins. His choice of wood, proportions of length, width, and depth, arching of the upper and lower plates, and quality of varnish — a juggling of seemingly infinite permutations — emerged as inspired perfection. Amati's violins had power, delicacy, and penetration. Their general proportions were slightly smaller and their f-holes more upright, open, and roughly carved than Stradivari's. Their scrolls were also somewhat different, in that Stradivari's violins had the curl of a perfect snail shell, while Amati's had a curl that stretched slightly into an oval, as if by centrifugal force.

The success of Amati's violins determined the fundamental characteristics of the violin family from then on. One of my violins, an outstanding new instrument made by Hiroshi Iizuka, has essentially the same dimensions as Amati's. George Nelson, who lectured about perfect design, once said that the bicycle, eyeglasses, and the umbrella were examples of items you could alter slightly but whose fundamental design could not be improved. With the exception of a few small changes, the violin has endured as a perfect design.

Andrea Amati had two sons, Antonio and Girolamo, who became violinmakers, and Girolamo had a son, Nicolò, who also followed in his grandfather's footsteps. Antonio died of natural causes in 1607, but Girolamo died of the plague that spread across

Europe in 1630, which killed more than 20,000 people in Cremona alone and effectively wiped out the other great center of Italian violinmaking, in Brescia. It is hard to imagine what course violinmaking would have taken if Nicolò had perished with his father in the plague; Nicolò was Stradivari's teacher.

I wondered what kind of sound would come out of the 437-year-old Amati. Airplanes are regularly pulled out of service because of metal fatigue. Was there no such thing as wood fatigue after four centuries of use? I chose Massenet's "Meditation" from *Thaïs* for its slow and voluptuous sonorities. A stream of robust but penetrating sound filled the Hall of Violins. Whereas Il Cremonese offered a big, beautifully organized sound, the Amati's was slightly smaller and more rough-hewn, as if its disparate elements were still clamoring for dominance. The "Meditation" came to an end, and I handed the violin back to Mosconi. Neither in Italian nor in English could I express the reverence I felt for these instruments. As we stood at the entrance to the Hall of Violins and prepared to leave, Mosconi smiled at me, shook my hand, and said, "Arrivedurci."

Our Cremona adventure had come to an end. To celebrate, Francis took us to Caffé La Crepa in the nearby town of Isola Dovarese. The café boasted an ancient wine cellar on three levels, the earliest dating from the thirteenth century. We wasted no time in ordering several bottles from down below. *Storioni* means "sturgeon" in Italian, and as luck would have it, sturgeon was served during the course of the meal. The coincidence was irresistible. I tapped my wineglass for attention. "Friends, yesterday I played my Storioni, today I am eating it, and tomorrow . . . tomorrow . . ." But the wine had gone to my head, and I could think of nothing more to say. "Yes, tomorrow. Let's drink to tomorrow," they chimed in, smiling indulgently at me.

Tomorrow. Mark Wood, whom I would describe as a heavy-metal violinist, plays a seven-string electric violin he calls the Viper. It lights up in the dark. Perhaps therein lies the violin's future. People have made earthenware, metal, and leather violins. They have cooked up trumpet violins, pear-shaped violins, and five-stringed violins; yet the old model endures. Old man Amati made it smaller, Stradivari broader and longer, Guarneri del Gesù flatter, and Storioni more rough-hewn, but so far George Nelson has been right. You can only tinker with, not improve on, something that is perfect.

Early the next morning, Dorothea, Jan, and I drove out of Cremona. We were all in good spirits and smiling broadly, having spent three days doing little other than eating, drinking, and reveling in the city's glorious violins. My Lorenzo Storioni was comfortably stowed in the back with our luggage, home at last. I turned in my seat to get a last glimpse of Il Torrazzo, the tallest brick bell tower in the world. "*Arrivederci,* Cremona," I said, as the tower receded into the distance.

CHAPTER 16

A Concert Hall for the Gods

THE PRESIDENT called me the other night. It was in a dream, but one so vivid that the memory of it has lingered for days. The president asked me to meet with him in the White House. Overwhelmed by the magnitude of this unexpected request, I agreed immediately. A government helicopter picked me up in front of my New York City apartment and whisked me onto the White House lawn. In a heartbeat I was standing in the Oval Office before the president of the United States. He came around the desk and put his arm around my shoulders. "I'm so glad you came, Arnold," he said with great feeling. "I need you. The United States needs you."

For the life of me, I could not imagine why my services were so valued.

The president continued: "I want you to accept a job of utmost importance for your country. I want you to be my point man."

The president's arm continued to rest on my shoulders, and he gazed expectantly into my eyes. What exactly was a point man? I wasn't sure, but the honor being bestowed on me swept away any doubts about the job. In any case, how could I refuse the president of the United States in service to my own country? I accepted.

"Thank you. Thank you," said the president. He gave my shoulder an extra squeeze and then vanished behind a bevy of Secret Service men, who rushed me back into the helicopter. The pilot flew to New York City and deposited me on Broadway near my apartment.

I wandered in a daze into the nearest restaurant. There sat John Dalley, my fellow violinist in the Guarneri String Quartet, and his wife, Nancy. I told them what had just happened.

John burst out laughing. "Point man? You accepted a job as point man? Do you realize what you're in for?" I had to confess I didn't. He turned to his wife. "Nancy, tell him what a point man does."

Nancy, looking embarrassed and uncomfortable, explained. "A point man is . . . well, the one who, you know, gets the coffee and doughnuts in the morning, makes travel arrangements, orders the takeout pizza — stuff like that."

My heart turned cold. What had I gotten myself into?

"And our quartet concerts? What's going to happen to them?" John asked.

I hadn't thought about that when I accepted, or for that matter about my own concerts. This was a disaster. Obviously I could not be the president's point man and a performing musician at the same time.

As in so many of these anxiety dreams, I awoke with immense

relief. The terrible pickle I had gotten myself into was only the mischievous work of my nocturnal scriptwriter. I was still a live, working musician.

Later that season the Guarneri Quartet flew to Denver for a concert. Richard Replin, a member of the Denver Friends of Chamber Music, kindly picked us up at the airport and drove us to our hotel. As we checked in, he inquired whether any of us would like to go on a little drive into the foothills of the Rocky Mountains. The others declined, preferring to relax before the evening concert, but I accepted, figuring that a little sightseeing would do me good after the long trip we had just made. "Fine," said Richard. "But only if you bring your violin." No amount of prodding brought forth an answer as to why I had to take the fiddle along, but Richard was adamant. "No violin, no trip," he said firmly.

I deposited my luggage in the hotel room and returned with the violin. What could Richard have in mind?

Richard avoided the subject entirely as city eased into country and country gradually sprouted rolling hills. Instead he played a succession of avant-garde works on his CD player for me. Richard was a passionate music lover with an uncommon interest in new music. The music and conversation briefly diverted my attention from the changing terrain. When I looked out again, giant brick-red monoliths made of layered sandstone and shale carved by millions of years of erosion suddenly appeared, strewn far and wide across the landscape. A few minutes later a sign appeared announcing Red Rocks Park, and we pulled into a parking lot. Richard turned to me. "We're here. Bring your violin."

We began to climb a series of steps, with no end in sight. "So where exactly are we, and what's going on?" I asked, unable to contain my curiosity.

"You'll see" was all I could coax out of Richard.

After mounting several hundred steps, we came upon an enormous seven-thousand-seat natural amphitheater set among enormous tilted rocks wedged into the landscape like sinking ocean liners. Originally formed on the flanks of the ancestral Rockies, the layers of rock surrounding the seats were pushed up along the mountain's flank some 50 million years ago, when the present Rocky Mountains were formed. "The Beatles once performed here," Richard informed me dryly. "Now it's your turn."

So this was what he had had in mind. Without further prompting, I walked onto the stage area, which looked out at space and rock of uncommon scale. I opened my violin case, picked up the instrument, and briefly tuned it. The violin's sound floated effortlessly across this cavernous open-air cathedral. Six or eight tourists appeared from among the rocks and took seats: the smallest audience in the biggest concert hall I had ever seen. Without a moment's hesitation about what to play, I plunged directly into Bach's Chaconne, the opening chords seeming to set the amphitheater into vibration like a giant tuning fork. The Chaconne, grandchild of a dance that had traveled from South America to Spain and across Europe before coming to rest in the imagination of Johann Sebastian Bach, had now arrived in the Rockies. Would Bach in his wildest dreams have pictured the Chaconne, his cathedral, being played in this cathedral?

As I played the Chaconne, I thought of old Arthur Loesser dancing it, of Isaac Stern dissecting it, and of Maria Barbara Bach, now almost three hundred years old, resting in her grave as I presented Bach's gift to her in a command performance. And then I thought of the president's offer. What job could be better than the one now under way — a trinity of violin, violinist, and the most moving of violin music taking place in a concert hall meant for the gods? My body began to sway with the music before an audience of sightseers and outsized ancient rocks whose story unfolded in geological slow motion. Just as Bach had taught me in a dream at Petra's house, I was dancing the Chaconne.

Epilogue

I OFTEN WRITE DOWN my dreams. I'd probably forget them otherwise. Occasionally I'll pull the little dream journal out of my desk and read from it. Saddam Hussein serves me pizza. A psychiatrist asks me what key an oversized replica of a strawberry is in. The notes on my music stand turn into abstract paintings I have to interpret and perform before an audience. Amusing. The unfettered imagination is a marvel of free association. Sometimes the dreams turn serious. Then I feel like the German musicologist Helga Thoene, who looks for secret meanings embedded in Bach's Chaconne. A nugget of truth that I might profit from may lurk within a dream. The dreams are usually easy to figure out, but not always.

I dreamed I moved back to my birthplace, Los Angeles, and had to find a place to live. To my surprise, a real estate agent showed me the very apartment I lived in as a child. We walked through all the rooms, ending in the second and last bedroom. I loved the apartment and told the agent that I was eager to take it. "Excellent," she said. "The rent is three hundred and fifty thousand dollars a month." I could not believe my ears. The agent, ignoring my strenuous objections to the exorbitant cost, strode purposefully into the bedroom closet and opened a concealed door in the back. To my astonishment, it led to a dizzyingly huge, hangarlike area. "*This*," she said triumphantly, "is why the apartment is worth every bit of three hundred and fifty thousand dollars a month. Imagine what you can do with the space — build a factory, a skating rink, a department store. Why not, say, a Bloomingdale's West? This place has *enormous* potential."

I found the dream interesting, but its meaning eluded me. Why my old apartment? Why secret doors? Why giant spaces?

Not long afterward I took my son, Alexander, with me to visit my mother in Los Angeles. Mother and I decided to show him the old neighborhood where we had once lived. As luck would have it, there was a FOR RENT sign in the window of our apartment — the very one I had dreamed about — and the super let us in to look at the place. When we arrived at the second bedroom, I opened the closet door and told Mother and Alexander about the dream. We looked at the small, enclosed space, furnished with only a few forlorn empty hangers. Almost wistfully, I examined the back wall. There was no secret door. The closet led nowhere.

Then a thought hit me. I had stored my very first violin in this closet — the violin that opened my eyes, ears, and heart to music, the violin that set me on a journey I am following still. I felt exalted. The real estate agent was right: enormous potential.